"Often, it can feel like our problems are intractable. Rob Fersh and Mariah Levison demonstrate that it doesn't need to be that way. They explain why overcoming division is vital to solving problems and help readers understand why they need the mindset—the will—for constructive engagement as well as the building blocks and process—the skills—to move forward productively. Their hopeful, well-written, and engaging book provides a roadmap for anyone with an appetite for collaborative problem-solving."

—Congressman Derek Kilmer

"Through creative storytelling, the authors walk us through practical steps to find shared solutions that might seem impossible. It should be required reading for all our elected officials! The long-term impact of this book should influence how those making policy can deploy this experience in these days where, as the authors say, we need to look across the aisle and not see enemies but partners for change."

—Margery Kraus, Founder and Executive Chairman, APCO

"As a conservative in the policy world I learned long ago that for true reform to be achieved and sustained we must be willing to listen, and try to understand each other's values, goals, and perspectives. Helping strange bedfellows to do that is what Convergence does. In this book, Fersh and Levison share the techniques that produce success."

—Stuart Butler, Senior Fellow in Economic Studies, Brookings Institution, and former director of the Center for Policy Innovation, The Heritage Foundation

"Conflict is all around us and cripples our urgent efforts to respond to urgent threats to our climate and communities. This book uniquely combines research on collaborative responses to the problems of the commons with practical mindsets, skills, and tools to practice collaborative problem-solving in a wide array of settings. Strongly recommended for instructors committed to using real-world applications of effective collective problem-solving."

—Lawrence R. Jacobs, Director, Center for the Study of Politics and Governance, University of Minnesota

"As a growing lack of trust in institutions and each other threatens to destabilize societies across the globe, Levison and Fersh have given all of us a major and timely gift. They make the case we can achieve more durable and wise solutions to any number of thorny problems by opting out of the zero-sum game of competing interests, and instead turning toward each other. Even better, their book walks us through exactly how to value and work across our differences."

—**john a. powell**, Director, Othering and Belonging Institute; Robert D. Haas Chancellor's Chair in Equity and Inclusion, University of California–Berkeley

"I've been involved with Convergence since Day One and sat as a stakeholder in one of its projects. People of widely divergent backgrounds and viewpoints, including political perspectives, can put these ideas to use to solve problems effectively without compromising principles important to them. Now more than ever we need to find ways to constructively and respectfully engage with others to solve problems where differences stand in the way of progress. This is the way."

—**Kelly D. Johnston**, Former Food Lobbyist; 28th Secretary of the US Senate

"If you have thrown up your hands and decided there's no way to talk to or understand 'the other,' don't give up just yet. The path forward is in this book. Insightful, easy to read, and packed with memorable stories, this book shows the authors' advice in action and inspires you to give it a try yourself. The perfect book at the perfect time on how to resolve our differences with respect for each other's humanity."

—**Linda Lorelle**, Journalist and Entrepreneur; Host of *Our Voices Matter* Podcast

"Drawing upon decades of personal experience, Levison and Fersh have produced an accessible and practical toolkit for people who want to solve problems, not simply argue about them. Using examples stretching back to the Constitutional Convention through to their own frontline experience with modern debates, Levison and Fersh demonstrate that a healthier, happier, more just America is entirely available to us."

—**Shamil Idriss**, CEO, Search for Common Ground

"The farther removed the 'other' is from our own dinner table, the harder it is to navigate conflicting ideas. Yet if we cannot find ways to bridge our conflicts, our democracy will fail. That's why this book—outlining a step-by-step procedure for finding convergence around solutions to our most serious problems—is absolutely essential."

—**Mickey Edwards**, Former Congressman; Lecturer at Princeton School of Public and International Affairs

"*From Conflict to Convergence* is a thoughtful guide for anyone seeking to forge lasting solutions to tough problems in a polarized world. Drawing on sound research and their extensive experience, Fersh and Levison offer practical strategies for fostering collaboration among people with different perspectives—a requirement for tackling the greatest challenges in society today."

—**Brian Hooks**, Chairman and CEO, Stand Together

"In this much-needed book, two experienced practitioners show that even in times of intense polarization, 'collaborative problem-solving' can produce agreement on difficult questions. As I can attest from personal experience, the process requires patience, trust-building among longtime opponents, and the willingness to consider new evidence and unfamiliar arguments. It's more than a feel-good exercise, because it can lead to breakthroughs that improve the lives of millions of Americans."

—**Bill Galston**, Senior Fellow, Brookings Institution

FOREWORD BY AMANDA RIPLEY,
BESTSELLING AUTHOR OF *HIGH CONFLICT*

ROBERT FERSH

MARIAH LEVISON

From Conflict *to* Convergence

COMING TOGETHER
to SOLVE TOUGH
PROBLEMS

WILEY

Published by John Wiley & Sons, Inc., Hoboken, New Jersey.
Published simultaneously in Canada.

For general information on our other products and services or for technical support, please contact our Customer Care Department within the United States at (800) 762-2974, outside the United States at (317) 572-3993 or fax (317) 572-4002.

Wiley also publishes its books in a variety of electronic formats. Some content that appears in print may not be available in electronic formats. For more information about Wiley products, visit our web site at www.wiley.com.

Library of Congress Cataloging-in-Publication Data is Available

ISBN 9781394198566 (cloth)
ISBN 9781394198573 (ePub)
ISBN 9781394198580 (ePDF)

Cover Design: Wiley

SKY10076938_060624

For my sons, Soren and Everett. May they and their peers grow up in a world that recognizes that we all have so much in common, that the differences we do have are a source of strength, and that solutions are wiser when they meet the needs of all involved.

And for my beloved husband, Kyle, and my wonderful former boss, Commissioner Josh Tilsen, each of whom, in very different ways, played an essential part in the creation of this book.

—Mariah Levison

Above all, to two women who have had the greatest influence on my life—To my late mother, Blanche Fersh, who did so much to instill in me the values that guide my life. And to my extraordinary wife, Sharon Markus, who has been an indispensable partner in leading our lives true to those values.

And to my dear children and their partners and children, with the humble hope this book will contribute in some small way to a better world for them.

—Rob Fersh

Contents

Foreword

Wherever I go as a reporter, I meet Americans who are exhausted by our politics and yearning for something different. I see it in school board meetings, churches, statehouses, newsrooms, and libraries. I see it when people come up to me with tears in their eyes to talk about estrangements in their families, alienation from their neighbors, fears for their children, and public problems that never seem to get solved.

This longing is *intense*. And here's the irony: almost everyone, from all sides, cares deeply about the country and the future, and they desperately want another, less excruciating way of being in conflict.

So why, I often wonder, don't they have more options? The demand for a less poisonous civic life is skyrocketing. And yet this craving is utterly unfulfilled. Isn't that a little odd?

I know, of course, that there are many forces that benefit from our intractable conflicts, financially and psychologically. There is an entire outrage industrial complex that feeds and perpetuates our current culture of fear and blame.

But it's also true that we live in one of the world's most open and competitive marketplaces for ideas and innovation. America contains literally millions of risk takers and storytellers, thinkers and advocates. We are not afraid to try new things, and we are nothing if not opportunistic.

So why don't we have better options by now?

One reason (among many others), I think, is that we have a lot of people *talking* about the need for a more dignified way to disagree, and almost no one *showing* us what that looks like. We are inundated with examples of dysfunctional conflict in our news and social media feeds, but we have very few examples of what *functional* conflict looks like. The examples we do get tend to be poorly told and forgettable. In this void, it can feel like our only choice is to join the melee—or withdraw from the arena altogether.

That's why it is so important what Mariah Levison and Rob Fersh have tried to do with this book. They have chronicled vivid examples of Americans who have met their enemies face to face and done something radically different. And, just as importantly, they have given us a clear guide to creating useful conflict like this in our own organizations and towns. The emotions are unvarnished and believable; the methodology is specific and doable. We need more examples like this—where Americans share raw truths about what happens when we break free from the trance of polarization and dare to get things done. I hope everyone who reads this book will share their own stories far and wide, so we can finally imagine what might be.

—Amanda Ripley
Best-selling author of *High Conflict,*
Co-founder of Good Conflict,
Columnist for the *Washington Post*

Introduction

How do we treat each other across our differences? Is it with derision, dismissal, or avoidance? Or is it with respect, decency, and engagement whenever possible? We believe the path to better solutions and a better society will virtually always be found through respectful dialogue. Whether you're addressing festering family issues, workplace disagreements, thorny community decisions, or contentious public policy challenges, we have enormous—and, in too many cases, unrealized—potential for resolving problems, large and small.

Having differences of opinion, including those that lead to conflict, is a normal part of human life. The world would be a boring and far less productive place if we all thought the same things. Disagreement can be a big positive, producing a creative tension that elevates thinking to a new level. Especially when aired respectfully, disagreements can broaden our horizons and generate new understanding and insights.

When disagreement leads to conflict, however, problems can arise if we're not skillful in how we deal with them. While not all conflicts can be resolved amicably, this book is about how we can handle conflict and disagreement constructively in our personal and public lives to address problems and find breakthrough solutions. The main challenge we face in an increasingly divided world is not that conflict exists, but rather in how we think about and respond to it.

COLLABORATIVE PROBLEM-SOLVING

Thankfully, we've seen firsthand that there's a proven way to approach conflict more effectively. This approach not only reduces unnecessary strife but also creates better solutions to tough problems by having people come together to find obscured areas of genuine agreement without compromising principles. The approach is called collaborative problem-solving, and we've spent much of our careers supporting people to employ its power.

Collaborative problem-solving addresses conflicts and issues by bringing together the collective knowledge, experience, and influence of the people needed to solve a problem, including those who are in strong disagreement, and convening them in a dialogue designed to elicit rich and respectful exchanges on the issues at hand. These conversations create a community of concern and a culture of respect that often lead to agreement on a set of solutions that meets the most important needs of everyone taking part. Having shaped the solutions, having a stake in their success, and knowing that the solutions have broad support, more often than not, motivates the participants to put the solutions into effect. It also generally results in ongoing collaboration over time.

One special benefit of collaborative problem-solving is that it can have an impact right away. It can help to arrest a downward slide toward increased division, hopelessness, and gridlock by increasing the number of people who, despite major differences in background and perspective, can work together effectively. While some conflicts, such as those dealing with fundamental differences in identity or religious belief, can be especially tricky to resolve, most conflict is driven by honest disagreement about things people care about and by our inability to navigate those differences well. When people see they can work well together, the experience has a unique ability to heal wounds and divisions. Communication gets better and people form bonds through the experience of accomplishing something together, like a sports team.

The importance of learning how to collaborate effectively is heightened today as more and more people have less exposure to other points of view. Increasingly people choose to live, work, worship, and play mostly or only in places where others are likely to think like them. And because we all choose our own information sources, many of us have no familiarity with even entirely reasonable points of view held by people who see the world differently.

FROM CONFLICT TO CONVERGENCE

We're practitioners of what we preach. Since the early 2000s, we've both been directly involved in projects around challenging national, state, and community issues where collaborative problem-solving was the gateway to shared solutions and joint action. We've worked on tough issues in the public domain, ranging from elementary and secondary education to the selection of public art; from rising rates of obesity and diabetes to long-term care for elderly and disabled persons; from police–community relations to tribal treaty rights; from increased economic mobility for lower-income people to improved reentry programs after time in prison. In these and many other cases, the fundamental mindsets, building blocks, and process steps of the collaborative problem-solving approach led to new ways of working together and addressing the issues.

Mariah has spent her entire career facilitating conversations across differences, first among individuals and communities at several non-profit dispute resolution centers, then for ten years leading the Minnesota Office of Collaboration and Dispute Resolution, where she worked on local, state, and tribal governmental issues. In 2022, she joined the Convergence Center for Policy Resolution. There she now focuses primarily on national issues.

Early on, Mariah recognized that people's poor behavior in conflicts was, in almost every case, a misguided attempt to fulfill one of their basic human needs—security, dignity, or belonging. Like a child who acts out to gain attention, adults do things like unquestioningly accepting bad ideas to remain part of a group that helps them meet their need for belonging, or lashing out at a colleague when they feel the person's feedback threatens their sense of competency. This key insight led her to realize that most conflicts, from the interpersonal to the international, could be solved by finding ways to meet the most important needs of everyone involved. This set her on a course to facilitate people's ability to understand others' core needs and develop solutions that integrate as many of those needs as possible.

For Rob, who started his career decades before Mariah, the work to solve big problems collaboratively came at mid-career. He had already spent over two decades as an advocate working on national policy issues. For a long time, he believed his "side" held the truth, and it was his job to get others to see the world the way he did. But at heart, he is a mediator, and his bipartisan work for congressional committees as well as his experience leading a national group working to end hunger in the US reinforced this instinct. These experiences exposed him to the decency and thoughtfulness of countless people who did not see the world in the way he did. In particular, working closely in the US Senate with Bob Dole (R-KS) and Patrick Leahy (D-VT), and then in the House of Representatives with Leon Panetta (D-CA) and Bill Emerson (R-MO), Rob broke through the stereotypes he held about people whose orientation to policy issues did not match his own. As time went on, Rob became convinced that no one side or perspective held all the answers. He became increasingly aware of the limits of what he knew, and the limits of *any* orthodoxy or ideology, to provide complete answers. It became important to him always to hear the "other side" of policy arguments because virtually everyone had something valuable to add.

These experiences led Rob to believe that something was missing from our capacities as a nation to take on issues of consequence: the ability to skillfully integrate the wisdom and experience of people with differing backgrounds and vantage points. While various task forces and other entities had successfully resolved differences on an ad hoc basis in the past, these efforts tended to be episodic, and very few people and groups were systematically applying the best available techniques for collaborative problem-solving to a wide array of problems. Building on the work of organizations like the Consensus Building Institute, the North Dakota Consensus Council, and the Montana Consensus Council, Rob brought together a politically diverse set of colleagues to establish a new organization that could systematically take on major national issues where divisions and disagreements stood in the way of progress. After successfully incubating this approach at the international conflict transformation organization Search for Common Ground, Rob founded the Convergence Center for Policy Resolution in 2009. Convergence's approach and experience animate many of the unique, firsthand stories shared in this book.

We're often asked about the "magic" or "secret sauce" of what we do at Convergence and our wider work as collaborative problem-solvers.

This book is intended to demystify the magic and let our secrets out of the bag.

We want to share our approach because we passionately believe that widespread employment of collaborative problem-solving can lead to a more civil and functional world. Taken to scale, it can be an important antidote to the deepening divides in civic culture. Collaborative problem-solving is a powerful and proven response to the growing doubts in the US and elsewhere that people who see things differently can work cooperatively to achieve important gains.

THE WORK AHEAD

Although it reflects the findings of leading researchers and practitioners, this book is not academic or theoretical. Instead, it's offered as a story-driven roadmap for using collaborative problem-solving in a wide range of settings to successfully understand and integrate differences in viewpoints and temperaments. We offer practical and flexible ways to help you employ collaborative problem-solving to address issues of concern, grounded largely in our own work and the parallel experiences of others, complemented and supported by relevant science and research. We don't ask you to change your personality or opinions wholesale; that would be in contradiction to the essence of this approach to collaboration. But to do this work well requires intention and practice.

Collaborative problem-solving often requires organizers and participants to move out of their comfort zones to engage people who are very different from, or at odds with, themselves. It takes courage for most people to go into rooms where they know they will meet disagreement. It can be challenging to convene and facilitate conversations that touch a nerve for just about everybody in the room. It also takes courage and open-mindedness to speak with others who know something you don't know, even when you're not in conflict.

You don't need extraordinary skills or talents in mediation or communication to have success with it. Most of us find ways to regularly resolve differences and get on with our lives. In these highly divided times, it's good to remember that many of us continue to work together effectively across differences—in our local communities, our places of employment, our schools, our houses of worship, and even our seats of government. We should take time to celebrate these demonstrations of our human capacity and desire to collaborate. Belief in this capacity is a vital foundation for putting into practice the mindsets, building blocks, and process steps that we share in the chapters that follow.

We also believe that collaborative problem-solving isn't an all-or-nothing package. Employing just one of the concepts we present, like nurturing trust or putting relationships at the center of your thinking, can make a remarkable difference in how you work with others. Whether you're a community leader in charge of a public project, a student confronting differences on campus, a manager trying to build a cohesive team, a politician looking for ways to get things done with the other party, or just a citizen concerned about growing divides in the country, our goal is to inspire and equip you to harness the wisdom and benefits of our approach so that you can resolve challenging problems that are critical to you effectively and amicably.

WE CAN DO BETTER

We hope you will take away from this book the fact that collaborative problem-solving is not soft or naïve. It's not a nice-to-have tool to employ on rare occasions, when conditions are right, or when only courteous people are involved. Rather, integrating the fullest range of needs and interests consistently achieves not-otherwise-possible results while also building positive relationships in the process. In turn, these relationships across differences often engender a virtuous cycle of continued collaboration and constructive results. That's the big dividend.

We recognize that collaborative approaches are not appropriate in all instances. It's not necessary or possible to find agreement on every problem, nor can we assure that every individual invited to join a dialogue will participate in good faith. There are times when differences run too deep, or minds are too closed, or potential participants are so ideologically rigid that they cannot participate effectively. Dialogue won't be successful if the people taking part aren't honest or willing to engage. And dialogue may not be an appropriate course if decisions need to be made so expeditiously that there's no time for meaningful exchange. Indeed, too much collaboration can test the patience of those who need prompt decisions to proceed in their endeavors.

Dialogue works to solve problems in a far wider array of settings and issues than commonly thought possible. No matter how irreconcilably divided we think we are, how much we think we already know the answers ourselves, or how skeptical we are of the "other side," we can all do a far better job of understanding how other people think; we can all do a far better job of working together to solve problems of mutual concern. Too often, we assume we know how and why others think the way they do and we fail to see the decency and shared aspirations of the people we view as dyed-in-the-wool opponents. Too often we fail to recognize that as smart as we may be, we never hold all the answers for solving tough problems. And too often we react to messengers who may have been strident or unreasonable in how they present their views instead of considering the reasonable arguments and good intentions of those who propose them.

Especially when it comes to public issues, there is a heightened challenge today of finding shared solutions. Many voices in the media and people in positions of power are fanning the flames of conflict, demonizing those who disagree with them, and putting everything in terms of winners and losers (and no one, it goes without saying, wants to be the loser). It may feel like it takes extra energy and effort to be collaborative when so much of the world is combative. Yet, despite deep differences and loud voices, the vast majority of people want to find ways to work together, and they're able to. Most people prefer to be in positive relationships with others. They want the same fundamental things—security, dignity, opportunity, and community. They may just disagree on how to achieve them.

Ultimately, this book is about how we treat each other and what kind of society we want to have. As modern-day living raises increasingly complex and daunting challenges for each of us to resolve personally, professionally, and in the public domain, the primary barrier to navigating these problems is often relational; it's when we lose our trust in each other that problems go from hard to seemingly intractable. Creating positive relationships alone will not do the trick but, especially where issues are stuck, it's often the lubricant needed to get things moving.

This is hard work that's well worth the effort. And maybe, just maybe, as more of us choose to be collaborative problem-solvers, we'll forge more functional, caring, and resilient communities and societies and reach higher ground together.

The Path
to Higher Ground

Even when people are deeply divided, it's possible for them to work together to build effective and satisfying solutions to problems.

Those who participate in collaborative problem-solving have more hope and optimism for the future and benefit from finding themselves to be part of a larger circle of care and community. The biggest dividend is the ability, likely more than you've ever imagined, to develop wiser and more enduring solutions to issues that deeply concern you.

Over the years we've found, and polling confirms, that most Americans share key goals—things like free speech (81%), equal justice under law (80%), ensuring everyone has an opportunity to succeed (80%), working together toward the common good (76%), and personal independence and self-reliance (71%).[1] When done right, collaborative problem-solving isn't about splitting the difference among those with conflicting views. It's not about forcing yourself to sit with and compromise with people whose views are so extreme you cannot abide engaging with them. It's about creatively finding higher ground, which entails generating solutions that work for all perspectives of the people involved in pursuing an important goal they share.

We believe you don't need to pick between advocating for a social cause and engaging with others collaboratively. In fact, when a shared goal can be found, even where there is deep disagreement on how to achieve it, we've seen people use collaborative action to transform their conflict into a constructive opportunity. They *can* find a way to meet the needs of a wide range of people and groups and reduce tensions between sides along the way. It's not about watering down your ideas but rather integrating competing ideas into a shared vision. Having a shared vision can achieve stronger and more durable solutions than any individual or group had at the start.

It's also not about getting people in a room to preserve the status quo and delay change. Done properly, collaborative problem-solving actively seeks out and creates space for divergent perspectives, including those who are ignored, minimized, or undervalued. It embraces the views of those who lean toward keeping the status quo as well as those who are passionate about making change.

It's about raising thinking and generating breakthrough shared solutions that engage the full range of perspectives. Because that's what leads to more effective, longer-lasting problem-solving.

CHAPTER 1

Why Solve Problems Together?

One day in November 2006, during the lunch break of an all-day meeting, Carla Willis grabbed a moment to chat with Rob, one on one.

Carla had been taking part in a series of two-day meetings over two years with leaders from organizations representing the nation's doctors, hospitals, drug manufacturers, insurance companies, employers, consumers, and workers. They were joined by policy experts from left, middle, and right. The formal name of the project was Health Care Coverage for the Uninsured. Sometimes the participants referred to it as the "strange bedfellows on health care" project.[1]

They'd all come together to work out how to insure as many Americans as possible who didn't have healthcare coverage, as quickly as possible. Every person at the table had come with their own ideas, interests, assumptions, and proposals. In fact, most of them disagreed, and quite a lot—some for years, others for decades. It had been a long haul. Rob, who was directing the project, had worked with the project team to ensure that the widest possible range of stakeholders were seated at the table. This day marked session number 11.

AGREEING ON THE PROBLEM

At the start, the group agreed on one thing: they were trying to tackle a major challenge. Stuart Butler, then director of domestic policy at the Heritage Foundation, the leading conservative think tank in

Washington, DC, who was at the meetings, remembered the acrimony hanging in the air:

> This was a nearly hopeless situation. Remember that this was just a few years after the Clinton health care plan fiasco. There were stakeholders who thought the government should take over health care and that health insurance companies and pharmaceutical companies were the "Great Satans." . . . You had people campaigning for "Free care for all." You also had people on the right who wanted to go in exactly the opposite direction, with only market-based approaches. Employers and their unions generally resisted any change in the current employment-based system in the US, where large portions of the population get their health care coverage through their workplaces. Everyone was angry and it seemed that divisions were irreconcilable. So it was hard to imagine how these fiercely opposing sides could ever come together.[2]

Carla, knowledgeable and engaging, was principal economist at the American Medical Association (AMA), one of the organizations at the table representing doctors. She and the rest of the AMA team in the meetings knew the scale and urgency of the issue. It was estimated by federal agencies that over 40 million Americans—one in eight people—didn't have any form of public or private healthcare coverage year round. Many of these Americans didn't qualify for Medicaid, the federal–state program helping to cover medical costs for low-income households. They didn't qualify for Medicare, the federal government program for people aged 65 years or older or those who are younger who meet certain disability guidelines. Many were working, but their employer didn't offer healthcare coverage as a job perk or they felt their employer's plan cost too much, or they were self-employed and felt they couldn't afford the cost.[3]

More worryingly, a large proportion of those uninsured were children. Indeed, about one in nine children in the US didn't have healthcare coverage, though 80% of them had at least one parent working.

Without healthcare insurance coverage to help pay for medical expenses over time, regular checkups often get skipped and health concerns can get pushed to the side in the hope that they'll clear up, either on their own or with a big bowl of chicken soup. But sometimes things didn't clear up, or symptoms went unnoticed by an untrained eye. In those cases—and the number of those cases seemed to be growing every year—a patient would show up at an emergency room without insurance, needing urgent care and having no clear way of paying for it. That emergency care was very costly—in terms of dollars and cents and in terms of health and human lives. Nearly half of households filing for personal bankruptcy reported they'd done so because of medical debts,[4] and about 18,000 people were estimated to be dying from preventable and treatable diseases each year simply because they didn't have insurance.[5]

The AMA recognized this as a "Tough Problem"—capital T, capital P. Everyone who'd come to the table for these meetings did. They just didn't agree, at all, on how to solve it.

For their part, Carla and her colleagues at the AMA had spent a lot of time and effort crafting a solution. They'd been especially focused on how healthcare coverage was tightly linked to people's jobs. Most doctors' practices couldn't afford the administrative time to set themselves up with every health insurance provider, so when patients changed jobs, they often changed coverage; too often they were forced to stop getting care or move to a new doctor, though they didn't want to. The solution to both issues—the startling number of uninsured Americans and an emerging crisis in continuity of care—was to delink coverage from jobs, the AMA argued; give patients the power to choose and buy their own health insurance. In March 2004 the president of the AMA had published a plan for shifting the "ownership" of health insurance from employers to individuals by creating a system of tax credits that could be used to purchase coverage.[6]

Some in the healthcare sector had applauded the AMA proposal. Many others were skeptical; some were openly hostile. One doctor, presumably an AMA member, wrote that "expanding insurance through tax credits appears to be an attempt to save a sinking ship by finding more buckets instead of doing something to hold back the water."[7] In addition, several groups were on the record as being opposed to market-based solutions to uninsurance. They preferred "single payer" approaches, like those employed in the UK, Canada, and other Western democracies, where healthcare coverage is paid through taxes and where healthcare is often described as a fundamental right of citizens.

In the US, however, any option that didn't include market players like the health insurance companies was sure to meet intense resistance. The debacle around the attempts to reform healthcare coverage in the 1990s had made that clear.

A BREAKTHROUGH ACHIEVED

At the early meetings of this effort to extend healthcare coverage to uninsured Americans, Carla and the other AMA team members confidently and enthusiastically presented their ideas. The representatives of the other groups and interests at the table piped up with their proposals, too. A dialogue developed as the group grappled with the diverse issues and interests being raised. Now, at the 11th meeting, the group had gathered to ratify some big areas of agreement that they'd painstakingly developed. Having spent many days together over a two-year period building the trust needed to find solutions that satisfied the wide range of stakeholders' visions and values, they seemed ready to reach an agreement, and Rob was optimistic.

However, Rob had noticed that Carla had grown quieter and quieter, month by month, during the meetings. Had she become disillusioned by the discussion, impatient with her fellow participants, frustrated by the process, or annoyed that the AMA plan wasn't being adopted in full? He didn't know. So he was a bit concerned when Carla came over to him at lunch and, with a smile, blurted out: "Rob, you have *ruined* my life."

Rob tried to keep it light. "I hear all the time that I've ruined people's lives—I do have four kids, after all. How in particular have I ruined yours?"

Carla didn't hesitate in answering. "I came into this process thinking the AMA and I really had the right answers on how to provide healthcare coverage for all Americans. We had done our homework researching and considering the options," she said. "But, for the last two years, I've been listening to thoughtful and well-meaning people with widely different perspectives who made points and arguments that never crossed my mind. *I just can't see the world the way I used to.* My whole understanding of the issues and potential solutions has changed."

Later that afternoon, the groups at the table did agree on a set of recommendations for how to expand healthcare coverage in the US. Some needed to bring the agreement back to their organizations for formal approval, but breakthrough consensus proposals had been found and the participants had made a plan to work together to get them approved and adopted.

They'd each come to the meetings with differing beliefs, backgrounds, and understandings of the problem. To help them reach a new, higher ground, several key principles had been put in place to guide their discussion.

First, the participants had been invited to take part in a dialogue rather than a debate. People were encouraged to get curious about what other people had to say, to move from superficially knowing the other participants' stances to gaining a deeper sense of who they were, what they believed in, and why. No one was asked to sacrifice their principles. Instead, they were asked to see where their principles aligned with others'.

Second, they had agreed early on about how to engage with each other, such as keeping confidentiality and communicating respectfully. The participants themselves created and agreed to ground rules, which helped to keep the dialogue moving forward when tempers could have flared and conversation could have come to a halt.

Third, expert facilitators helped to keep the process on track and ensured that everyone got a chance to share their perspectives and truly be heard. Having a neutral person shepherd the discussion promoted the feeling that the outcome of the meetings would benefit all participants. They all could gain by taking part.

Fourth, the process put as much emphasis on building mutually respectful relationships as on getting to an agreement. Many forged new, rich collegial, and friendly relationships, built on trust and understanding. And as they did, they discovered a lot more intersection in what they wanted to achieve than they'd expected before the meetings began.

The Heritage Foundation's Stuart Butler had spent decades working on healthcare and knew many of the players at the table before he joined the dialogue. He shared the goal of greatly expanding healthcare coverage but preferred to rely more heavily on market-based solutions, many of which were included in the final report. "Just getting these people in the same room to begin with, no less getting them to agree on a package, was an enormous breakthrough," Stuart told us. For this policy expert, the key to breaking the deadlock on healthcare this time was in the relationships formed between participants. He said that while many of the people involved were already acquainted, "they really did not *know* each other." Over the course of the meetings, people not only began to understand each other in ways not previously achieved but also developed a newfound respect and even affection for one another. These deeper relationships, in his view, were the crucial lubricant. They smoothed the path toward principled agreement on shared goals they could all buy into.

Together, they'd decided that the utmost priority—something that everyone was committed to, ethically and pragmatically—was getting healthcare coverage for all children. This could be done by expanding the existing State Child Health Insurance Program (SCHIP, now just CHIP), making it much easier for eligible kids to be enrolled, and creating a tax credit to make private-sector coverage more affordable to families at income levels above but still relatively near the poverty level. Ensuring that all kids could get timely healthcare would support children's development, education, and long-term health, reaping dividends for them as individuals and for the communities in which they live and work. Plus, because healthcare typically costs less for kids than for adults, it was affordable. They called it the "Kids First Initiative." The "first" was a signal. After these initial plans were in place, the group generated ideas for extending similar initiatives to make healthcare coverage available to most uninsured adults in the future.[8]

To get there, the group had taken the best ideas from their dialogue; the AMA's tax credits were part of the solution, but they were only one part. For instance, arrangements to pool the costs of insurance for those with preexisting, expensive medical conditions were also included—a feature that wasn't in the AMA's proposal. As Carla had realized, as had others at the table, no one has a monopoly on good ideas, and when it comes to tough problems, solutions are likely to be found by bringing approaches together rather than by insisting on one right answer.

In their agreement on recommendations, the group had succeeded in overcoming a major hurdle, articulated at the outset of the process by Ron Pollack, who was then executive director of leading health consumer group Families USA: many groups had been fighting for decades for their own ideas to cover the uninsured, and most viewed their "second choice" as maintaining the status quo. When they began to engage again on each other's views and ideas, they'd carefully restricted their focus to health coverage, setting aside discussion of other important health issues, like costs. Doing this allowed them to move beyond decades-old logjams that had been blocking meaningful reform. Most important, because the agreement had the backing of a range of different players in the field of healthcare, it stood a better chance of coming to fruition. The Kids First Initiative helped inspire changes within a couple of years that significantly expanded health-care coverage for children.

The ability of this disparate group of stakeholders with competing ideas and interests to come together and converge on common ground wasn't some happy accident. The entire process had been designed to help participants realize that their most important goals and needs weren't mutually exclusive but instead could be woven together in creative ways to develop practical and actionable solutions none of them alone could have come up.

Indeed, whether a problem's big, like healthcare for uninsured Americans, or smaller, like a dispute in your neighborhood association, having strong differences is never the main stumbling block to solving it. The issue really is how we deal with our differences. Do we come together, build trust, bridge differences, listen to others, uncover our obscured commonalities, and develop creative solutions that meet the most important needs and concerns of all involved? Or do we resist this and just fight for our preferred solutions, thinking that our way, or something close to it, is the only way?

WHAT WE'RE UP AGAINST

Unfortunately, today it feels as though too many of us are abandoning the concept that reasonable people can disagree while also working side by side, or that you can disagree while at the same time respecting each other's motives. The less we know and interact with each other, the more we grow apart. This makes it more likely that we'll choose clashing over collaboration, especially when faced with tough problems.

As bad as things seem now, it's important to remember that human beings have always faced challenges in resolving differences of opinion. It's nothing new that people may choose to not listen to those who offer new or different views from themselves.

Groucho Marx and his famous brothers used one of their classic comedies, *Horse Feathers*, to poke fun at this very human habit. In the movie, Groucho plays the fictional Professor Wagstaff, the dean of a college who is assailed by a battery of ideas for reforming the curriculum from the school's trustees. Because this is Groucho, as the professor contemplates all these different ideas, he chews his cigar and breaks into song, regaling the audience with his firm stance that, no matter the idea, "I'm Against It."[9] It makes no difference to Professor Wagstaff if the idea is good or bad, or if the person peddling the idea has changed their mind, not even if they've made a complete U-turn in the dean's direction; he'd be against it. Wagstaff's opposition isn't about the quality of the ideas being suggested to him but that those ideas hadn't sprung from his own head.

We probably each have a little bit of Professor Wagstaff in us. We resist changing our mind, and we like to be right—especially if we're dealing with an area where we've got expertise. We often react to others' ideas by closing off conversation. If the person or group suggesting the idea isn't on "our side," whatever that side is, we're against it. Yet when we don't listen to anyone who sees things differently from us, it makes it hard to resolve the problems that are holding us back from achieving so many of our goals and aspirations.

As the good professor's song and dance routine displays, clashes in interests can arise even where divisions in belief and worldview don't exist. Instead, the clashes are caused by lack of openness to others' experience and expertise. For example, you may be reluctant to engage with those with whom you disagree for fear that you'll be proven wrong or asked to give up long-held beliefs. Or you might fear you lack the skills to navigate a difficult conversation—to manage the strong emotions that can get stirred up. And it's true that you might find yourself stuck at loggerheads if you try to engage someone in a conversation about an area of disagreement without a clear, shared game plan and set of tools for choosing collaboration over clashing. If you've had bad experiences engaging with people in the past, it might seem easier to walk away from the conversation, in the mistaken belief that a conflict that isn't voiced will fade away. This resistance is a normal human tendency. But when it shapes how we interact with each other, our tough problems are left to fester.

Of course, people have long disagreed and clashed over the issues of great importance to them, whether these are embedded in their morals or other beliefs or needs. Multiple and sustained wars mark human history, and many of them have been fought over principles. Whole new religions and countries have been born because of differences of opinion. Over the centuries, and long before the recent rise in "toxic polarization," we've proved ourselves to be remarkably skilled at building up a story of the righteousness of our particular way of doing things, sometimes grafting our morals onto entrenched disputes.

This may be why people often have a hard time putting differences aside to work to forge solutions that meet the needs of many. Whether it's debates over zoning rules in a community, confrontations between business and labor, tensions over whether to prioritize economic growth or environmental sustainability, divisions in deeply held beliefs about abortion or race, or differences of opinion about how to deal with crime or immigration, we're often clashing. Even in the ivory towers of academia where one might think civil conversation is the norm, people fall into adversarial ways of interacting. Columbia political scientist William Wallace Sayre used to say, "The politics of the university are so intense because the stakes are so low."[10] It seems no human enclave is immune from contentiousness in reconciling differences of opinion and needs.

In those cases where people deeply at odds with each other have decided to go their separate ways, disagreeing groups don't actually find themselves freed of the need to reconcile differences of opinion and needs. They still have to think about how they can get along, both with those in their new "like-minded" community as well as with those who are outside of it. We live next door to each other. We share streets, neighborhoods, offices, governments, one planet. There's value in finding ways to work together to resolve problems rather than resort to battling each other, figuratively or literally. There's benefit in collaborating rather than going it alone or working only with those who agree with us.

Indeed, there are other challenges to effective problem-solving that don't involve obvious hostile clashes. Sometimes the inability to solve problems simply grows out of a lack of coordination, not a matter of deep disagreement. It's the classic problem of silos.

People who work in different units or departments of a business, organization, educational institution, or government agency aren't always communicating, or communicating well, when they're each responsible for just one aspect of a large, cross-cutting problem. They may not fully understand what others are doing and so create inefficiencies in how they're working toward their common purpose. Some individuals or groups may be so consumed with their day-to-day workload, or so strapped for resources, that they don't have the will or capacity to break outside of their team to collaborate.

In these instances, just as in situations where there's already a clash, it is helpful to commit time and energy to pull together the expertise and experience of everyone involved if we want to resolve problems effectively and durably. We need to engage in open and constructive conversations with each other so that collective wisdom informs our way forward.

THE CHALLENGE OF POLITICAL POLARIZATION

There are countless problems that people face in their organizations, communities, and families where political polarization is not at play. Yet stark political differences can seep into these settings, with a corrosive effect on how people relate and cooperate. This is why the rise in political polarization in the US and elsewhere is so troubling. This rise has been well documented, so we're not going to attempt to provide a full explanation here of its extent or causes.[11] However, we'll briefly cover how it relates to collaborative problem-solving.

A survey by the Associated Press and NORC (the National Opinion Research Center) at the University of Chicago captures people's growing unease, with nearly 9 out of 10 Americans stating that they consider political polarization to be a major problem.[12] Fox News similarly reports that more than 8 in 10 Americans are concerned about political divisions within the country.[13] There's a very good probability that you're among this vast majority, and if you're not, that one of your neighbors or colleagues is.

We're worried about how we treat each other. We're worried about how we speak to each other. We're worried that the problems that face our communities and our nation can't ever be solved, or won't be solved effectively, because we're stuck in confrontation. Although some students of history say it has been this bad before, many people cannot recall any instance in their lifetime when we've been more separated and polarized as a society.

To make matters worse, people don't merely say they disagree with opposing political beliefs. They now tend to talk about opposing beliefs as a serious threat to themselves and their way of living. For example, before the 2022 mid-term elections, NBC News asked voters if they felt the opposing party's agenda would "pose a threat that if not stopped will destroy America as we know it." That's a loaded question, of course, but it's nonetheless distressing that 81% of Democrats and 79% of Republicans said they agreed at least somewhat.[14]

The increased fragmentation of mainstream media has contributed to feelings of rising political tribalism. People often read or tune in to only those outlets that provide perspectives they agree with and get a large dose of the views of a handful of powerful influencers who dominate the conversation—and steer it more toward the extremes. Social media in particular has exacerbated this problem because of the lack of fact-checking standards, which are more of a norm in traditional media institutions. In our technology-driven world, virtually anyone can create a platform and gain a following without clear signposts as to whether they're reliable sources of accurate information. People who have grown up with social media are especially susceptible to being influenced online. The Pew Research Center has found that half of Americans in this age group put trust in the information they get on social media, nearly as many as trust information from national news sources.[15] Living life primarily online minimizes our ability to engage directly and deeply with others. It makes in-person dialogue feel more foreign, and potentially uncomfortable. The next generation of collaborative problem-solvers will face an additional hurdle of learning how to interact constructively with people who differ from them when it comes time to come out from behind screens.

The way in which US political candidates are chosen is also fueling increased division.[16] Using primaries to pick party candidates often rewards the most extreme politicians, people who play to the "base" of their party who are more likely to turn out to vote, thus outflanking more moderate candidates who may more fully reflect the collective views of voters in that district. With influential actors on both the left and right watchdogging the statements and votes of political leaders, politicians are fearful of saying something potentially at odds with the orthodoxy of their camp, let alone walking across the aisle to come up with a solution that's also agreeable to the opposing party.

People's trust in institutions has also been falling. It's not just that people on average have less trust in the media or in politicians, which they do. They also have less trust in the medical system, church and organized religion, public schools, financial institutions, big business including big technology platforms, and the courts and criminal justice system.[17]

Increased economic inequality, stagnation in middle incomes, and rapid demographic change are also playing a role, stoking anxiety and anger around losing stature in what many perceive to be the zero-sum hierarchy of modern society. According to researchers, this isn't unique to the US; it's happening all around the world.[18]

In addition to these factors—our disruptive media landscape, distortions in democratic processes, erosion of trust in institutions more generally, and economic changes—we're experiencing a *relationship crisis*. Many of us are sorting ourselves into tight groups, stuck in our ideological silos and "othering" people who disagree. According to the Pew Research Center, 41% of Americans have *no* friends who support the other side's candidate; another 36% said they had "just a few" friends who did.[19] Not interacting with people holding different ideologies or supporting different candidates makes it easier for us to dismiss and even dehumanize them. When a tough problem appears to be deadlocked, it's almost always for both structural and relational reasons.

However, the outlook is not all bleak. These statistics about polarization and sorting ourselves into ideological groups mask a shared, underlying belief that we're in this together. The majority of Americans rank "uniting the country" as the most important national priority.[20] And three in four Americans agree with the statement "It is still possible for the U.S. to achieve the ideal of our national motto 'E Pluribus Unum': 'From many people, one.'"[21]

Far from being hopelessly divided, Americans share core values. In a survey conducted by NORC and the not-for-profit Starts With Us, 9 in 10 among both Republicans and Democrats said the following values are very or extremely important to them:

1. A government that is accountable to the people it serves
2. Rule of law
3. A representative government
4. Learning from the past while working to improve the country's future
5. Personal responsibility and accountability
6. Mutual respect across differences[22]

Most Republicans and Democrats don't see how much they agree, however, with only about 3 in 10 saying that members of the other political party would also consider the first four values on this list to be important.

The last two values—personal responsibility and mutual respect—are essential to coming together to resolve tough problems, and this is where there's a chasm between perception and reality. Republicans grossly underestimate the importance Democrats place on personal responsibility, with only 32% of Republicans saying Democrats value this, when in reality 91% of Democrats do. Similarly, Democrats underestimate the importance Republicans place on mutual respect across difference, with only 27% of Democrats saying Republicans think this is important, when actually 90% of Republicans do.[23]

It will be impossible for Americans to move from clashing to problem-solving until we look across the aisle and see not enemies but potential partners for change. Opening our eyes to our shared fundamental values creates a basis on which we can being working together to get our shared problems resolved.

Some people may be too ideological, too committed to hating others based on their identity, or too convinced that only they hold "the truth" to effectively engage with others. But there is ample evidence that most people and groups can find significant common ground and build a sense of community in the process, even when they've long been at odds.

It's also worth considering how getting people to work collaboratively and well on issues of concern for them can counteract the rising tides of political polarization. According to researchers, getting something done together provides tangible and undeniable evidence to all the parties involved that they're not as different or divided as they thought they were.[24] The experience of working on issues together has the potential to bind people to each other even more robustly than conversations that focus only on reducing tensions or breaking down misconceptions.

A WAY FORWARD

What if what happened with Carla Willis and the other participants in the Health Care Coverage for the Uninsured dialogue could be replicated in all sorts of settings with a wide range of people, addressing all manner of challenges—in government, businesses, communities, places of worship, schools, families, and other settings? What barriers to communication might come down if we could create a safe space where people, including those seen as adversaries, can really talk and develop trust in each other? What new doors could open for creativity when people feel comfortable easing off a belief that they're right, and others wrong, about an issue that concerns them? How would the tenor of conversation shift if they knew they could speak freely in a setting where no one is playing "gotcha"? What benefits would accrue if more people had opportunities to listen, learn, and expand their worldviews, without worrying that they might be forced to relinquish their fundamental principles? What would it mean for our ability to solve problems if people who saw themselves as opponents could engage in respectful conversation and collaboration around tough subjects and emerge saying, *I can't see the world the way I used to*, even if their perspectives changed only a little?

What happened with Carla and the others in the meetings on healthcare can happen for you, your family, your neighbors, your coworkers, your community, and the other organizations that you're part of and that represent you—including, from our experience, Congress. Each of us, as individuals, have to put our mind to building up new ways of working with one another—sometimes on our own, sometimes with the help of others who bring skills in facilitating constructive conversation and who don't take a stand on how to solve the issue being tackled. It takes commitment, but we can communicate and work together in ways that are more constructive and more considerate. We can all be collaborative problem-solvers.

Today, as much as at any time in recent memory, it feels like we need more collaborative problem-solvers among us. In the next chapter, we'll introduce you to the methods for reaching convergence.

CHAPTER 2

How to Reach Convergence

Wat would happen if more of us expanded our problem-solving skillset, gaining stronger capability in listening, learning, and inviting other voices to inform and challenge our worldview? What if we cultivated the ability to identify our own and each other's core needs and the capacity to then develop solutions that integrate the essential needs of all sides so that our solutions are more effective and more widely supportable over the long term? Imagine how our world would improve if we could create spaces where people, including those who see themselves as adversaries, can openly and safely talk, develop trust, and generate more agreeable, more enduring, and wiser solutions.

As idealistic as this might sound, these kinds of shifts are possible. Both of us, Rob and Mariah, have seen that respectful dialogue around shared concerns can achieve important goals in a range of conflicts—from the process to choose what art should be displayed in a state capitol building to the discovery of shared beliefs and goals between a prison reform advocate and an executive at a private prison company, as well as scores of others. In some instances, we've convened people who thought they couldn't even talk with each other, no less find ways to work together, and saw surprising results when they came to know and trust each other and collaborate. When challenging conversations are structured in better ways, people can solve problems more agreeably, wisely, and durably while also reducing tensions and temperatures into the future. Adopting a collaborative problem-solving approach can make each of us an effective problem-solver.

We've broken this approach into three elements, which correspond to the why, what, and how:

1. **Mindset.** Start at the foundation, with *why* you're ready and willing to truly engage in problem-solving, because you're choosing to be in a collaborative and constructive frame of mind.
2. **Building Blocks.** Pick up *what* you need to know to work constructively with others—the collaborative problem-solving skills, tools, and tactics that can be applied to building the solution to tough problems, together.
3. **Process.** Learn *how* to set up an effective collaborative problem-solving process, even as this will vary as you adjust it to meet differing circumstances.

The rest of this chapter outlines each of these three elements, while the chapters that follow will explore each of the elements in greater detail, including very concrete advice and tips for how to organize and conduct collaborative problem-solving successfully.

YOUR MINDSET

While solving tough problems requires a wide range of skills and processes, having a collaborative problem-solving mindset is the foundation on which everything else is built.

We all have mindsets, though we may not be consciously aware of them. A mindset is an established set of beliefs that shapes how you interpret and respond to situations. Your mindsets shape how you put new ideas or events into perspective. They underlie your interactions with other people and every decision you make. Your mindsets can inspire you to collaborate with other people and support the development of problem-solving skills, or they can goad you toward quarreling and clashing.

To solve a problem in a wise and enduring way that attracts widespread support and doesn't leave the parties spoiling to fight in the future, we must cultivate mindsets that help to achieve this. If we see the world as inherently adversarial—where for you to win, others must lose—then we limit our capacity to generate mutually beneficial solutions and relationships.

In Part II, "Mindsets," we look at five mindsets that support collaborative problem-solving, along with exercises to help you cultivate them:

1. **Conflict Can Be Constructive.** Most people, most of the time, think of "conflict" as being negative—something to be avoided. But, we'd argue, conflict is necessary and healthy for human beings. Indeed, the creative tension of differing points of view can push people's thinking to a new, more productive level. How can you change your mental script to welcome the opportunity to work through disagreement?

2. **Everyone Gets the Benefit of the Doubt.** A key to collaboration is staying open-minded about the views, motivations, and intentions of other people, especially those you disagree with. In practice, giving the benefit of the doubt can be harder than it sounds, especially when you're in conflict. That's why we've dedicated a chapter to learning how to develop this mindset.

3. **Curiosity Is the Cure.** When you're skeptical or unsure about other people's ideas, motivations, or intentions, you can choose to be curious rather than cautious or confrontational. By parking fears and asking questions, you'll often discover important information you hadn't been aware of, as well as unanticipated commonalities with those who see the world differently from you. How do you push past your natural defenses to cultivate a mindset of curiosity?

4. **Relationships at the Core.** While substantive conflicts will always exist, those with whom we disagree need not be enemies; they can—and, many times, should—be our partners in solving problems. Building relationships of mutual respect leads to more openness and creativity in working on any issue. It also has the likely added benefit of improved communication and cooperation over time. When you put your focus on forging relationships rather than persuading people, conversation blossoms, as does the potential for collaboration.

5. **Seek Higher Ground.** The first four mindsets support better relationships across differences; this final mindset is at the heart of moving beyond good relationships to solving problems in a manner that meets disparate needs. It's the belief that people of widely differing views and ideologies can agree on solutions without

compromising their principles. We describe how to reframe your thinking to believe that mutual gains are possible, and a wise solution is more important than winning.

You might be wondering, *What's the big deal about these mindsets?* They may seem obvious. You may already believe in them and practice them. If so, that's great. However, our experience strongly suggests that these mindsets get sorely tested once you're trying to find a solution to a tough problem with people who don't share your views. It takes continual dedication to maintain these mindsets in the heat of the moment. In the chapters on each mindset, we explore why that is; how you can recognize when you're falling into old, antagonistic habits; and how to get back into a collaborative state of mind.

There are other reasons you might feel resistance to collaborative mindsets. You might be concerned that taking a collaborative problem-solving approach requires you to sit down with people whose views you find morally repugnant—for example, someone who has different beliefs than you about abortion. Or you might worry that talking with your opposite on an issue will inherently dilute your efforts to pursue a strongly held agenda—a deeply held religious belief, social justice cause, commitment to action, or other principle that feels deeply non-negotiable to you. This is understandable, especially if you believe those advocating for dialogue actually have an unstated agenda of indoctrinating their worldview rather than entering into an honest exchange of ideas.

In Part II, we meet Gisèle Huff, one of the nation's most spirited advocates for transformation of elementary and secondary education (K–12) through school choice and increased use of computer technology. Having spent years of her early childhood hidden in southern France to survive the Holocaust, which took the lives of 18 of her family members, Gisèle is the first to say that she has little tolerance for talk where action is called for. When she was invited to a project on K–12 education convened by Convergence Center for Policy Resolution, she told us she "had no illusions about the work product being anything worthwhile," but she decided that she needed to be at the meetings. Above all, she wanted to advocate for making technology an integral part of the curriculum in schools. She didn't want to leave the discussion to organizations, such as teachers' unions, that she saw as adversaries to the change she favored. By the end of the process, she says, she was a believer in the power of dialogue to create effective change—and, as with Carla Willis and Health Care Coverage for the Uninsured, this wasn't because Gisèle had persuaded everyone that technology was the main path forward. Gisèle's journey, as well as the experiences of others who have cultivated a collaborative mindset, is testimony to how much can be achieved simply by shifting your frame of mind.

Here it's important to note that these five collaborative mindsets pave the way for creative problem-solving where the goal is to meet the needs of as many people as possible. So long as there is a shared goal as well as an honest, equitable exchange of views, there's no conflict between collaborative problem-solving and pursuing faith-based policies, social justice, or other causes.

Some people worry that collaborative problem-solving is about civility for civility's sake, requiring participants to censor their strong views and sacrifice their principles. Some even fear that it is a Trojan horse for maintaining the status quo and won't help us build the fair and just society that our diverse country needs. These folks suspect that only adversarial advocacy can achieve these outcomes. However, as international peacebuilding expert Shamil Idriss and democracy preservation scholar Rachel Kleinfeld stated in the *Chronicle of Philanthropy*:

> We know that in polarized societies, change only endures when championed by diverse coalitions, while adversarial advocacy yields victories that last just long enough for opponents to organize and generate backlash. . . . Adversarial approaches lead people to see each other as the problem rather than bringing together unlikely allies with diverse constituencies to solve shared problems. Similarly, bridge-building efforts that convene the most willing participants for polite conversations fail to fix unjust systems. We know from history that there is a better way: strategies that use dialogue to spark collaborative actions that advance justice and peace together.[1]

Collaborative problem-solving, when done well, is this better way. It's not about civility for civility's sake but rather a challenge to build a better society that won't be undone by the inevitable fallout triggered by adversarial approaches. As Idriss and Kleinfeld write, "The debate between civility and adversarial advocacy ignores the power of collaborative action to transform conflict. . . . Such collaborative approaches yield a dual benefit: meaningful progress toward social justice and improved trust between otherwise opposing groups. Activists who facilitate collaborative action do not treat justice and peace as a trade-off but integrate the principles of both in their activism."[2]

A survey by the Philanthropy for Active Civic Engagement shows that Americans recognize that justice and pluralism are not competing priorities but rather go hand in hand in creating a society that works for all of us. The poll asked a representative group of citizens to think about two values that many people say are important to society: "First, consider racial equity, defined as the state of being just, impartial, and fair to people of all races, and ensuring that systems and structures provide equality of outcomes. Next, consider pluralism, defined as the ability of people to live together and cooperatively solve problems in a diverse and tolerant society. When it comes to advancing racial equity and pluralism, which, if either, do you think needs to be prioritized first in order to strengthen society?" Every race, age, gender, political party, and education group was most likely to say, "Both, at the same time."[3]

Our experience mirrors these views—answers typically lie in "both, at the same time." We find that the more people and perspectives that are involved, the more we strengthen society. Solutions reached through comprehensive and engaged collaborative problem-solving often achieve what the participants consider to be answers that were better than those they started with. Better yet, coming to a collaborative solution often opens the door to future collaboration, and even friendship, across conflicting viewpoints.

Of all the tools in this book, the collaborative problem-solving mindsets are the most broadly applicable. Whether the issue is within your family, your workplace, your school, your place of worship, your community, or your government; whether you're just worried about how to resolve a contentious conflict or you're in a position to lead your group in finding solutions to a tough problem; whether you're taking part in a formal problem-solving process or just using a collaborative problem-solver's approach with an issue; you can bring these mindsets to bear on the situation. They'll help you to work with others in any type of disagreement in any type of setting without need for outside expertise. They don't even require buy-in from the other people involved (though of course that's nice to have). Having mindsets that support collaboration and problem-solving reduces antagonism and helps to build interpersonal bonds, which makes it more likely that you'll be able to identify ways of thinking about and tackling a tough problem that are agreeable to everyone with an interest in it.

YOUR BUILDING BLOCKS

We want this book to encourage collaborative problem-solving among a wide range of individuals and organizations, whether they're engaging with each other informally or undertaking a full-blown collaborative problem-solving process with a convener and expert facilitator. That's why we've put together the building blocks. They're the skills, tools, and tactics to help turn any meeting of disparate minds into a collaborative problem-solving session, whether the engagement is formal or informal. These basics apply across a broad range of time, budget, and buy-in conditions.

In Part III, "Building Blocks," we walk you through the five building blocks that support collaboration and problem-solving in practice:

1. **Map the Terrain.** To tackle tough problems, you need to be cognizant of everybody who has a stake in the solution and where they stand. Who needs to talk to whom to create a solution that will last? Who has the knowledge, experience, and influence to move things forward? Not everybody will necessarily be willing or able to come to the table for problem-solving, or you may not have room to include everyone, but you need to know who all the stakeholders are and to represent as many of them as possible. How you implement this will vary depending upon whether you're addressing an internal organizational issue or an issue of public concern, but either way, this is a necessary step to set the stage for effective collaboration.
2. **Nurture Trust.** In collaborative problem-solving, trust is the essential lubricant to make relationships work. There needs to be

trust above all among the stakeholders, but also between the stakeholders and those who have organized the effort to solve problems
collaboratively. Trust is built among stakeholders when they recognize the obscured reality that they do in fact have shared values and
goals and have much more in common—on both the issues and
who they are as human beings—than they've realized. When you
have a wide range of conflicting viewpoints, things can get heated
quickly, and trust helps to weather those storms. Trust isn't generated just once. It must be actively and continuously created, fos-
tered, and fed, and here we explain what works well to do this.

3. **Really Hear Everyone.** Too often, stakeholders see the world,
or at least the issue at hand, in binary terms that lead to an attitude of "I'm right and you're wrong." The more that you can complexify how people are seeing issues by actually hearing how and
why others think the way they do, the greater the opportunity to
break up stereotypes and misattributions of motives and crack
open the door to possible higher ground. You can learn a lot by
reading articles and books or listening to podcasts, but there is
no substitute for hearing directly from people whose views differ
from your own. We describe some ways you can structure conversations to encourage dialogue and deeper engagement with other
perspectives.

4. **Generate Options for Mutual Gain.** A key to successfully solving tough problems is creating solutions that meet the needs of as
many stakeholders as possible without people feeling as though
they're compromising what's most important to them. In the par-
lance of the field, this is known as *integrative problem-solving*.
This chapter gives you the tools to get attuned to the underlying
needs and concerns of others to create options for reaching higher-
ground solutions together.

5. **Take Your Time**. While it sometimes helps to have a deadline
for solving a tough problem, the normal impulse to go straight to
solutions or hash out disagreements head-on is often counterproductive. Sure, it takes time to build trust, understand others' viewpoints, and fully process what you're learning, but it takes much
less time than it takes when you're stuck at an impasse! It's worth
it to create the time and space you need for collaboration and effective problem-solving.

We call these skills "building blocks" because, like a Lego set, these skills, tools, and tactics are individual pieces that can click together in any number of ways to create the architecture for collaborative problem-solving. If you only have the time or capacity to use one of the blocks, that's okay. You don't have to use every block in the set. However, the more blocks you use, and the more times you use them in different ways, the more you'll be able to build robust problem-solving structures, solutions that will stand up longer and taller even if they experience a few knocks.

The building blocks also click together more securely when you've got a collaborative frame of mind as your foundation. We can see that in the experiences of Marc Howard, professor of government and law at Georgetown University and the author of *Unusually Cruel: Prisons, Punishment, and the Real American Exceptionalism*, and Daren Swenson, the vice president for Reentry Partnerships and Innovation at CoreCivic, the leading provider of private corrections and detention facilities and services in the US. Both men believe in dialogue and respectful listening—key qualities that serve collaborative problem-solving. But when they first met during a project to talk about prison reform, the divide between them seemed incredibly large. How did they get to the place where they not only agreed on a set of reforms to better support people returning to society after time in prison but also now call each other when they need a sounding board about their very different work to improve prisons? As we explain in Part III, the building blocks helped them to learn from each other and later pursue opportunities for further collaboration.

THE PROCESS STEPS

In Part IV, "Process," we lay out a more comprehensive set of steps for engaging in formal collaborative problem-solving, including guidance on how to carry out these steps, so that people engaging in the most complex problem-solving activities, such as addressing issues at the local, state, or national level, can understand what may be entailed. Depending upon the complexity of your issue—whether it's organizational or public policy, whether you've got time or resource constraints—you can pick and choose from these steps as you deem appropriate. Even if you've decided that an informal approach is the better way to go, we find that it's helpful to consider each of these process steps, because adapting them to your situation may very well help to maximize the chances that you and your fellow stakeholders will achieve higher ground.

We've distilled these down to three steps, each of which are underpinned by the collaborative mindsets and building blocks:

1. **Discovery and Design.** These steps help you to prepare for convening people to engage on problems they are seeking to solve. The level of thoroughness needed here will depend upon the nature, complexity, and locus of the problem at hand. The discovery portion of this step is supported by the building block discussed in Chapter 8, "Map the Terrain." It helps you to identify who needs to be around the table, what roles they'll have, and how to frame the problem in a way that's inviting to the parties who will be invited to get involved. During the discovery phase, you consider the frequency, duration, and location needed for meetings and a timeline for engagement. Everything that's learned in the discovery phase is then converted into a concrete design for the problem-solving process. In many cases, writing up what discovery interviews and other research have revealed about the issues, the stakeholders, and optimal participants, and then sharing the proposed design, is useful in persuading potential participants to devote time and energy to the problem-solving process. Doing this also builds trust that a wide range of views have been heard and recorded.

2. **Dialogue and Destinations.** These process steps lay crucial groundwork for successful engagement and deliberation on the issues. Identifying a shared "destination"—a goal that all participants buy in to, despite differing views on how to achieve it—is key to creating a sense of shared mission and also for building trust that everyone is on the same page about where they want to go. Based upon the shared goal, it's often very useful to get agreement on broader principles everyone can get behind even if there are important differences in people's views about how to apply them to the issues at hand. These principles become useful yardsticks by

which to evaluate options that are generated as possible solutions. After the problem-solving group discerns their overall shared goal and develops guiding principles, the next step is to generate a range of options that can meet varying stakeholder needs. Skillful facilitation can help a group move toward the options that achieve mutual gains.

3. **Achieving Consensus and Impact.** In this crucial final step of a collaborative problem-solving process, participants review the proposed options the group has generated and, through frank and well-facilitated exchange, identify those ideas that truly meet the needs and interests of diverse stakeholders and generate shared enthusiasm for moving forward with them. This includes identifying what kinds of impacts the group wants to have and who has responsibility for carrying out any consensus recommendations. Understanding the leverage points and agents for change helps participants to craft a shared plan for achieving impact, which may include convening some or all of the group over a period of time after agreement is reached to help coordinate ongoing efforts.

As these steps suggest, running a formal collaborative problem-solving process involves recruiting a number of people into roles and sustaining an ongoing dialogue with the support of skilled facilitation and other tools. Sometimes a formal process, convened by an authority or other interested party with influence, is necessary to bring together groups where dialogue has broken down. That was the case in Minnesota when Governor Mark Drayton called for a process to address issues at the Minnesota Security Hospital, a facility serving individuals convicted of crimes who also have a mental health condition. Scott Melby, chief operations officer of Minnesota's Forensic Mental Health Program, remembers thinking that the process offered a chance to reset relations between management and staff at a critical moment. Having come together on a shared vision for the hospital's future, they were then in a position to secure the support needed to improve how the hospital cared for its patients. In Part IV, we describe the process with the hospital's key stakeholder groups, as well as other processes, to show the power of this approach in practice.

WORKING SIDE BY SIDE

We think most people would be shocked at how reliably collaborative problem-solving works. It isn't that it's easy. It takes a lot of effort, time, skill, and commitment. Yet it does work, consistently. And it works in a wide range of situations—from deciding if a new park should have more recreational equipment or natural space, to working out whether and how two departments might be consolidated into one, to solving how to extend healthcare coverage to uninsured Americans. People who have been at odds can forge mutually beneficial solutions to tough problems of shared concern, and they can build a sense of community in the process.

You don't have to take our word for it. In the chapters that follow, we show abundant evidence for the power of collaborative problem-solving. In addition to the experience of Carla Willis on healthcare coverage, Gisèle Huff on K–12 education, Marc Howard and Daren Swenson on incarceration, and Scott Melby and others involved in the Minnesota Security Hospital process, we'll introduce you to a host of other people who have engaged in collaborative problem-solving, including:

- Becky Pringle, the current president of the National Education Association, who joined with Gisèle to create a transformative vision for the future of K–12 education
- Michael Sodini, a third-generation firearms industry professional, and psychologist Sherry Davis Molock, who came together around the issues of mental health and gun awareness in the context of suicide prevention
- Melanie Leehy, a resident of Falcon Heights, Minnesota, who became co-chair of the city's task force on inclusion and policing after the shooting of Philando Castile in the community
- Julie Ring, executive director of the Association of Minnesota Counties, and State Representative Dave Baker, who worked together to ensure that Minnesota received its full share of a national opioid settlement
- Ellie Bertani, formerly a Walmart executive, and Judy Conti, a workers' advocate with the National Employment Law Project (NELP) and long-time critic of the retailer, who took part in a group of stakeholders who generated a series of ideas that supported greater economic mobility for workers at Walmart and elsewhere

Healthcare. Education. Policing. Prisons. Opioids. Mental Health. Guns. Economic mobility. These aren't easy issues. But in every case, the collaborative problem-solving approach got people talking and working together. It moved things forward.

The work of collaborative problem-solving involves stepping back from seeing those with whom we disagree as antagonists and instead investing ourselves in fostering mutually respectful relationships with them. The model works best when its processes include the full range of voices and all concerns are heard and seen. When that happens, it's possible to get a handle on all angles of a problem and work to craft higher-ground solutions that gain wide-ranging support. We've seen how well it works, and we want to help others to deploy the collaborative problem-solving approach to whatever problems they're facing. That way, we can *all* work side by side more effectively—and live side by side more happily.

The path to convergence is not merely about finding common ground where possible and agreeing to disagree about everything else. It involves concrete skills and guidelines that support effective collaboration that anyone can develop and use on a regular basis to reach the higher ground of mutual benefit. In the following chapters, you'll see "Try It Out" boxes. These contain exercises to help you gain the mindsets, building blocks, and process know-how you need to succeed at collaborative problem-solving. We're closing this overview of collaborative problem-solving with the first of these exercises because we're confident that, no matter what problem you think of, whether it's big or small, tough or easy, you'll start to see how the approach we recommend can change your way of seeing the issue and open the door to new relationships and solutions as you apply the mindsets, building blocks, and process steps to it.

Try It Out

Think about a divisive problem you're facing. If you can't think of something you're personally involved in, maybe you can think of something that's going on in your neighborhood, your workplace, your school, your place of worship, or local, state, or national politics. Summarize the problem in a sentence or two and write it down.

As you go through the chapters that follow, we'll bring you back to this issue so that you can practice applying what you're learning to a real conflict and potentially make some progress in solving it.

As a start, think about rewriting your sentence or two through the lens of collaborative problem-solving. Have you simply stated the problem, or have you included some of the big-picture goals that a solution would achieve? Have you framed it in a way that invites a range of views about the problem and solutions? If not, try to reflect another individual's or group's perspective on the issue.

Once you've done this, you're on your way from contentious conflict to convergence around a solution.

Despite the way it seems in the media, in our experience most people long for a way to get along better with others, to solve problems amicably, and to live and work in settings that have less tension and antipathy. People are looking for ways to put their personal values and their desire to be in positive relationships with others into practice, but too often they don't know how. Too frequently, people find the challenge so daunting they throw their hands up in frustration, losing hope that they can break a cycle of dispiriting distrust and debate. It doesn't have to be this way.

Together, we can create meaningful breakthroughs and provide a great deal of something else that is sorely needed: hope that we'll be able to foster kinder, less contentious, and more functional communities, sectors, and societies now and in the future. Whether you're a local community or campus leader, a faith leader, a PTA president, a business or nonprofit leader, an elected or appointed public official, or just an interested citizen, the concepts in this book will help you become a more effective problem-solver.

At a minimum, we hope you'll leave this book more hopeful that people can solve important problems together more regularly and effectively. We hope you'll see that together we can create a culture of collaboration that serves as an antidote to the all-too-common belief that we can't come up with solutions that will work for everyone. We need not respond to conflict with the reflexive instinct that we might as well fight or withdraw and retreat into our respective camps. We can work together.

Yes, some of our differences run deep, and some of our differences may be irreconcilable. But every one of us has the power to change the tenor of our interactions. We can each change the way we relate with one another. We can adopt a path that takes our conflicts from clashes to convergence, because this approach isn't about changing a person's core values; it's not about compromising principles. It's about finding our shared concerns and humanity in service of meeting each other's needs. It's also not about being nice or polite, although that often happens, too. It's about getting results that are not otherwise possible. It's about reaching higher ground in service of everyone's needs.

No matter where you live, what you do for work or play, or your life circumstances, we hope you'll find value in what we present. Collectively, we all can help to create a more functional and amiable world by employing the accessible and proven practices and approaches in the chapters that follow.

II

Mindsets

Your mindset is a set of beliefs that shape how you make sense of the world and yourself. It influences how you think, feel, and behave in any given situation. As people encounter different situations, their mind triggers a specific mindset that directly impacts their behavior in that situation. And, according to research by psychologist Carol Dweck and others, your beliefs play a pivotal role in what you want and whether you achieve it.[1]

Some mindsets support collaboration and a problem-solving approach to working with people with whom you disagree. Other mindsets put a wrench in the works. Having the right overall mindset is the fundamental starting point for effective collaborative problem-solving.

Over the years, we've watched as hundreds of people from diverse walks of life gather to tackle a thorny problem or issue and reach agreement on how to move forward together. As part of our commitment to being collaborative problem-solvers, we've gone out of our way to bring together people who *don't* agree, because if you only ever talk with the people you agree with, it's less likely that you'll find the best possible answers and more likely that you'll continue to face resistance over time from those who see things differently. From our own experience, we've seen how employing five mindsets can widen your ability to resolve tough problems—both collaboratively and without compromising deeply held principles.

The five collaborative mindsets are:

1. Conflict Can Be Constructive
2. Everyone Gets the Benefit of the Doubt
3. Curiosity Is the Cure
4. Relationships at the Core
5. Seek Higher Ground

In this part, we walk you through why these mindsets make such a big difference and how you can develop the habit of thinking about problems, conflicts, and other people's perspectives in more collaborative ways. We urge you to try them on for size.

CHAPTER 3

Conflict Can Be Constructive

After the American Revolution, the leaders of the 13 colonies were facing growing disagreement. They couldn't see eye to eye on how the debt for the war would be repaid, who would protect and control the western frontier, or what role the state governments should have compared with the federal government. There was open debate around the possibility of breaking up the new nation, with some people wanting to rejoin England. By and large, we're still living with a number of these tough issues today (though few would say they want to return to being a colony!). But a small group of problem-solvers—James Madison, Alexander Hamilton, John Jay, George Washington, and Benjamin Franklin—saw an opportunity.[1] This conflict could be *constructive*. They could gather together and rethink the founding principles of the nation.

They didn't have to work together this way. They could have decided that the former colonies were better off as 13 countries, or a handful of countries formed from colonies that shared ideas about how to organize their government. And when the conflict really started to boil up, it was the summer of 1787—hot, sticky, and muggy, the sort of weather that gets people in a quarrelsome mood. Yet by that September, the 55 delegates from the 13 colonies had settled on the basic outlines of the Constitution of the United States, a visionary document that artfully, if imperfectly, created the structure for our lasting experiment in democracy.

They did this by finding higher ground—identifying areas where they all agreed. This started foremost with their belief in wanting to be a nation. (The people advocating a return to English rule hadn't come to the convention.) Even in the darkest days of their meetings—in late June, when Madison and his bloc of nationalists were ready to walk out, and everyone was in an ill temper—Benjamin Franklin, widely known as a deist, rose to his feet and proposed that each day's session be opened with a prayer to inspire the delegates to work together.[2] Without a higher purpose, he said, "We shall be divided by our little partial local interests; our projects will be confounded, and we ourselves shall become a reproach and a bye word down to future age. . . . I therefore beg leave to move—that henceforth prayers imploring the assistance of Heaven, and its blessings on our deliberations, be held in this Assembly every morning before we proceed to business."[3] Though the delegates voted against having a daily prayer, over the course of the next few weeks, nudged by Franklin's appeal, they were able to set aside their "non-negotiables" and focus on what they could build together: "a more perfect union."

They chose to take this moment of contentious conflict and make something awe-inspiring out of it.

FLIP THE CONFLICT SCRIPT

When confronted with conflict, most of us don't think first about its potential for positive impact. How do you feel when you think about conflict?

What words first came to mind? We bet they aren't positive ones. Now think again.

What are some of the positive words you could associate with conflict? Change, growth, transformation? Those are some pretty powerful words. For most people, it's harder to think of the positive aspects because we mainly have negative experiences with conflict. Plus, research shows that we remember the negative more easily than the positive.[4]

Yet for problem-solvers, in most situations, the creative tension of differing points of view generates answers that are wiser, more creative, and more enduring than those favored by any one party before they engage with each other. This is true not only for America's founders but for all of us. We can choose to respond to conflict constructively. We can choose to see the positive potential of it.

At some level, despite the strong negative associations that most of us have with the word "conflict," we all know in our gut that conflict is a normal and expected part of life. Many conflicts flit past us as part of our day to day, hardly noticed and leaving no lasting impression— you and your sibling fighting over that last piece of pie, you and your spouse disagreeing on which movie to watch, or maybe you and your neighbor gently sparring over what kind of fence would best go between your yards. Every day, we all work through differences that amount to conflict. Mostly we get them resolved, or learn to live with them, and move on.

However, when conflicts arise on issues that are really important to us, or that touch on deeply held beliefs, conflict can become quite upsetting and distracting. It can trigger anxiety, anger, or fear. This is because we've been groomed by evolution to protect ourselves whenever we sense a threat—what's called the fight, flight, or freeze response.[5] We may no longer fight off predators like bears and badgers, flee like squabs and squirrels, or play dead like opossums, but our basic impulse to protect ourselves is automatic and unconscious. We have a hard time controlling it.

What happens, exactly? When you first perceive the threat of a conflict, the part of the brain that regulates our emotions and behaviors sounds an alarm, releasing a cascade of chemicals. Stress hormones like adrenaline and cortisol flood your body, giving your arms and legs the catalysts to punch or run or flop down to ground. Your heart rate and breathing speed up so you can take in more oxygen if you have to. Your face might flush with heat. You might feel your jaw clench tight and hear your voice quiver. You're in the grip of a highly efficient, prehistoric set of physiological reactions designed to move you into action to save yourself.

These reactions are known as "amygdala hijacking" for the part of the brain that sets it off.[6] Unfortunately, the amygdala also shuts down access to the part of the brain that regulates empathy, complex decision-making, and problem solving—your prefrontal cortex. So while you're trying to protect yourself from a threat, you also lose some of your decision-making capacity and your ability to see other people's perspectives. You're more likely to think, *I'm right and you're wrong*, even when you ordinarily see more perspectives.

From here the thalamus, your brain's perception center, starts to work on interpreting what exactly is going on. In your compromised emotional state, it usually gets things wrong. As your attention narrows, your brain oversimplifies the story, focusing like a laser on potential dangers and ignoring any information that muddies your understanding of what's happening. Complexity collapses even more. Your memory is also compromised, which makes it hard to recall information that might help you calm down or solve the problem—even really fundamental information, like your love for the person you currently want to murder for once again forgetting to pay the electric bill on time. Worse, you're not making new memories very well, so you won't accurately recall what's happening when you try to do so later. This is why misunderstandings are such a common theme in conflict.

Luckily, amygdala hijacking just takes our prefrontal cortex offline for a short time. The prefrontal cortex is standing ready to help you respond productively to conflict—to help regulate your thoughts and emotions, cooperate, navigate differences, and accomplish other complex tasks. You just have to get it back online.

There are proven ways that we can all give our prefrontal cortex the boost it needs during conflict. These include exercises to build greater awareness of the unconscious physical changes that happen in the body during the fight, flight, or freeze response, as well as exercises to balance and override amygdala hijacking. Instead of fighting, fleeing, or freezing, we can learn how to stay present, regulate our body's protective reactions, and eventually develop new, more flexible, and more constructive ways of interacting with each other.

Try It Out

When confronted with and reacting to conflict, here are some tools to help you better manage how you respond:

- **Stay present.** We all have physiological reactions; the key is to notice yours. When you're in conflict, pause and scan yourself. Is your heart racing? Is your voice raised or trembling? Are your palms sweaty? Are you pounding the table when you make a point? Is your jaw clenched? Get to know how your body reacts to conflict.
- **Breathe.** It helps to breathe—not just to get air in and out but to slow down your breathing. Even a few short moments of

focusing on the pace of your breath can stop the cascade of cortisol and adrenaline in your body. There are many techniques, such as counting for a few seconds when you inhale or exhale, that effectively use your breathing to calm yourself. Resources on this are readily available with a minimum of internet research on your part.

- **Refocus on your body.** Now that you've slowed down your breathing, focus again on what's happening in your body. Take a few moments to note the different parts of your body where sensations are occurring—what's tight, shaky, tingling, or hurting. As you pay attention, you'll start to restore your prefrontal cortex's ability to process information, making it easier to make decisions, listen, and relate to others.

Understanding and learning to manage how your brain and nervous system react to conflict won't prevent you from feeling distressed or angry. That's not the point. Indeed, according to social scientists, the emotion of anger can be good for conflict resolution and even for repairing relationships.[7] It's a dense form of interaction that communicates more information more quickly than our other emotions. It does an excellent job of forcing us to listen to and confront problems we might otherwise avoid. Anger can also be a powerful moral force that leads to social change and the pursuit of a more just world.

Instead, the reason to understand and learn to manage your reaction to conflict is to prevent you from feeling *outraged*. Outrage is an escalating cycle of blame, rumination, and ever-expanding fury for revenge. It can build when anger is not expressed and issues are left unresolved.

When you dare to express your anger in constructive ways, you can use it as a force for problem-solving. You choose to make conflict constructive.

WORTHY DISAGREEMENTS

In settings where passions are running high, there can be understandable trepidation. You might be aware of how your amygdala is hijacking your reactions, but what about the other people in the room? If you've had experiences in the past where you left a conflict wounded, you might be inclined to avoid conflicts with certain people or groups, or over certain issues.

Indeed, a lot of us, especially in these deeply polarizing times with divisive media and political figures making a lot of noise, may have a hard time imagining a scenario where we're amicably sitting down with people who see things very differently than we do. Because conflict feels uncomfortable, many of us are conflict averse, at least much of the time. Often, we might prefer to establish a temporary truce rather than face a conflict head on. In some instances, we may view others as so off base that we don't see the point of engaging with them at all. It can seem like a waste of time and energy to try working together when you're so at odds. It's natural to think nothing's going to come from it.

Education activist Gisèle Huff found herself having to deal with such a scenario when she was invited to take part in the Education Reimagined project convened by Convergence. In fact, she said that when she agreed to take part, she "had no illusions about the work product being anything worthwhile."

Gisèle is a self-described "force of nature." When she feels passionately about a topic—like the importance of rethinking the way we educate children—she punctuates her ideas with a gentle punch to the table; you can hear it in podcast and radio interviews she's done. This passion is deeply tied to her own experiences in the US education system after the Second World War. Having survived the trauma of the war and losing family in the Holocaust, she and her mother emigrated to New York. They had $400, and neither of them spoke English, "other than a few standard sentences . . . learned from a French-English dictionary."[8] She was enrolled in her local elementary school in the Bronx and, even as a youngster, couldn't believe how little the students were expected to learn. She pushed and pushed to get the education she wanted to pursue a professional career.

She leveraged these experiences to inspire her to work for meaningful change in the education system. Yet by the time she'd dedicated herself to promoting school reform, she'd come to see conflict as a barrier to change. Working by committee to resolve issues didn't work, she said, and she had little tolerance for talk when what was needed is action. The few times she'd joined groups to discuss ways to reform education, she'd found them to be inefficient and a waste of time. When she was invited to participate in the Education Reimagined project, she'd only turned up because she felt as though her perspective on technology in schools wouldn't otherwise be represented.

When we don't cultivate a mindset that conflict can be constructive, we can lose interest and lack incentive to turn conflicts into change-making tools. Instead, we sweep our differences under the rug and swallow our concerns, or we go off and work in a silo, doing only what we can, when we could do much more by joining forces with others.

Of course, there are times when you have no choice but to engage in an adversarial manner. You may be confronted by people who don't operate in good faith, who have blind biases against you that make it hard to work together, or who are so committed to their own set of beliefs that they're unwilling to engage with others they see as adversaries or enemies. Some people in a conflict may just be disagreeable or litigious by training or nature, and relish having a fight, so that they don't see collaboration as means for resolving issues. And many societal norms encourage people to seek victory over those with whom they disagree.

Sometimes you might not be aware of how your own mindset is shaping how you think about the possibility of solving problems together. Gisèle remembers looking at the list of the other people invited to Education Reimagined and thinking it was "a group of people mired in the status quo." She felt they were bogging down the transformation of education that she wanted to get going.

In these instances, you have a choice. You can insist on your own way. Or you can stay present, engaging in worthy disagreements in a way that doesn't burn bridges and leaves the road open for future collaboration. Gisèle joined in because she wanted to have a voice. She stayed and was able to shift her mindset because of three things: the group as a whole committed to step out of their present conflicts and step into a future that they could imagine together; she built relationships with people who had very different views but whom she realized were just as committed to providing all children with the kind of education they deserved; and she came to see that dialogue and negotiation with those people could create a transformative vision that stretched beyond her own views. She said, "By letting go of our animosities and ideological agendas, we were able to imagine a future for

K–12 education that would serve all of America's children."[9] She gave herself—and the conflict—time to breathe, refocus, and build something new and bold.

OPENING MORE DOORS

It's become rare that many of us see conflict as an opportunity, but in a surprisingly wide set of circumstances, engaging on conflict can be a doorway to achieving not-otherwise-possible results. Conflict is not only normal and necessary among human beings; it's also an opportunity to learn and grow.

Engaging with conflicting views forces us to grapple with new facts and perspectives we may have never considered before or begin to see them in a new light. None of us has full knowledge of all the possible factors and perspectives underlying any difference of opinion.

Embracing conflict often opens the door wide enough, even if just a crack, to find ways to create solutions even as major disagreements in worldview remain intact. Think back to the discussion in Chapter 1, "Why Solve Problems Together?" about Carla Willis's experience working on Health Care Coverage for the Uninsured. She didn't change her interests. She just saw more ways of seeing the problem and more routes for getting to a solution.

For those who seek to be collaborative problem-solvers, welcoming and understanding conflict has another practical value. In our experience, when conflict is swept under the rug in the interests of short-term agreement and collegiality, it may well come back later to haunt the participants. Eventually the conflict will resurface and likely unravel the earlier agreement. An unaddressed conflict can fracture a fragile peace and any trust built between participants. The story of the Constitutional Convention is inspiring to many, but we cannot and should not ever forget that the delegates did leave one very big issue unaddressed by allowing each state to decide whether it was legal for its residents to enslave people. By placing this great moral issue outside the scope of the national government, they set the country on the path to the Civil War.

During the Education Reimagined project, Gisèle chose to see conflict as a doorway. For many years prior, she'd been an outspoken critic of teachers' unions. She wasn't in the habit of asking the leaders of teachers' unions for their thoughts, and the leaders of teachers' unions weren't in the habit of asking for her thoughts either. They imagined that they didn't agree on anything much about what was wrong with education. But once the group was invited to imagine that anything was possible, they started a sustained dialogue that lasted about 18 months and has continued since then in a new organization that the stakeholders created so they could keep working together for their shared goals over the long term.

As their dialogue unfolded, Gisèle and her counterparts from the teachers' unions were surprised to learn that, despite their oft-conflicting views, they agreed on quite a lot. When they started to broaden their perspectives, giving themselves the breathing space to take in other points of view, they found that, together, their differing views and experiences could contribute to a far more creative and compelling vision for the future of K–12 education than they had before they started to talk with each other.[10] And because this vision was shared across a variety of advocates and organizations, it was stronger. It had more champions, more people committed to translating their dialogue into action. Reflecting back, Gisèle says, "I can't stress enough the importance of overcoming ideological barriers to reach a shared goal."[11]

When the initial dialogue on education concluded, one of the teachers' union representatives who took part lamented that she was losing a vital forum for the warm, respectful, and productive exchange of views. Sitting in her usual professional circles and mainly talking with people who shared her educational worldview had failed to provide the frank and honest critiques that she had come to value in the Education Reimagined project. Nowhere else could she share with, and learn so readily from, people who operated from assumptions and experiences different from her own. Her understanding of the issues and possible solutions had been greatly enhanced by hearing perspectives that made her think afresh.

Such positive experiences start by having a mindset that conflict can be a force of creativity. Reframing conflict as something that can be positive is a cornerstone of being an effective collaborative problem-solver.

CHAPTER 4

Everyone Gets the Benefit
of the Doubt

A thousand years ago, the philosopher Moses ben Maimon (Maimonides), who served as judge to Cairo's Jewish community as well as physician to the ruling Muslim court, considered how best to weigh the words and deeds of the diverse people he met in his daily work. "Judge every man to the side of merit," he started, quoting an oft-debated line from the Talmud. "This refers to when you are unsure about a certain individual, whether or not he is righteous or wicked, and you witness him doing an act or saying something that may be interpreted as either good or bad. In such a case, judge favorably and do not think he is doing something wrong."[1] When you don't know the person, he said, judging favorably is always the right course.

Maimonides had a reputation, even in his day, for espousing controversial ideas, and it's quite possible that some of his neighbors and colleagues dismissed his approach out of hand. Those within his own religious enclave would have known that his family had been forced to flee Spain after the invading Berber caliphs told non-Muslims they must convert or leave—or face death. His family had wandered for nearly 20 years before settling in Egypt.[2] How could he set aside all those years of persecution, hardship, and opposition? How could he give everyone, even Cairo's Muslim rulers, the benefit of the doubt?

For Maimonides, however, there was only one justification for skepticism: if someone is widely known for repeatedly harming others, it's natural to be cautious, he explained—to be alert to the possibility of bad intentions but still to approach the situation with a fair mind. We should seek out the good in everyone, because in doing so, we'll encourage everyone—ourselves included—to treat each other with respect and to live well, side by side.

Once you've started to see conflict as something that can be constructive, the next step is to extend the benefit of the doubt to others—starting with the belief that, like you, everyone around the table wants to solve the problem, not make it worse. Giving the benefit of the doubt requires a generosity of spirit. It's making every effort to hold others in positive regard. And what a difference it makes.

FIND THE GOOD

Too often, we assume we know other people's motives, especially when we consider them our adversaries. Too often, we don't have a grasp of the work or life experiences that have led people to see things the way they do. And far too often, we get caught up in systems that bring out our worst competitive, "survival of the fittest" instincts, and we're unable to see each other's underlying decency and laudable intentions because we're so ready for a fight. When we assume those with whom we disagree are nefarious or ill-intentioned, it's rarely possible to find shared solutions to problems with them. We become invested in our belief that we're right and anyone on the other side is wrong.

But, as Maimonides gleaned, very few people get up in the morning wondering, *How can I make the world a worse place today?* Most people, most of the time, do what they believe is best.

Of course, some people do some things that are not kind, ethical, or productive. When this is intentional, you may decide that it's not possible to engage with them. Generally, however, people don't do these things out of malice; they're not intending to harm you or make matters worse. Instead, they probably have a different view of the situation and don't understand that their actions or words have a negative impact. They're just doing what seems right and good according to their worldview and circumstances. That doesn't make them horrible people with horrible motives.

That makes them human.

To solve a problem with other people, it's essential to find and connect with the goodness in them, to think of them as fellow problem-solvers, even when their ideas for resolving an issue diverge from your own.

For most of us, finding the good in everyone isn't our default state of mind. Psychologists have studied the ways in which people view actions depending on whether they're the person acting or they're the person on the receiving end. We're prone to viewing our own misdeeds through the lens of the situation we're caught up in—that is, some external irritant has blocked our good intentions—while viewing the misdeeds of others through the lens of their character—imagining, in someone else's case, that they're personally and purposefully to blame. For example, if you snap at someone, you're more likely to attribute your behavior to being stressed out at work rather than to you inherently being a mean person. If someone snaps at you, you're more likely to think they're a jerk, especially if they're someone you're already in conflict with. Psychologists call this the *fundamental attribution error*.[3]

Note that this is an *error*; it's a mistake to think we're always kept from doing the right thing by outside forces while other people are doing the wrong thing because that's their nature. To correct the error, you have to take a moment to put yourself in the other person's shoes. For example, if someone snaps at you, you might immediately think they're a jerk, then pause to remind yourself that you sometimes snap at people when you're really stressed out at work, saying to yourself, *Maybe they're just under a lot of pressure with work today.*

When we're feeling under threat, as often happens in contentious conflicts, we tend to be guided by negative thoughts. Our brains jump to memories of unpleasant or harmful interactions, even when we've had just as many—or more—neutral or positive experiences that we could use as the frame of reference for understanding the situation we're in. In other words, when people disagree about how to do things, they tend to come to the table carrying a heavy load of negative experiences and assumptions. They think of other people as adversaries, other ideas as wrongheaded, and the potential to find a shared solution as a long shot, blind to the irony that this sort of pessimism can often be one of the biggest roadblocks to forging a solution.

WIDEN YOUR VIEW

In chronic conflicts we may *catastrophize*—that is, begin to imagine that the only possible outcome will be the *worst* possible outcome, and ruminate on that narrow, dismal future.[4] We develop a story that the other side is doing what they're doing not because of some situational limitation but because they're trying to frustrate us. We then look for evidence to confirm this story and disregard any evidence that contradicts it. This further distorts our view of what's going on. It closes off our capacity to see how conflict can be constructive and makes us less likely to want to engage with other viewpoints on a problem.

You may feel that you're already embracing the mindset of giving others the benefit of the doubt, perhaps because of the teachings in your faith or because of a personal commitment to being fair-minded. But even people who do collaborative problem-solving for a living can find themselves falling into these mental traps when they're in the midst of a contentious conflict. Indeed, in every group we've worked with as collaborative problem-solvers, the human mind's readiness to jump to evidence that confirms people's biases and ignore evidence that conflicts with them has cropped up. This is why we believe it's so important to consciously and actively develop your ability to pause judgment, to consciously draw your mind to alternate ways of seeing a situation.

Science backs up our experience that people appreciate it when you give the benefit of the doubt and they repay the largesse. We like being generous to each other. *Wait, that can't be true*, we can hear you thinking. *What about the news, crime, wars?* Perhaps you've heard the term *negativity bias,* which describes the human tendency to focus more on the negative because negative things can be a threat and we're hardwired for self-protection.[5] Our heightened attention to bad news might explain why more than half of what the media reports skews wildly negative.[6] But humans are complex creatures. We also naturally pay more attention to people who are kind. At just three months of age, babies spend more time looking at a puppet character that has previously acted in a nice way than at a puppet that has acted negatively. By six months, they reach out to puppets who have a history of behaving nicely.[7]

Some of the most compelling evidence of our hardwired sense of fairness and empathy comes from a study of rhesus monkeys. When the monkeys were put in a position where they could only get food if they pulled a chain and then they learned that pulling that chain would give an electric shock to another monkey, they stopped eating rather than harming their companion. One monkey refused to pull the chain for twelve days![8] Although humans obviously aren't rhesus monkeys, most primates share similar behavioral characteristics, and we can clearly relate to how these rhesus monkeys felt.

So although people sometimes do things that aren't kind or productive, perhaps because they lack the skills to navigate conflict, we're all naturally inclined to be fair, empathetic, and compassionate. Whether we're taking care of young or older family members, shoveling snow from the sidewalk, putting our trash in garbage cans rather than littering, or stopping at stop signs, each and every day the vast majority of us do many more prosocial than antisocial things. We're fundamentally cooperative. So it isn't naïve to give people the benefit of the doubt. On the contrary, it's an evidence-based best practice.

Try It Out

When you find yourself in difficult conversations with someone on another side of a problem, ask yourself, *Why do I think they're saying this?* If your answer involves a negative description of the person's character—for example, he's such a jerk, she's so narrow-minded— take a moment to check yourself. You may be falling into the trap of the fundamental attribution error.

Challenge yourself to imagine they are acting in good faith. What experiences or circumstances might be informing their behavior or view? Which external events or forces might be shaping their perspective?

If you can, ask them to explain their actions or beliefs to you— and don't embed assumptions in your questions. Instead, name the behavior or opinion you're unsure about and ask the person to help you understand it. For example, ask, "Why do you support a border wall?" rather than "Why do you not care about people fleeing violence?"

As you listen, push yourself: don't disregard what they say that contradicts the narrative you've got in your head. Then believe their story and intentions.

If you're not in the midst of difficult conversations, you can still practice this mindset. Scan your memory for a time when you felt sure someone was up to no good only to later realize this wasn't the case. What kept you from seeing the other person's challenges and needs? How did learning about their challenges and needs reshape your understanding of their intentions?

Even when we have deep disagreements, we're more likely to find a way forward when we start by giving each other the benefit of the doubt, understanding that the other person has legitimate reasons for their views, and that those reasons are often tied to their commitments to make the world a better place. We often want similar things and disagree on exactly how to achieve them. To solve tough problems, it's helpful to recognize this reality. Assuming good intentions at the start helps people to feel more comfortable sharing the experiences that have led them to hold a view or opinion. In turn, it hastens the process of building understanding and trust among the people who have a stake in a shared issue. When you keep an open mind about others' motivations and goals, you'll find it's easier to learn what's most important to them and factor this into how you approach solving the problem together. Other people are also more likely to return the favor of suspending judgment and taking your views into account when you've given them the benefit of the doubt.

If the benefit of the doubt ultimately proves to be unwarranted, you can adjust your approach based on the facts you've gathered. But in our experience working with numerous groups, when people give each other the benefit of the doubt, they discover that they're part of a community of well-intentioned individuals.

WIDEN YOUR CIRCLE

Extending the benefit of the doubt to everyone requires widening your view of who's part of your problem-solving community. Think of everyone who has a stake in solving the problem you're tackling, including those who, in the past, you might have met with skepticism or distrust. Foster feelings of generosity both toward people with whom you've previously been at odds and toward those whose background or experience is foreign to you.

This means taking a hard look at your assumptions about people's motives and character. A lot of assumptions are typically based on the groups people belong to, or that *we think* they belong to, including assumptions based on how people look or speak. Many of our assumptions about other people are unconscious but some are built into the fabric of modern life. As we noted in Chapter 1, "Why Solve Problems Together?" Americans today often live, work, and play with people who are mostly like themselves. We're less likely to interact with people who are different and so have few opportunities to see the many ways in which we're actually pretty similar. When people see each other as more different than we really are, we can start to lump people into perilous "us" and "them" camps.

Our tendency to see the world in "us versus them" terms is a product of human evolution.[9] We seek the safety of group membership, the deep-seated knowledge that our "family" or "tribe" will protect us if we're attacked. However, group membership hasn't solely evolved to help us when we're under threat; it's also there when we need extra sets of hands to build a shelter (think of a barn raising), gather an abundance of food to weather the long winter, or care for young children.[10] For millennia, we've reached out to a wide circle of kith and kin when we need more people to help out. We can use this aspect of group bonding to help us extend the benefit of the doubt to everyone.

The key is to expand who you think of as being in "your group." That means getting out of your bubble of like-minded folks and making connections with people who see the world differently than you. This requires an openness to embrace any point of shared connection, including your shared interest in solving a problem.

For example, one of the teachers' union representatives who participated in the Education Reimagined project was Becky Pringle, then vice president and now president of the National Education Association (NEA), the largest union in the US. Like Gisèle Huff, she rose to her leadership position in the field of education from modest roots—she's "just a Black girl from North Philly," as she has often said.[11] For more than three decades, Becky taught science to middle-school students in the Susquehanna Township public schools in Harrisburg, Pennsylvania. She's been actively involved in the NEA from early in her career. She believes deeply in the central role of public education in not only serving young learners but in ensuring we have a well-grounded democracy and society. She also believes deeply in the power of teachers' unions to make schools better places—for teaching and for learning.

When Becky agreed to attend the meetings for Education Reimagined, she, like Gisèle, didn't think much would come of it. She'd scanned the list of participants and recognized many of the names—some she'd only ever engaged with in adversarial debates, others who had regularly attacked teachers' unions as being the root of all problems in American education. She knew Gisèle's reputation for opposing unions. Becky felt that many of these opponents thought they knew what the NEA stood for, but, to her eyes, they didn't.

So Becky's main objective going into the project was to educate others about the NEA's mission—"our commitment to kids, our commitment to excellence, our commitment to building and sustaining a system that prepares every single student, and supporting those people who have dedicated their lives to educating every student." This was a challenge, she said. "Whether they were [or not], would I view them as allies, or having like-minded thinking, or not?" She felt skeptical but committed to seeing them as allies unless they proved her wrong.

There were rough patches, when she thought attending the meetings might not be a good use of her or the NEA's time. Here was Gisèle, a long-time proponent of vouchers and charter schools, talking about replacing teachers with technology. Becky had long considered vouchers to be a red line she'd never cross, because she believes they undermine the vitality of America's education system and leave behind the children who depend on public schools. How could she trust a partner who had once advocated so strongly for them?

A breakthrough came when the participants were asked to set aside old arguments and grievances about what wasn't working in the current education system and their own ideas for fixing schools and instead focus on a vision for K–12 education. The group facilitator asked the participants to put together skits portraying an ideal day in the life of a learner 25 years in the future. As they watched each other perform, they found that they all were envisioning a world where students are empowered to have more choice over what and how they're learning, with teachers providing guidance, balance, and exposure to content beyond students' chosen interests. These skits and other interactions made clear they had a core goal on which they agreed—creating schools where students' individual needs played a central role in shaping teaching decisions. This also helped them to enjoy each other's ideas, and reduce if not eliminate their doubts and fears about each other.

Becky's and Gisèle's experiences with Education Reimagined aren't unique. Time and again, when we've helped to bring groups together to tackle a tough issue, we've watched as people who thought they'd never, ever be able to talk civilly discover they have more in common than they'd imagined and—gasp!—even *like* each other. They learn from each other. They bounce ideas off each other as sounding boards and confidantes. They grow to become friends through collaborating while also disagreeing. Our former colleague Russell Krumnow at Convergence Center for Policy Resolution calls these "friendly surprises," because supposed foes become friends and fellow travelers. Friendly surprises reveal the fruitfulness of giving one another the benefit of the doubt: when you park your negative assumptions, you create space for both friendship and problem-solving.

THE BENEFIT OF MINDS MEETING

Michael Sodini took charge of the family business, gun company Eagle Imports, Inc., back in 2006. He hadn't planned to have a career in the firearms industry. He'd spent time working as a model and a real estate marketer.[12] But the family business was something he knew, and it let him be close to home. His uncle was president of the company when he joined, but a few years later, the uncle passed away. The person who stepped into the leadership, a friend, had personal struggles and died by suicide, using a firearm.[13] That's when Michael became president.

This tragedy hit Michael hard, but he also had a business to run. Eagle Imports was one of the largest gun import companies in the country.

By 2018, business was booming. One night, after Michael and his national sales manager had closed a big deal in New Orleans, they went out for a nice meal to celebrate. There was a woman dining alone at the restaurant and they decided to invite her to join them. As Michael recalled, "She sits down and, of course, when you sit down with two people from the gun industry, you've got fifty million questions, right? It makes sense. I have those same questions."

Over the previous decade, with the memory of his friend's death etched in his mind, Michael had noted with sadness the loss of life across the gun community. Troublingly, the rate of death by suicide among current and former members of the military and law enforcement was increasing. Nearly 70% of first responders who died by suicide had died by using a firearm, a much higher percentage than in the general population.[14]

Just as troublingly, mass shootings were increasing, too. In 2017, 60 people had been killed and more than 800 injured at the Route 91 Harvest musical festival in Las Vegas. Twenty-six people were killed and 22 injured at the First Baptist Church in Sutherland Springs, Texas. On Valentine's Day 2018, 14 students and three staff members were killed at Marjory Stoneman Douglas High School in Parkland, Florida; 17 were injured in that mass shooting.

Michael's dinner guest said she wasn't completely opposed to guns but the rise in mass shootings troubled her. She felt as though nothing was being done to make these crimes less likely. "What happens when there's a mass shooting?" Michael remembers her gently challenging him. He confessed that gun control advocates blame guns and the gun community blames mental health, "and then nothing ever happens."

Looking back on that moment, Michael says, "She asked one question and completely changed my life." All because a total stranger engaged with him in a difficult conversation about guns and neither of them walked away. After that conversation, Michael contemplated what could be done and, more importantly, what he could personally do.

Michael could see that supporting people's mental health was critical to ensuring fewer people were killed through the use of firearms. His national sales director suggested that, for every gun sold, they donate a dollar to mental health projects, and said he was sure others in the industry would donate, too. Michael liked the idea, but would any organizations working on mental health be receptive to hearing from a gun company, let alone accepting money from one?

By July 2018, he'd spent days researching mental health and gun violence, learning that only 5% of people with mental health issues are violent toward others.[15] "The knock-out punch," he said, was realizing the stigma "put on mental health is just as bad as the one put on the firearms industry." He believed that if organizations supporting mental health would be willing to talk with the gun community, they could work to provide funding for education, preventive services, and other outreach that would save lives. He began to set up a not-for-profit, Walk the Talk America, to address the misconceptions around both mental health and gun ownership. And then, before it was even incorporated, he emailed several of the top people working in the field of mental health to see if they'd be willing to collaborate, stating outright in his letter that he knew the gun industry didn't have a track record of supporting mental health initiatives. Two days later, the chief social impact officer at Mental Health America wrote back to invite him to meet. The benefit of the doubt extended both ways.

Michael goes into every conversation about guns fully committed to giving the other person the benefit of the doubt. They might not budge a bit. They might leave still saying they want to ban all guns. They might say they blame everyone in the firearms industry, including him, for gun violence. But he reminds himself that they have something in common with him: they "don't want people to die. That's it."

Of course, one need not continue to extend the benefit of the doubt to those who prove to be unworthy of it over time. But before withdrawing your generosity of thought, it's useful to reflect very hard on your own feelings and assumptions to ensure that the issue isn't a conflict-stoked inability to understand the other person's perspective or needs. Imagine the gains to be realized when the benefit of the doubt is extended openly and authentically. It can blossom into multiple positive relationships and achievements that could only have been accomplished by taking the initial risk to trust people on the other side of the issue.

Finally, there's a large body of evidence that all types of human behavior are contagious, with some studies suggesting that generosity is especially contagious.[16] So take the risk and give other people the benefit of the doubt. Our experience—and science—argue that they're likely to return the favor. We may not be able to bridge all, or even most, of our differences, but by opening up to each other, we can create room for some meeting of minds to occur.

CHAPTER 5

Curiosity Is the Cure

We've discussed the value of recognizing that conflict can be constructive and the advantages of giving others the benefit of the doubt. It's not always easy to practice these mindsets. Many if not most of us have to work hard to see conflict as a positive and people on the other side of an issue as having intentions as good as our own. The best way to cure our instinctual pessimism, doubts we have about others, and fear of threats is to practice being curious.

For most of us, curiosity comes easily—that is, it comes easily when we're eager to learn more about something we want to understand. When we're internally motivated to know the answer to a question, it's a pleasure to seek out unknown information.

It's harder to be curious in the presence of conflict, particularly with people who push our buttons. When we feel even slightly threatened, we must make an active choice to be curious—to seek information about unfamiliar or seemingly alien people, their feelings, their concerns, and their motivations.

Yet being curious is necessary if you want to solve problems. Curiosity allows you to learn about and see other people's perspectives, which in turn creates the understanding, empathy, and insight necessary for problem-solving. If we treat other people as though they're irrational, selfish, or stupid, they aren't going to engage in problem-solving with us; we need to understand why their story makes as much sense to them as our story makes to us. Understanding their story helps to reduce our feeling that they're trying to obstruct us, further encouraging everyone to engage in addressing our issues hand in hand. Not only is this a kind and respectful thing to do, but it also helps us to figure out what others need in order to consider a problem to have been resolved.

That's why we recommend you practice curiosity regularly, and especially when you don't feel like doing so.

Better yet, curiosity breeds curiosity. As you ask others about themselves and they sense you're starting to understand their point of view, they'll likely ask about you and how you see things. Your newfound wealth of wisdom and understanding about each other will put you in a better position to resolve tough problems amicably and wisely.

ASK MORE QUESTIONS

In her wonderful book *I Never Thought of It That Way*, veteran journalist Mónica Guzmán describes all the barriers that seem to divide people and how we typically think we might break down these barriers.[1] We imagine, she says, that getting other people to hear and see more "trustworthy" information will do the trick, forgetting that we each tend to trust our usual sources of information and distrust those frequented by people on the opposite side of an issue. We believe that, armed with the "right" information, we can persuade the "misinformed" to agree with us, forgetting that we're all susceptible to mental shortcuts like the *confirmation bias*, where we unconsciously gravitate toward stories and data that confirm our beliefs and disregard those that challenge us.[2] We may daydream that we could simply stop spending the time and effort trying to work with people we disagree with and just push our solutions forward without them, pretending that we don't live in the same community and country.

While you might have some success, some of the time, you aren't going to build durable solutions by approaching others (or avoiding them!) in these ways. Instead, Guzmán argues, "What we need are more questions."[3]

Since 2021, Guzmán has been senior fellow for public practice at Braver Angels, a not-for-profit organization committed to bringing together Americans who disagree so they can ask questions and get to know each other better, as real people rather than caricatures. "Nothing busts through walls we've built between us like a question so genuine and perceptive it cannot be denied," writes Guzmán.[4]

She says the one big question to ask, as often as you can, is "What am I missing?"[5] We all need to ask this question more frequently, and then listen.

LISTEN WITH INTENTION

It's hard to overstate the value of just listening—actually listening, intently, actively, and with respect. While there are no silver bullets when it comes to resolving contentious issues, listening is as close as it gets. A good curious, perceptive question is grounded in good listening.

You don't need to be a trained expert in listening—like a counselor or therapist—to reap the benefits. What you need is a mindset that the purpose of listening is *to listen*, not to persuade. The goal is to achieve *understanding*, not agreement. That's a big shift in approach for many people, particularly for those who have spent years working in a field like sales, marketing, or politics. In these professions, as well as many others, the point of listening is to gather information so you can pitch your product, idea, or candidacy to a person and convert them into a customer or supporter. This form of listening risks making people feel as though their disclosures are being exploited.

To be a collaborative problem-solver, it is helpful to recognize and respect the importance of identifying and meeting basic human needs. Being heard is a basic human need. When someone is truly heard—that is, not when the listener agrees with them but when the listener shows that they really understand the other person's concerns, fears, and needs—it can break down longstanding barriers to resolving conflict.

Being understood can shift people from focusing on being right or winning to focusing on finding a path forward. Sometimes, listening closely, in and of itself, is enough to resolve a conflict. A mutually acceptable solution suddenly becomes clear, or it turns out that just being understood is enough.

Many books have been written on the power of listening and how to do it well, so we won't retread that ground. Listening closely and attentively to others is often referred to as *active listening* or *deep listening*, and we'll use both terms in this book. If you'd like to take a deep dive into deep listening, you can find many resources in print and online, but you can gain a lot by following just four key tips:

1. Quiet your mind.
2. Listen for the heart of the message.
3. Confirm you've got it right.
4. Practice makes perfect.

Quiet Your Mind

Listening well is harder than it sounds, and it's especially hard when you're broaching a topic you have strong feelings about. So you need to prepare yourself first.

People with a practiced listening mindset quiet their mind so they're fully present while listening. Whatever helps you to quiet your thoughts and feelings will work. You want to stop the flow of your own stream of thoughts and let your mind rest peacefully. Some people work out, spend a minute or so taking deep breaths, or express their thoughts and feelings by writing or doodling in a notebook in the lead-up to difficult conversations. For some people, the practice of meditation or mindfulness is very helpful. While it helps to prepare yourself close to the time of a difficult conversation, it's even better to do this on a regular basis, because we don't always have the luxury of knowing when those conversations are going to happen.

Listen for the Heart of the Message

There's a common misconception that most human communication is verbal and directly stated. In fact, many of our thoughts and feelings are communicated nonverbally, through our gestures, body language, tone of voice, and emotional expressions.[6]

We also tend to assume that people are telling us the most important information when this is often not the case. People usually share facts, data, and demands because those things are more comfortable to talk about. They're more hesitant to reveal their feelings, fears, and needs—the information you most need to understand the person, particularly when you're in the midst of conflict. So it's important to go slowly and ask multiple open-ended questions to draw out the speaker's core concerns.

Many of the changes that happen in the body when we're feeling an emotion are similar from person to person. So the "Try It Out" in Chapter 3, "Conflict Can Be Constructive," that helps you notice your emotions and stay present can also help you recognize reactions in other people. For example, if a red-faced person with arms crossed hisses at you through clenched teeth that they're perfectly fine with something you've done, then you can deduce that the person is angry, and probably hurt, too, about what you did. Is the person's voice raised? Are they slumped or looking down? Are they trembling in fear? Use nonverbal communication clues, and a sense for your own feelings, to uncover the heart of their message behind their words.

Confirm You've Heard It Right

The active listening tool that gets parodied most often is *reflection*. In its simplest form, this is when you parrot back what people say to you. Reflection gets parodied because it can feel awkward and weird. It probably feels that way to you, and you're right to feel that way: parroting back everything someone says to you *is* weird and awkward. However, it's incredibly effective to reflect back, not word by word everything that was said, but rather the heart of the message—the feelings, needs, and concerns that you're observing through your deep listening.[7]

For those who seek to solve problems collaboratively, developing an ability to stay curious is invaluable. Employing reactions like "Tell me more," "Can you clarify what you mean?" and "I normally don't think about it that way, can you help me understand?" invites people to move from defensiveness to explaining their viewpoint, experiences, and motivations—the stuff that will help everyone move forward.

Another effective way to encourage open conversation is to repeat back parts of what the person has told you, in their own words, to confirm that you've heard the heart of their message. Briefly and thoughtfully sum up the feelings, needs, concerns, and goals that you've heard them express, then ask, "Did I get that right?" Once you've listened to their answer, ask, "Is there more you can share about that? I'd like to hear more."

Try It Out

Especially in conflict, it's easy to miss or misread the true messages being shared. The confirmation bias means we're primed to hear what we expect and ignore everything else. So it's essential to confirm that you've got the right message. Briefly summarize what you think you've heard and then ask, "Did I get that right?" and "Is there more you can share about that?"

These two simple questions are incredibly effective. You might even make a note of them on your phone memos app or a piece of paper tucked into your wallet, and revisit that note before entering conversations about tough problems.

Practice Makes Perfect

You'll likely find it useful to practice being curious. Practice with trusted friends, family, and co-workers—the sorts of people with whom you might have occasional conflicts that you're able to resolve day to day. We recommend not mentioning that you're practicing curiosity and deep listening skills. Just go for it. Their reaction will tell you whether they're feeling heard or not.

After reflecting back a few times, asking if you've got it right and inviting them to tell you more about something, the person will usually become more relaxed. Speakers in conflict often begin in the throes of emotion, speaking loudly, forcefully, and rapidly if angry, or very quietly and hesitantly if sad. Once they feel heard, they become calmer. Their pace and tone return to normal, and their body often visibly relaxes. Sometimes there are tears of relief. And as they feel heard, they'll usually start sharing deeper thoughts and feelings, including concerns and needs they might have been keeping from you, out of self-protection or embarrassment.

Eventually—though this may only happen after a few conversations— they may start to get more actively curious about your perspective, asking you if they've got it right and inviting you to tell them more about your thoughts and feelings about some matter. People can pick up the habits of deep listening through the act of conversation with deep listeners.

NO ONE HAS A MONOPOLY ON GOOD IDEAS

Deep listening is the groundwork for developing durable solutions to tough problems. That's because, to resolve longstanding, contentious issues, you need to identify solutions that allow all sides to get at least some of their most important needs and concerns addressed. If there isn't something in it for everyone, the folks who don't get their needs met will keep fighting the issue, one way or another.

Through deep listening, the people who have gathered to solve a problem come to understand one another's experiences, fears, principles, and perspectives. Even in cases where an issue cannot be resolved in a mutually acceptable manner, calmly taking in each other's point of view ordinarily increases mutual respect and lowers the temperature of any disagreement.

More important, however, listening allows you to see more aspects of the problem and more possible solutions, including issues and options that you aren't aware of. No one "side" in a dispute is always right or knows everything. No matter how brilliant, insightful, or decent someone is, no one person, organization, or political party has a monopoly on good ideas. That's why the Convergence Center for Policy Resolution and others in the field are dedicated to bringing together people with a range of viewpoints on an issue and giving them an opportunity to understand one another.

Convergence's work on the challenges of guns and death by suicide demonstrates the power of curiosity. In 2021, Convergence brought together a diverse group of leaders in light of research finding that 30,177 active-duty personnel and veterans who served in the military after 9/11 had, to date, died by suicide, compared with 7,057 service members killed in combat over the span of the same 20 years.[8] Michael Sodini from Eagle Imports and Walk the Talk America was at the table. So too was Sherry Davis Molock, associate professor of clinical psychology at George Washington University in Washington, DC. Sherry does research to develop ways to prevent suicide, particularly among Black young adults and youth through faith-based communities.

When Sherry was first approached about the project, she wasn't interested. Her first thought was, "Guns are bad." From her point of view, the easiest way to prevent death by suicide was to remove guns from the equation. From her perspective, the data were clear: countries with low gun usage and ownership had lower rates of death by suicide. She didn't understand why people insisted on having guns at home.

But when she thought about the invitation some more, she decided to take part. She knew the power of asking questions and gaining a better understanding of other people's perspectives. "Research is what I'm known for," she recalled.

There were people in the group who had lost a loved one to suicide using a firearm. There were also gun advocates. And there were people, like Michael Sodini, who fell into both groups. In listening to their stories, some of which conflicted with what she thought she knew, Sherry was able to see why some people opposed things she had thought were obvious solutions.

For example, she remembers being shocked to hear how protective orders work in the real world. These orders are issued when health or law enforcement authorities have identified someone as being in a mental health crisis, when they're at high risk of self-harm; the orders allow the authorities to remove weapons from the person's home. However, as Sherry heard from members of the group, in some cases protective orders become a lifelong punishment and stigma for being in crisis. "I didn't know that people could come and get your firearms and keep them forever. I didn't know that it was a record that could be used against you later. I thought people go get the gun, they store them safely, and when you're better, you can get it back." It made more sense why people resisted them.

A pivotal moment came for her when gun advocate and instructor Rob Pincus gave the participants a virtual tour of his gun collection. Pincus is the author of *Defend Yourself: A Comprehensive Security Plan for the Armed Homeowner* and a member of the board of Walk the Talk America. He's a strong believer in people's right to bear arms and in ensuring owners are trained to use their guns safely and appropriately. His gun collection is extensive, and he proudly pointed out the uses and strengths of the various firearms to the participants. Thinking back on it, Sherry still gets emotional. "For me, that was very scary; it felt really unsafe."

When Rob Pincus finished his presentation, Sherry had a choice: sit with her fear, or quiet her mind enough to ask questions. She recognized that some stereotypes were playing across her mind: here was a middle-aged White man with a bald head who owned what she perceived to be an "arsenal" of guns. She felt in her gut that if a Black man showed off a similar collection, people wouldn't applaud, like many of the roundtable participants had done. She thought about it and chose to share her reaction.

Pincus listened and acknowledged Sherry's reaction and feelings. That put Sherry more at ease, so she asked a curious question: "Why would you have all that kind of stuff? What are you getting out of having that many?"

His answer surprised her: "It's fun."

Over the years she'd tried to imagine why people want to own guns, and she'd come up with many ideas, but that answer had never crossed her mind. She wanted to learn more. In addition, she felt he'd really heard her when she said that if he were Black, like her, he'd be treated differently for owning so many guns.

No one person or group can possibly have considered all the different angles or all the relevant facts that might contribute to an effective resolution of a challenging issue. Spending time with gun advocates and asking them questions, she said, had opened her eyes. "I think it's probably one of the most meaningful things I've done in my adult life," she said. "There were just so many things I learned that I would not have learned by reading." Having curiosity-driven interactions defused tensions, built bonds, and allowed the group to come up with strategies that could be embraced by gun advocates and mental health advocates alike.

Many scientific studies support our experience that diverse groups produce wiser outcomes because they incorporate a wider range of views. It may also be that diversity drives curiosity. For example, a group of researchers across the Kellogg School of Management, Brigham Young University, and Stanford found that socially different group members do more than simply introduce new viewpoints or approaches; they also outperform groups where members think alike. The study found that diverse groups did better than more homogeneous groups both because they were able to harness a greater range of new ideas and because their differences triggered more careful information processing than in homogeneous groups.[9]

SEEING THINGS DIFFERENTLY

There may not always be the time or the interest to engage collaboratively with other points of view, but no matter the circumstances, there are always new facts and perspectives that can round out what we understand about the causes of tough problems and possible solutions. Realizing that there's knowledge and experience to be gained from people who see things differently can help prompt people's desire to be curious, learn more, and explore new ideas. Studies have found that when people are curious, they're more willing and able to tolerate uncertainty and embrace unconventional thinking.[10]

This doesn't mean you must accept an opposing point of view as being factual, or that you must agree with it. You simply need to see that it's part of the universe of concerns and needs attached to the problem.

Even if you're bristling or quaking inside in reaction to what you perceive to be bad motives or unfounded biases, getting curious about others can offer a doorway out of sustained conflict. If you allow yourself to stay open to learning new things, you'll probably learn something new, and this may uncover a shared need or concern, providing an avenue for tackling part of the problem with your perceived adversary. And if the response to your curiosity reinforces your worst fears about how unreasonable or dishonest the other person may be, you're no worse off than when you started. Indeed, if you find you're unalterably opposed, you may still learn something new that allows you to strengthen the argument for how you see the world. At a minimum, both parties can feel more assured that they're not jumping to conclusions about each other's needs, concerns, motivations, and beliefs.

More often than not, however, you'll leave the conversation enriched by a more interesting and nuanced view of the problem and maybe, just maybe, you'll have started down the path to developing mutually beneficial solutions with a new friend.

CHAPTER **6**

Relationships at the Core

On July 6, 2016, Philando Castile was killed by a police officer during a traffic stop in Falcon Heights, Minnesota, a small city bordering the state capital, Saint Paul. Castile's girlfriend, Diamond Reynolds, and her young daughter were in the car at the time. Moments after the shooting, while still in shock, terrified, and upset, with her boyfriend bleeding next to her, Reynolds shared a live video stream on Facebook. The video gained national attention.

In the wake of the shooting, emotions in the community were raw. The next several city council meetings in Falcon Heights were overwhelmed by concerned citizens, many of them frustrated and furious. They demanded that the existing contract for policing services from a neighboring town's police department be scrapped. The mayor and the city council, feeling ill-equipped to productively address people's anger, abruptly called a heated council meeting to a halt.

Among the people demanding answers and actions was John Thompson, a close friend of Castile's. He left the meeting aghast and seething. He felt that no one cared about his friend's death or was interested in changing the way traffic stops were handled so people wouldn't die unnecessarily in the future.

The community leaders in Falcon Heights hadn't intended to stir up emotions, but by ending the meeting that night, they'd made people angrier, and they'd made it harder to forge a way forward. When they realized their mistake, they set out to invite members of the community to join a new task force on inclusion and policing. As a first step, they asked the Minnesota Office of Collaboration and Dispute Resolution, along with partners including the Center for Integrative

Leadership at the University of Minnesota, the Dispute Resolution Institute at Mitchell Hamline School of Law, and Metropolitan State University, to design and facilitate the task force meetings and a series of wider community conversations.

A task force and "community conversations" might sound like a weak response—talking instead of acting in the face of a tragic death. But the conversations opened the door to new relationships, and putting relationships at the core of their response allowed Falcon Heights to address the issues with policing and begin to think about how the city could become a better community for all.

PEOPLE BEFORE PROPOSALS

Most of us respond to conflict by focusing on solutions first. We think about how to marshal facts and allies so we can prevail in seeing our preferred solution implemented as soon as possible. But in many situations, a "fix things first" mindset doesn't lead to a durable solution. It just leaves some of the parties—the people whose facts and allies weren't enough to sway the day—spoiling for a chance to get their proposals enacted in the future. And the problem remains.

As soon as she heard about Philando Castile's death, Melanie Leehy knew she had to be involved in how Falcon Heights addressed the aftermath. An ordained minister, she'd moved to Falcon Heights in 2005 and remembered what it had felt like to be one of a handful of African American families living in the city. She recognized that the city was becoming more diverse year by year and she was already leading a volunteer group to help make the city feel welcoming to everyone who chose to make a home there. The morning after the shooting, she'd immediately picked up the phone to try to reach the mayor or city staff. When she wasn't able to get through, she'd made her way to City Hall. "I'm here to do what I can. I'm here to serve" was her guiding principle.

Because of her extensive professional and personal experience, Melanie was invited to serve as co-chair of the task force set up after the city council meetings had unraveled. When city leaders suggested that another person of color be named as the second co-chair alongside her, she was steadfast in pushing back: she believed the task force co-chairs needed to embody different perspectives. Ideally, she thought, someone from the city council would come on board. That would demonstrate the city's commitment to the task force's work as it evolved.

Revising the policing contract, rethinking policies around traffic stops, and requiring police officers serving Falcon Heights to go through regular racial equity training were potentially useful changes. They might even be quick to implement, and some people in Falcon Heights were impatient to get things fixed, fast. But Melanie knew that those sorts of changes, enacted in a vacuum, could also divide their community. For example, some residents felt that Falcon Heights needed a police force that would aggressively stop drivers who were speeding near the local elementary school; in fact, that had been the most heated issue of debate at city council meetings before the evening of Castile's death. Telling officers that the city had zero tolerance for race-based traffic stops might encourage them to avoid stopping anyone, including people who were speeding in the school zone. This could easily lead to increasing conflict over the city's policing and priorities.

What they needed as a community weren't immediate policy changes. It wasn't about winning one fight in a way that started another. Instead, what they needed was a way to make more connections between people in and across Falcon Heights. They needed to create a tighter sense of community. They needed relationships.

Melanie and Falcon Heights mayor Peter Lindstrom felt it was vital to have John Thompson take part in the task force's community conversations. Having someone who was both a friend of Castile's and a vocal participant in the protests and initial city council meetings would ensure the community was hearing the full range of voices with a stake in making life safer and more welcoming. Thompson was skeptical at first. "I never wanted to come," he said. "I thought the city was just checking a box." But Melanie and the mayor kept calling him and finally Thompson agreed. "I was seated at a table with Mayor Lindstrom. I had never talked to him before. I just yelled at him. Now I see he is crying and I realize that he is young and a new mayor," recalled Thompson. "I lost Philando and that was all I was thinking about."[1] Sitting together and talking about the shooting allowed them to see each other as human beings, each touched by Castile's death in different ways, each committed to trying to ensure that another person would not die unnecessarily.

Melanie and the other task force members had understood that the community needed to channel people's anger and animosity into empathy. That didn't mean Castile's family and friends had to forgive the officer who had fired the fatal shots; it meant setting aside blame long enough that people affected by the death could get to know each other and learn what they had in common. It meant gathering together for a concert to remember Castile and beginning the process of healing. And eventually, it meant gathering for an annual meal to celebrate the friendships forged through the community conversations and other events. In other words, they needed to build a culture of change where relationships, as much as policies or data, are central.

"I go for heart issues because that impacts the core of who you are," Melanie explained. "If you think of it in a physical sense, if you're not taking care of your heart, if you're not taking care of your core, then the rest of the extremities aren't doing well. And if someone is in a crisis situation, everything's going to rush toward their core, keeping their core warm and functioning properly. Only when the core's functioning properly can you heal the rest."

IT'S A PEOPLE PROBLEM

Whatever tough problem you're facing, it's primarily a people problem.

Of course, there are meaningful differences of opinion and belief, and these differences matter a lot to you and everyone else. But when you come across a seemingly intractable issue, it's worth checking to see whether, when people have tried to solve it in the past, they've done so focused solely on the substance and not the relationships. To solve the toughest problems, you must first get to the heart of things: the human elements.

Jonathan Haidt, a social psychologist who is Thomas Cooley Professor of Ethical Leadership at the New York University Stern School of Business, underscores how people's opinions are formed primarily through gut reactions, well before their rational minds go to work to find evidence of the correctness of these intuitions. We discussed this propensity to look for evidence that lines up with our intuitions, the confirmation bias, in the previous chapter. Haidt makes the point that, because we ordinarily have no trouble finding evidence to back up our opinions and beliefs, rational argument often doesn't lead to a meeting of minds or a cooling of antipathy. One thing Haidt says changes that dynamic is relationships. When people in opposition start to see and hear each other in new ways, the relationships of understanding and trust open new ways for people previously in opposition to see and hear each other differently. It's a side door that allows people to enter new, previously unexplored spaces where they can shift the perceptions they have about each other and the issues. People they previously discounted as possible partners for change become fellow travelers, crossing the threshold into collaboration, too.

You may be at odds with others or view them with suspicion, but you can build the basis of a relationship that moves beyond your disagreements. You can learn to appreciate each other through the things you have in common. Once you learn that you both have children the same age, or love baseball, or follow the same musical groups, or are members of the same faith, or are taking care of elderly parents, you've found the first dimension of your shared identity. Starting from these touchpoints of experience and interests, you'll be able to see each other, and your perspectives on your problem, in a new light. You're unlikely to walk in lockstep, but you'll create greater opportunities for some meeting of both hearts and minds to occur.

We can get daunted by the prospect of reconciling our differences through relationships because it can often feel emotional and messy. But if we don't think of the people around the table as our colleagues and neighbors, and potentially our friends, we can get stuck, fanning the flames of conflict rather than working together to tackle our shared problems. By putting relationships at the core of our thinking, we can lower temperatures and tensions and forge the bonds needed for solutions to last for years to come. This is what Abraham Lincoln appealed for in his first inaugural address: "We must not be enemies. Though passion may have strained, it must not break our bonds of affection. The mystic chords of memory . . . will yet swell the chorus of the Union when again touched, as surely they will be, by the better angels of our nature."[2]

We've found in this work that it's essential to seek out what you have in common and nurture relationships with a wide range of people, in both your area of conflict as well as your wider life. This is something that every aspiring problem-solver would do well to dedicate substantial personal attention to. And it can be hard. But if you put effort into relationships with people who differ from you, including those who differ with you about the solutions to a problem, you'll be far more likely to develop shared solutions that respect your differences.

Those who only know another person as an adversary will keep up their defenses and feel resistance to what others have to say. Yet it's possible, through simple exercises that help you find shared identities, to form connections that open minds and warm relations, at least a bit.

Try It Out

The Greater Good Science Center at the University of California–Berkeley brings together research on practices that can increase our sense of meaning and purpose, and in turn, our individual well-being and compassion as a society. This science-based exercise, which we've adapted from the center's resources, can help you to find shared identities with others.[3]

Think about someone in your life who is very different from you. It doesn't need to be someone with whom you have a conflict, just someone with different beliefs, goals, or experiences.

Now make a list of the things you may have in common. Do you live in the same community, or work or worship at the same place, or go to the same school? Do you like the same sports or hobbies? Do you both have children? Have you both lost a loved one who was important to you? If you don't know much about the person, imagine what you might have in common.

Next, challenge yourself to focus on the things on your list. We're all more complex than the first impression we make or the conflict we're in the midst of. You and this person very likely have shared interests, values, and identities in addition to your differences.

BREAKING BREAD

You're probably familiar with the saying "to break bread with someone." The phrase implies so much more than sitting down to a meal together, as its origins in the Bible make clear. For millennia, breaking bread has been about sharing food and friendship, being intimate and cooperating, transforming the act of providing physical sustenance into a moment of deep emotional connection.

It's fitting that the documentary about Nof Atamna-Ismaeel, the first Muslim Arab to win Israel's twist on *MasterChef*, is entitled *Breaking Bread*.[4] After winning her cooking competition, Atamna-Ismaeel founded the annual A-Sham food festival, through which pairs of Arab and Jewish chefs have gathered in Haifa to collaborate in preparing traditional regional dishes for the public as part of the 22nd Holiday of Holidays, a poignant celebration of Jewish–Arab coexistence. Atamna-Ismaeel believes that food can help to open the soul to connection in ways that conversation alone can't, even if only to help people "to see things from a different angle."[5]

Researchers have also found that you're likely to find a conversation with a stranger to be less awkward if you avoid shallow topics—like the weather—and allow yourself to be open about deeper disclosures—things like your background, family, interests, and passions. When people feel safe enough to offer comments of a personal nature, surprising friendships and connections often emerge. In a Convergence project on how to pay for long-term care for elderly persons and people with disabilities, a hard-bitten group of policy experts and advocates bonded unexpectedly as they recounted their personal experiences providing care to their relatives. At one point, there was not a dry eye in the room as one participant, known for being a policy wonk, shared his frustration at not being able to provide the care his father so sorely needed.

We underestimate how interested people are in who we are, what we've been through, and what we care about. People tend to be interested in other people, including people they disagree with. And closing yourself off from making these sorts of personal connections tends to amplify misunderstanding and increase conflict.[6]

In more intimate contexts, adopting the attitude that you're willing to sit down and break bread can be pivotal to creating connections with people when arguments are heated. In March 2011, at the height of the fight over contract terms between National Football League team owners and the players' association, the owners locked out the players, closing all training camps and shutting down all communication between coaches, team doctors, and the squads. The owners had little reason to rush into terms they didn't like, because TV broadcasters were on the hook to pay $4 billion for rights whether or not any games were played in the calendar year. The players were up in arms, as were retired pros who knew their healthcare plan and other retirement benefits depended on a full season of play. Emotions were running high when a judge ordered both sides to mediate their way to a solution.

The two sides began to find a way forward when NFL commissioner Roger Goodell and NFL Players Association head DeMaurice Smith got together to break bread. Arthur Boylan, the mediator, "found a quiet place for the three of them to grab a bite to eat and they talked about their families and background—everything but football."[7] It was such a success that they made a regular habit of it as they worked out contract terms that satisfied both the players and the owners. According to Boylan, "The whole thing about mediation is finding common ground, even if it's something unrelated. You can find camaraderie in anything."[8] Sure, both sides wanted a profitable season, but to get there, they had to get to know each other personally and build a foundation of trust and shared understanding of each other.

There's something special about breaking bread. It may be related to the activation of the rest and digest system, which in many ways is the alter ego of our fight, flight, or freeze reaction in the face of threats. The act of eating a meal—and we do mean a meal, not a quick snack on the run—stretches the lining of your stomach, sending a signal up a bundle of nerves that runs from your gut to your brain, which responds by releasing a cascade of calming hormones. These hormones slow down our heartbeat and our breathing rate, settling us into a relaxed state.[9] On a physiological level, rest and digest gives our body the time and energy it needs to absorb nutrients and otherwise rejuvenate. On an emotional level, it gives our mind the time and energy it needs to connect with others—that is, to find the shared identities and connections that we might not see immediately.

THE GOLDEN RULE

Put another way, this chapter is about how practicing "the golden rule"—treating others as we ourselves would like to be treated—is essential to collaborative problem-solving. Too often people think that the wisdom and reach of the golden rule only applies to our personal lives, even if not perfectly practiced there. In our experience, when people practice the golden rule, they're far more likely to develop trust with each other, understanding of each other, and affection for each other. These are key accomplishments if your goal is to avoid unnecessary conflict and to find answers that authentically meet a wide range of needs. In our view, the golden rule is a good basis for anyone who wants to live in a more functional and peaceful world.

The golden rule is also highly relevant to our collaborative mindsets. Who among us wants our motives questioned or attacked? Who among us wants to be treated with disrespect? Who wants to be excluded from conversations on topics of great importance to them? We all appreciate being understood before being judged or criticized. When passions run high, applying the golden rule can help us to pause and check the impulse to berate or belittle others.

In our work over the years, it's become strikingly obvious that most people greatly prefer and are relieved to be in positive, affirming relationships rather than at odds with others. Science once again backs up our hands-on experience. In fact, beyond the fact that humans are social, arguably the most robust finding in the history of social psychology is that the single greatest contributor to our well-being is the strength of our relationships.[10] We're social animals; like wolves or elephants we need our pack or herd. Our need for belonging and relationships is a potent power when it comes to resolving conflicts. It can motivate us to make the effort to work through our differences.

If belonging and relationships are so important, why then is it so hard to form or maintain relationships with those we disagree with?

One reason may be that people need five positive interactions to balance out every single negative interaction they have. (This goes part and parcel with negativity bias, which we talked about in Chapter 4, "Everyone Gets the Benefit of the Doubt.") Psychologists John Gottman and Robert Levenson saw this in studies where they asked couples to solve a conflict in their relationship within 15 minutes and taped what ensued.[11] The couples who were able to weave five or more positive moments into the conversation were much less likely to be divorced when the researchers followed up with them nine years later.

Think about that. When you're in a contentious conflict with someone, how often do you think you achieve that "magic" five-to-one ratio?

Fortunately, these positive interactions don't have to be heroic. Gottman and Levenson included simple things like paying attention, expressing appreciation, empathizing, apologizing, taking the other person's perspective, and finding areas of agreement when they tallied up the positive interactions between the couples they observed.

Try It Out

Next time you find yourself in a disagreement, see if you can create five positive moments for every one negative moment. Afterward, take some time to reflect. Notice how the other person reacted, how you felt, and how creating many more positive moments impacted the outcome of the disagreement.

Most people long for a way to get along with others, to solve problems amicably, and to live and work in settings that have less tension and antipathy. We want to have positive, not negative, relationships, but too often we don't know how to go about it when emotions run high or strong opinions are flowing. The first step is to have the mindset that you can find a shared identity, experience, or values with anyone. As you discover other things you may share and do share with each other, you'll be more able to see that here could be the beginning of a host of beautiful friendships.

CHAPTER 7

Seek Higher Ground

Every one of the four previous mindsets we've covered—how to think about conflict, motivations, differences, and relationships with other people—provides a foundation for collaborative problem-solving. They're each invaluable to forging more amicable bonds with people with whom you may not see eye to eye, or who are new to you. But to get things done—to problem-solve—you have to push beyond being open to and building relationships with others. You need the knowledge that your problem is *shared* with others. And here it's most helpful to understand that life need not be a zero-sum game.

The concept of "common ground" often comes up in negotiations and other problem-solving efforts. Common ground can often be found by focusing just on those things where you agree and putting your differences to the side for someone else to fix some other day. Sometimes common ground can be found, but parties may still feel bothered by compromises they made in achieving it, and their commitment to the agreement over time may waiver. Finding common ground is a worthy goal, and collaborative problem-solving certainly looks to achieve it where it makes sense. But we think it's too limiting as an ambition. Unresolved differences or solutions that are not deeply satisfying to one side or another can quickly pile up to cast a long, deep shadow over what can turn out to be a temporary truce rather than a lasting meeting of minds.

Instead, the wisest and most enduring solutions come from seeking higher ground. This is where you rise to the occasion of integrating the perspectives and meeting the competing needs of everyone who has a stake in your problem, and you do so without requiring anyone to relinquish their fundamental principles or beliefs.

BEYOND SPLITTING THE DIFFERENCE

When people who aren't yet collaborative problem-solvers first hear about this approach, they may fear it inherently means making compromises that lead to uninspiring, split-the-difference solutions. While some compromises may be useful and appropriate, if they require one or more participants to swallow something deeply distasteful to them, it's far less likely that you'll accomplish durable change to resolve your differences. People will be less inclined to take the proposed path ahead with you because they'll see it as a journey that leaves them at least somewhat dissatisfied. Even if they do join in to help, they'll be less likely to put in full effort to ensure any agreements or recommendations are put into action. And over time, they may eventually renege on the agreed plan and sink back into an adversarial stance.

The solution isn't to make "compromise" a dirty word, nor is it to avoid compromise at all costs. Instead, we urge you to reject old-fashioned zero-sum thinking—that for me to win, you have to lose. Even around issues of principle, where people feel strongly that compromise isn't acceptable, mutually beneficial solutions are usually possible while also honoring issues of deep principle. This is how you seek and gain higher ground.

Having a higher ground mindset is similar to the "win/win frame of mind and heart" eloquently described by Stephen Covey as a key habit in his bestselling book *The Seven Habits of Highly Effective People*. The term "win–win" is often misconstrued to mean that everyone gets everything they want. A better way to understand win–win is to see it as an approach for creating mutual gain among affected parties. As Covey writes:

> Win/Win is a frame of mind and heart that constantly seeks mutual benefit in all human interactions. Win/Win means that agreements or solutions are mutually beneficial, mutually satisfying. With a Win/Win solution, all parties feel good about the decision and feel committed to the action plan. Win/Win sees life as a cooperative, not a competitive arena.[1]

Solutions that find higher ground integrate the views and meet the needs of the widest range of actors involved.

The very act of including more views and needs means these solutions are more durable and often also wiser. For example, imagine a dispute over whether a new park in a local community should be designed to promote natural landscapes or provide a children's playground. The higher-ground solution is a park that's full of trees and creeks *and* designed for children to play in. It's a solution that's better and more satisfying to both sides than having one side prevail. Seeking higher ground puts everyone in the business of searching for and creating answers that aim to satisfy all the interests at stake.

The goal of meeting the widest range of views and needs in the most satisfying way creates a culture of cooperation where everyone is looking out for each other. Have you explained your views and needs? Has everyone else done so? Who hasn't had their views and needs addressed? A feeling of shared investment in solutions develops.

Imagining that higher ground is possible also helps you to bring more people to the table to help you tackle an issue. Who wants to join a group in which they expect to feel pressured into agreeing with an idea or plan of action at odds with what they hold sacrosanct? You'd probably say no thanks or, if you have no choice but to go—say, because of your role at your company, school, or place of worship—you might resist taking part in any meaningful way. Some might even be tempted to throw some wrenches in the works in protest. When higher-ground solutions are your goal, you're more likely to speak and behave in ways that convey cooperation rather than competition. Fewer people will walk away from the experience feeling disappointed, angry, or spoiling for a fight.

THE VALUE OF MIND SHARE

Many people go into a conversation around a contentious conflict saying they want to find a resolution while also thinking there's no way for their interests to be served and their needs to be met by means other than their own approaches or positions. They've assumed that fixing a problem involves winning an argument in some marketplace of ideas. However, as Dawna Markova and Angie McArthur point out in their book *Collaborative Intelligence*, what's needed is a "shift from a market-share to a mind-share mindset."[2]

Once you're able to stop thinking in competitive terms, you're more likely to find higher-ground solutions to your problem. This is the difference between joining a group to share "your ideas" versus joining it to consider "our ideas." It's the difference between asking "who is right and who is wrong" versus asking "what could be possible."

We've seen this again and again in our work. In the Education Reimagined project in which education technology advocate Gisèle Huff and union leader Becky Pringle took part, many participants arrived with preconceived notions about how to fix America's K–12 schools. Some argued for greater use of computers, others for more social and emotional learning, and still others for school choice and charter schools. Each thought they had the silver bullet for the educational system. None of them did. That's because every school system and community in the US has its own unique challenges—and every learner does as well. What the group needed, instead, was an overarching solution—a vision—that could be used as a guide for deciding how approaches to transforming the K–12 experience could be most successful. "This country has been built on universal, free, quality public education," Becky reflected. "So how do we get to the quality part?"

The group stepped back and shared their own stories about the impact of education on themselves and their communities "from a place of caring and compassion and eagerness to learn" as Becky described it. They heard from Gisèle about her shock when she arrived in New York and discovered her school was mostly focused on keeping students out of trouble, from Becky about her experiences of discrimination, and from many others. After a deeply searching series of conversations, they found their higher ground in a vision of "learner-centered education." In the future they envisioned, schools and school systems begin from the belief that all children want to learn and are capable of learning, that there are many different ways to learn, and that standards and requirements that reflect society's goals for learners have to be integrated with the individual aspirations, challenges, and talents of each learner. Participants continue to believe that this vision, along with its principles of individualized, competency-based, socially grounded, experiential learning, will be a powerful improvement on our current system, where children sit in age-based classes to try to absorb information in preset, one-size-fits-all packages called courses. To create their vision of learner-centered education, the participants each had to let go of their market-share thinking and shift to a mind-share approach, asking what could be possible to make sure all children leave K–12 education with the tools, knowledge, and social skills they need for success in life, whatever path they take.

The participants in the Education Reimagined project humbly acknowledged that their proposals were a starting point to be improved upon over time, by both the people taking part in the group and others brought on board going forward. But what was remarkable was the degree of consensus on the big ideas they came up with across organizations long at odds on how to improve the education of young people. They saw the value they'd created by sharing ideas and making connections.

Their vision statement has become an enduring guide for many in setting priorities in education reform. "We ultimately developed a purpose for public education that I use to this day," Becky told us. All of the stakeholders in Education Reimagined were excited to get behind it because it served their common interest—serving kids.

RESPECT MORAL FOUNDATIONS

When you seek higher ground, you honor the reality that there may be issues of deep principle—moral, religious, or otherwise—that people feel are above and beyond the realm of compromise.

You might be thinking, *How can a book about collaboration be saying I have to defer to other people's principles?* The point isn't that you *have to* defer; it's that you aren't going to have any success trying to force others to bend on their deeply held principles, any more than someone else would have success trying to force you to do so. Understanding why people have principles they're unwilling to give up can help you as a collaborative problem-solver to find higher-ground solutions that have staying power.

It may help to take a step back and think about why moral principles are held so deeply. Social psychologist Jonathan Haidt and his colleague Jesse Graham have described five moral foundations, which, they argue, are rooted in our evolution—meaning they're hardwired into all of us, to a greater or lesser extent:

1. **Care (versus harm).** This is connected to our ability to feel—and dislike—pain being experienced by others. It takes years to raise a child to be self-sufficient, and for most of human history, it has taken a village to do it. The care foundation underlies motivations to be kind and nurturing.

2. **Fairness (versus cheating).** This is our sense of the need to keep things in balance and not unfairly advantage anyone, particularly when resources are scarce or limited. If you take more than your share, we as a group will see to it that you get short shrift in the future, to even things out. The fairness foundation drives ideas of justice, rights, and autonomy.

3. **Loyalty (versus betrayal).** This is related to our long history as tribal creatures who survived and thrived by forming coalitions (and shifting them when it benefits us). It's active anytime people think, *One for all, and all for one.* The loyalty foundation is behind the virtues of patriotism and self-sacrifice for your group.

4. **Authority (versus subversion).** This involves our deference to social hierarchy—obeying the rule of the dominant silver-backed gorilla, the chief, the monarch, or the president. The authority foundation animates the virtues of both leadership and follower-ship, including respect granted to authority figures and traditions.

5. **Sanctity (versus degradation).** This arises from our automatic reaction of disgust to pollution and contamination. It underlies religious notions of striving to live in an elevated, less carnal, more noble way and the widespread belief that the body is a temple that can be desecrated by immoral activities—an idea that's not unique to religious faiths.

While everyone is concerned with these five moral foundations, Haidt's research suggests that people who identify as liberals typically prioritize care and fairness over loyalty, authority, and sanctity, while conservatives tend to be equally attuned to all five foundations.[3] This might make it appear as though you're further apart on an issue, or lead you to think that the "other side" doesn't have much in the way of principles, but the opposite is true: it isn't that people have different morals but rather that they express their principles and priorities in different ways with different weights.

Whenever you're having a hard time understanding someone's perspective and priorities, remind yourself of these shared moral foundations, dig deeper to understand the other side's principles, and then think about the ways in which you're both looking out for your community—just in slightly different ways. This will help you to see that higher ground is possible and allow you to return to working on a set of solutions that can satisfy as many principles and people as possible.

Try It Out

Think of a hot political issue that is close to your heart. It could be the issue you chose for the "Try It Out" in Chapter 2, "How to Reach Convergence," or it could be something else. Which moral foundations most drive your perspective and principles around this issue?

Now think of someone on the other side of the issue. It's great if you can think of someone you know personally, possibly someone you've had disputes with. If you haven't met someone on the other side of your issue, think about some of the groups advocating for the other side. Which moral foundations do you think most drive them?

Finally, look at your two lists side by side. Where is there overlap? Where is there difference? Can you imagine some solutions that would satisfy the moral foundations important to both you and the other person or group? Push yourself to see the higher ground that you could share.

DISAGREEING ON SOME THINGS ISN'T DISAGREEING ON ALL THINGS

Morals and principles inevitably involve red lines—the boundary beyond which someone isn't willing to travel because this would trespass their most deeply held beliefs. It's important to tease out where the red lines are. Having a respectful attitude and open mind helps.

In some instances, it may seem inconceivable that you can find higher ground with those with whom you're at odds. You might even consider their views or behavior to be morally unacceptable or repugnant under your own codes of conduct. But just because you're generally at odds, that does not mean that you'll never find ways to work together. So while you could choose, on a principled basis, to avoid associating or collaborating with people whose views or behavior you find unacceptable, in the interest of solving problems, it's good to keep in mind that useful and productive agreements can be made among people with very different positions and beliefs so long as concerns and needs are shared. Meaningful higher ground can be found in important areas even where major disagreements remain around other issues, so long as those disagreements don't intrude on the areas of higher ground already found.

In 2009, Convergence kicked off a project to bring together a diverse group of people to address rising rates of diabetes and obesity in the US. Consumer advocates for healthier eating, long skeptical that major food companies cared about anything beyond profits, were concerned about the participation at the table of food company representatives, including those making products widely seen as unhealthy. One food company executive predicted trouble: he'd rarely been part of any discussion about creating healthier diets that did not end with public health advocates walking out in protest over the views and actions of the food industry.

Then, shortly before the first meeting for the project, almost on cue to stoke concerns, one of the leading consumer advocates scheduled to take part published a piece critical of "Big Food" in a medical journal. He wrote:

> It is an important time to reflect on the ways that the public and global health communities can engage with the food industry. . . . Many political bodies, foundations, and scientists believe that working collaboratively with the food industry is the path for change. The assumption is that this industry is somehow different than others, and that because people must eat, the industry is here to stay, and like it or not, working with them is the only solution.

Based on my 30 years of experience in the public health and policy sectors, I believe this position is a trap. When the history of the world's attempt to address obesity is written, the greatest failure may be collaboration with and appeasement of the food industry.[4]

The piece went on to call out a $10 million donation by soft drink makers to a Philadelphia public hospital, suggesting it was a public relations tactic meant to curry favor while the city was debating a tax on sugary drinks.

Some representatives from the food companies who were set to attend the meeting howled in protest. They were insulted by the insinuation that they couldn't be authentic and trusted partners in the goal of reducing the incidence of diabetes and obesity. One food industry participant called for the article's author to be disinvited from the project. The invitation stayed open and he attended.

Unsurprisingly, tensions ran high in the early hours of the group's first meeting. But over the next day and a half of conversation, where everyone was encouraged to set aside their assumptions and hear what others had to say, the mood in the room transformed. Representatives from food companies, including fast food companies like Burger King, expressed their strong commitment to healthier eating, citing their desire to protect the health of their own employees and reduce the costs incurred from lost workdays and medical treatments. They also talked about worries they had for their own families' health, with many having children or older relatives who had health risks related to diabetes or obesity. They were happy to acknowledge that, yes, they were looking to make a buck. But they also wanted to derive profits in a way that contributed to better nutrition and health for their customers, family, friends, and community.

Hearing—and, at least provisionally, accepting—the commitment of these food company representatives to improve public health was hugely important. It allowed the stakeholders to pivot together to work toward a principle that their work should improve public health. The central goal of the project became the joint pursuit of making healthier eating more profitable, where companies and consumer advocates could work together to increase consumer demand for healthier diets.

They saw an opportunity to create a virtuous cycle where food companies could invest even more in developing healthier food options, devote even more resources in marketing these options, and be supported by the endorsement and praise of public health advocates, rather than face the normal criticism and skepticism about their morals and motives. Importantly, the author of the article critical of the food industry, while not fully backing away from his views, conceded that in light of the meeting, he wanted to think afresh about how consumer advocates and the food industry might work together.

Finding areas of agreement in the midst of disagreement is a huge accomplishment. Sometimes, that's all that's possible. However, much more often than you would think, it's possible to find higher ground, if you set your mind to it.

THE GREATER GOOD

The collaborative mindsets we've shared in Part II of this book fly in the face of widely held worldviews. They undermine assumptions that the news often reinforces—that we live in a zero-sum world, that differences in political ideology, religion, and ethnicity are intractable, that those whose businesses have a profit motive cannot also work for a broader public interest. They contradict the notion that one side could hold the full truth. And finally, they challenge the all-too-pervasive feeling of resignation and stalemate that seems to hang over so many people, who see little or no hope in bridging divides. Too many of us have stopped believing that people with conflicting interests or differing political philosophies and worldviews can find productive ways to work with each other despite our differences.

Yet, in a surprisingly wide array of settings and circumstances, we can establish norms and practices that are likely to lead to effective cooperation and collaboration. Just as highly competitive or autocratic leaders often create cultures around them that mirror their own qualities, fostering environments of respect and civility can and does draw out people's "better angels"—the empathy, self-control, reason, and moral sense that the psychologist Steven Pinker says "orient us away from violence and toward cooperation."[5] When a group of people choose to set their sights on the North Star of higher ground, it changes the tenor and ambitions of their work together. Even when, inevitably, an individual or the group as a whole falters in meeting all of their ambitions, they're ready, willing, and able to be called back to the table because of their collaborative mindsets. Unity is acting together, not thinking alike.

It probably hasn't escaped your attention that cultivating these mindsets requires a lot from you. Like anything of such great value, it's worth the effort. We've shared some exercises that can help you turn these ways of thinking into a habit. When you've made them part of your life, you'll find it's not all work. And these mindsets aren't simply useful for collaborative problem-solving; they also confer positive effects such as widening your circle of potential friends and loved ones, feeling more optimistic, learning new things, feeling more comfortable in interpersonal conflicts, and much more.

When you're exercising your collaborative mindsets, you'll be better prepared to enter into effective dialogue across differences, no matter where they arise. In Part III, "Building Blocks," we turn to what you can do to ensure that a collaborative problem-solving mindset leads to action.

III

Building Blocks

Over the years, we've figured out some core elements that make the collaborative problem-solving process work so well. We call these elements building blocks.

Like the collaborative problem-solving mindsets of Part II, these building blocks can be applied in many contexts to many different sorts of issues. They're flexible, hands-on tools and ways of understanding and working with a group of people with divergent views. We've seen them work in dozens of cases. They've been designed to help individuals bridge divides and solve problems in ways that satisfy the widest range of needs and concerns.

The five building blocks are:

1. Map the Terrain
2. Nurture Trust
3. Really Hear Everyone
4. Generate Options for Mutual Gain
5. Take Your Time

Any one of these building blocks can prove to be helpful on its own, even when it's not possible to apply them all.

Whatever your position or role in solving a problem—whether as a formal or an informal leader in your organization, school, or community; as a policy-maker; or just as someone impacted by an ongoing conflict or failure to communicate across silos—you have the power to step into the role of collaborative problem-solver by introducing one or more of these building blocks into the way the people involved approach the issues. And we hope you will step into this role, because our communities, our nation, and the world at large need more collaborative problem-solvers.

CHAPTER 8

Map the Terrain

Understanding the full contours of an issue is the essential first step in collaborative problem-solving. Sometimes this can be quite challenging, especially when an issue feels huge and sprawling—like the question of how to improve the work of prisons and community groups to help people leaving prison succeed once they return home.

In the US, there are currently about 1.2 million people in prison.[1] Every year, about 600,000 people are released from prison and about 4 million people are on parole or probation.[2] When one also considers the family and friends of those in prison or on parole and probation, there are many millions of people affected by prison policies and programs relating to getting people fully ready for their return. One of the most discouraging aspects of America's criminal justice system is that about 40% of all those released are back in prison within three years. This contributes significantly to the already high rates of incarceration in the US compared to other countries and the attendant costs.

The intention and hope, of course, is that every individual who has served time for a crime will return to be a full member of society—not just law-abiding and productive but healthy and engaged in their community. Researchers on justice issues have found that individuals who have been given strong support for healthcare, education, and social welfare needs are better set up to remain out of prison. Ignoring the supports that are needed for reentry into society after prison creates what sociology professor William R. Kelly has called a "nearly perfect recidivism machine."[3]

In 2016, Convergence Center for Policy Resolution looked at these statistics and saw a tough, longstanding problem in need of durable solutions. But to have the best chance for success, the team at Convergence

101

first needed to identify the people and groups with a stake in the issues and what had been making it hard to improve reentry systems in the past. So the team asked: who and what might be enlisted to help create the paths needed to ensure more people in prison are ready to return to their community, and do so successfully?

EXPLORE THE STAKES AND STAKEHOLDERS

When you're faced with a problem, your default response may be to think of an immediate solution, and perhaps even impose it. That works fine for simple problems. For complex and contentious problems, however, this approach can actually make things worse, because typically you can't go it alone, and you're not the only person, or a member of the only group, with an interest in how things get resolved.

To ensure that you land on a successful solution, you'll want to get the setup right. This involves taking care in mapping the terrain of the problem: identifying who you need to engage, and gaining understanding of where all the differing parties stand, and why. You'll be in a better position for collaborative problem-solving once you've learned:

- Who the stakeholders are
- What they consider to be their core issues and needs
- What's driving divisions, including whether misunderstandings might be playing a role

It can be tempting to think you know all you need to know about an issue and the people involved, or if you don't, that all you need to do is bring a skillful facilitator on board to overcome differences of opinion and resolve the conflict for you. This can be especially tempting when you're tackling an issue you've been involved with for years or you're working to resolve a conflict in an organization you know well, like your workplace or place of worship. We urge you to avoid this trap. Based on our experience, no one ever knows everything they need to know about an issue at the start, especially if they haven't previously taken a collaborative approach. Doing the homework of understanding the stakeholders, their core needs, and the true nature of the divisions will be invaluable in laying a strong foundation upon which a shared set of solutions can be built.

It can also be tempting to think that your problem is so pressing that there isn't time to do this homework. This can be true, but in most cases the reality is just the opposite. The time spent mapping the terrain will enable you to create a plan for problem-solving that will ultimately prove faster than tackling the problem head-on and then running into unseen obstacles and impasses along the way.

GET TO KNOW STAKEHOLDERS

You can map the terrain of your tough problem in two main ways: reading about it and interviewing people with a stake in the issue.

Because you may not immediately know who else has a stake in your issue, it helps to start by reviewing the landscape, learning what you can about the scale, scope, and history of the problem and past attempts to solve it. When reading about your issue, whether you're reviewing internal documents of an organization or existing articles and reports on a public issue, we urge you to seek sources that cover the full range of views on your topic. For a national issue, for example, be sure to read and listen to media outside your usual media bubble. Watch Fox News if you regularly watch MSNBC and watch MSNBC if you regularly watch Fox News—and aim to do this with a mindset of curiosity and openness. See if there's a local newsletter or message board that you can learn from. Consider if there are leaders at local organizations who have written or talked about the problem or potential solutions from their perspective.

Reading widely and deeply about an issue will give you a better sense for what lies ahead, but remember that when you do research this way, you'll only be able to learn what people have felt comfortable sharing publicly, or what they've been asked about. Rarely do internal documents or stories written by reporters provide the full story behind the positions people take on an issue. This is why interviewing stakeholders, and potentially others with relevant knowledge and expertise, is vital.

We suggest this list of questions as a good place to start interviews:

- What are your views on _____?
- What personal experiences have shaped your views on _____?

- What is most important to you about _____?
- What, if anything, has been tried to address _____?
- Have things been getting better or worse?
- Are there any ways in which you feel you or your side are being misunderstood?
- How do you think people on other sides see this issue? What do you think is most important to them?
- What, if any, common ground, or potential for higher ground, do you see?
- Is there anything that I haven't asked you about _____ that I should know?

As your conversations with stakeholders unfold, really lean into being curious. Actively engaging in this way will help ensure that you understand each stakeholder's perspective. Asking follow-up questions that show that you're actively listening and engaged in their story will also allow you to tease out specific strands of historic division and potential areas of higher ground in the future.

STAKEHOLDER INCLUSIVITY MATTERS

When done well, including the fullest possible range of stakeholder views will lead to more effective, more comprehensive, more enduring, and wiser outcomes that meet the needs and concerns of more people.

Including the fullest range of perspectives is particularly important because, in today's world, the power to enact change is often thinly distributed. When individuals and groups feel shut out of developing a solution, they may be moved to disrupt it or stop it from being implemented. They can easily launch a campaign to "cancel" a solution before it gets off the ground by a variety of means—legislation, lawsuits, or putting pressure on other stakeholders to abandon the plan. Engaging with potential "spoilers" as part of your collaborative problem-solving will help you to head off such issues down the road.

For example, in 2019 representatives of the United Methodist Church (UMC) from around the world voted on whether to allow same-sex marriage and LGBTQ+ clergy within the church. The vote was close, with 53% voting to continue the ban and 47% voting in favor of lifting it. UMC leaders decided that the best course was to split into two separate churches. The challenge was to make it a peaceful split; when the Presbyterian Church and the Episcopal Church had split on similar grounds, there had been long legal fights over everything from ownership of church properties to naming rights.

In selecting people to come to the table to discuss the terms of the split, the UMC ensured that all the various factions—church progressives, traditionalists, and centrists—had a seat. With the assistance of mediator Kenneth Feinberg, who had served as special master of the September 11 Victim Compensation Fund, they brought together representatives who could voice their concerns and needs but were also open to finding common ground with others. Sixteen UMC leaders met over three months and agreed to establish a new traditionalist denomination supported by $25 million in church funds. Individual churches now had the opportunity to choose to join whichever faction aligned better with their viewpoints, an arrangement that satisfied everyone.[4]

In some cases, such as decisions affecting an organization like a school or place of worship, it may be possible to engage everyone or almost everyone who needs to be involved. For most public issues, even local ones, that usually isn't true. There are just too many people with a stake in solving the problem. In these cases, your goal should be to figure out who you need to talk with to understand the fullest range of views around the issue and foster buy-in from the key individuals and groups.

Here you'll start to draw the details of the landscape on your initial map of your problem's terrain. You start by looking at your list of key stakeholders and thinking about any gaps in your list. This is called *stakeholder mapping*. Ask yourself, *Are all the individuals, organizations, stakeholder groups, and others who care about or might be impacted by the issue and solutions represented?* In a full collaborative problem-solving process, the person or organization that's convening meetings invites as many stakeholder groups as feasible to be interviewed as part of their initial homework on the issue and then invites a representative sample of these stakeholders to participate in the problem-solving process of deliberation. If you're not going to engage in such a formal process, you can simply spend time with people representing as many perspectives as possible, learning about their concerns, goals, and needs.

The more views, the merrier. It's important to seek out stakeholders with very different views from your own because, as we saw in Part II, "Mindsets," it can be very hard for people to grasp perspectives and experiences unlike their own. If you're having trouble reaching and engaging with stakeholders with very different views, we urge you to take other steps to understand these perspectives rather than assuming that these people or organizations aren't concerned about the issue or don't care about finding solutions. You might look back at the reading you did about the issue and see if you can learn more about the views you're not hearing in your stakeholder outreach. You can also simply push hard to put yourself in the other person's or group's shoes, by imagining what might be most important to those stakeholders and why, and then noting where you might have made incorrect assumptions.

Nothing beats talking with people. Short of that, trying to think through their point of view is much better than not giving them any consideration at all, especially if you want to find solutions that will get all the key stakeholders on board by satisfying their most important needs and concerns.

STRETCH BEYOND PRECONCEPTIONS

For the Convergence dialogue on how to better prepare prisoners for their return into society, the team started with the statistics, and then read and listened deeper, learning more about contending views on prison management and reform. From this, we learned there were a range of stakeholders, inside and outside the criminal justice system, who agreed that people who had been in prison needed to be better prepared to return to their community; they just disagreed on how. We could see that we needed to include a wide range of perspectives, including prisoner rights advocates, prison managers, former prisoners, public health agencies and other support providers in the community, and law enforcement. Each of these groups held a piece of the puzzle, and in most instances they had not put together a plan where their collective efforts could be combined and coordinated for maximum positive effect. All would need to collaborate in implementing successful approaches to helping prisoners be "Reentry Ready," the name Convergence found for the project through this wide-ranging stakeholder research.

Among the people Convergence reached out to were Georgetown University professor of government and law Marc Howard, and Daren Swenson, then vice president of Community Corrections at CoreCivic, the leading provider of private corrections facilities in the US. Although there were a number of other perspectives at the table, these two men help to demonstrate the singular importance of mapping the terrain to ensure a wide range of views are being included as you consider potential solutions to a problem. They also show why it's so important to interview key stakeholders and ask them not just about their position on an issue but the journey they took to get there.

Marc is a passionate advocate for prison reform and has described himself as at times strident in his arguments against mass incarceration. He first got involved in the issue after a childhood friend was wrongfully convicted of double murder and sentenced to life in prison. That friend's experience spurred Marc to go to law school; he wanted to prove his friend's innocence and help him gain his freedom. After his friend's exoneration and release, Marc continued to represent wrongfully convicted individuals and work for changes in prison systems across the US. At the start of the Reentry Ready project, he was skeptical of, and somewhat resistant to, including private prisons at the table. In his view, private prisons were mainly concerned with making a profit, and their bottom line would be adversely affected if fewer people were in prison. He couldn't see how investments in programs to reduce recidivism would serve these companies' bottom-line interests. That would be akin to an ambulance-chasing lawyer spending money to fix uneven sidewalks.

For his part, Daren was equally skeptical that any stakeholders who hadn't spent time working in a prison could understand his views and experience. How could people with no experience running a prison gain an understanding of the challenges of running a safe and secure facility? He'd worked in prisons for 30 years, starting as a frontline corrections officer before being promoted to serve as warden at three different prisons. He'd since been promoted to a more senior role overseeing all of CoreCivic's community reentry facilities designed to assist incarcerated individuals to successfully transition from prison to their communities, and to divert some people from incarceration altogether by allowing them to remain in their community and maintain family connections, housing, and employment while serving their sentence. In Daren's view, CoreCivic and other private prison companies served as expert partners to government clients. He and many of his colleagues were confident that they were delivering an important public service, and doing so in a way that relieved governments from significant financial and administrative burdens. He knew many in the private prison industry who were driven by the mission of "corrections" and wanted to support people to have a successful return to their community and was concerned that he wouldn't get a chance to explain this outlook.

Daren's and Marc's perspectives were so seemingly divergent from each other that initially it was difficult to imagine making much progress in bridging their views in the Reentry Ready project. Marc's opposition to private prisons appeared to be a red line. Then Daren heard about Marc's research and outreach in a variety of prisons, including the education and other reentry programs he was developing, and shared how CoreCivic had had some success in cutting through red tape in reentry pilot programs. Marc and other prisoner rights advocates in the group began to push beyond their preconceptions to see the value of having the perspectives, knowledge, and experience of people operating private prisons among the people taking part in the meetings. Marc's red line began to blur as he saw potential opportunities to collaborate with unexpected allies.

Marc and Daren, while skeptical of the other side's willingness to work with them, were open to considering each other's perspective. They brought a curious collaborative mindset to their conversations.

However, in some cases, you may find that a few stakeholders continue to insist that their preconceptions are right and there's nothing to learn from the other people with a stake in the problem. Indeed, we're often asked how inclusive problem-solvers should be—should absolutely every side be asked to participate? Often this is followed by the question of whether it's possible to engage "extremists" in collaborative problem-solving. Here's our response: Because of how the brain operates in conflict, people are often too quick to dismiss those with whom they strongly disagree as being beyond engagement.

Given the importance of including the full range of views to the development of wise and durable solutions, we encourage you to stretch beyond your comfort zone and include individuals about whom you hold some skepticism. We've worked with many individuals who could easily be labeled "extremists" by their opposites who went on to pleasantly surprise their detractors and did excellent work to forge shared solutions with them.

That said, to participate constructively, the members of the group must share the goal of working together to solve a problem. If someone is so extreme that their presence would be deeply disruptive, or they refuse to collaborate under any circumstances, then including them may very well be counterproductive. You want people who are engaged in solving the problem.

AUTHORITY CHECK

In addition to mapping the full range of stakeholders and perspectives around your issue, it's important to map the contours of power—that is, who has the influence and leverage to enact change. This is sometimes called *power mapping*. Power mapping will help to ensure that all the hard work you and your fellow problem-solvers have done to develop collaborative solutions comes to something.

Some of the people with influence and leverage to create change around your issue may agree to take part in your collaborative problem-solving group, which is all to the good. If they can't take part because of time commitments or other obligations, you can still engage with them by learning about their perspectives and exploring their openness to supporting higher-ground solutions.

After posing stakeholder perspective questions like the ones listed earlier in this chapter in the "Get to Know Stakeholders" section, you'll then want to explore how they'd feel about collaborative solutions, framing them in a way that might pique their curiosity about getting more involved. We've found this handful of questions can help problem-solvers engage those with influence and leverage:

- If we're able to find a solution that's acceptable to both group X and group Y (where these are very different stakeholder groups), would you be interested or excited about that? Why or why not?

- Assuming we're able to find a consensus across a wide range of stakeholders, how willing would you be to work with me and those stakeholders to see those solutions implemented?
- Who else would be important for us to get invested in solving this problem?

In some instances, you may feel you need to do little to no power mapping to engage people or groups with the influence to implement solutions. For example, if the CEO of your organization is seeking a collaborative solution to a problem, you might be fine skipping this power mapping exercise, knowing the CEO has the power to implement the solutions you develop. However, even in a case like this, some amount of power mapping and engagement is prudent. What if there are potential spoilers opposed to your solutions among the membership of the leadership team or board? How can you anticipate the influence of key stakeholders outside the organization? You'll want to engage with these individuals as you're developing your solutions.

Try It Out

Think about the issue you identified in the "Try It Out" in Chapter 2, "How to Reach Convergence." Now, think carefully through how you might map the terrain by conducting an initial review of the landscape.

- **Research.** If it's a public issue, think about which respected media outlets, online forums and blogs, and news and community videos are good sources of information about the issue. If it's an internal organizational issue, what historical information, memoranda, or strategic planning documents might illuminate how different stakeholders see the problem? Note what side or sides of the issues these documents might cover. Are you missing some perspectives? Where else could you go for information?
- **Interviews.** Identify a few key stakeholders whom you could talk with to develop a deeper understanding of the issue. Again,

be sure to include individuals who hold a variety of views. Make a list of the individuals or representatives of stakeholder groups who you would need to talk with to understand the full range of views on the issues.

■ **Change agents.** Finally, make a list of the people who hold the levers to enact change. They could be people in a position of authority or those with some influence in some area related to the issue. They might be community and business leaders, politicians, or civil servants. Think beyond the usual suspects, too. A widely respected member of the community can sway a lot of people.

Your ability to realize change through collaborative problem-solving comes not just from the influential people involved but also from the credibility born of including the divergent perspectives of individuals with direct experience or deep knowledge of the issue you're tackling. Especially when the problem relates to members of the public, you'll want to be sure to spend time gathering the perspectives of individuals with lived experience of the issue and work to include them at the table where possible. They may or may not have influence or leverage to enact change, but they'll be critical allies and bring needed perspectives.

In Reentry Ready, it wasn't possible to have people in prison take part directly in the problem-solving dialogue, but several participants were formerly incarcerated people and others were prisoner rights advocates. In addition, the project organizers also spent time talking with people in prison about their experiences so they would have firsthand exposure to their views to help them understand the issues.

Once you have a good sense of the landscape of a problem, including the points of convergence and divergence across the full range of stakeholders, you have the first building block to collaborative problem-solving in place. Next, we turn to how you can nurture trust among these key players.

CHAPTER 9

Nurture Trust

Once you've mapped the terrain of your problem, you may feel like you've got everything you need to take the plunge into developing solutions. However, knowledge about the issue and stakeholders is only one set of the tools that you'll need on this journey. You'll also need to create a strong sense of common cause and, ideally, camaraderie with the wide range of stakeholders you've asked to join you in your problem-solving group.

Absent trust, the parties will be less open to hearing each other's ideas—even the good ones. So first take time to nurture trust between them. Opportunely, perhaps you started to do this simply by including them while mapping the terrain of the problem. But there's more trust-building work ahead.

US, UNITED

Humans are hard-wired to form groups. This tendency stokes much mistrust when we feel like we're on one side of an issue and someone else is on the other—for example, labor versus management, liberals versus conservatives, new lecturers versus tenured professors. When social identities are boiled down to just two categories, they often harden into "us" the in-group versus "them" the out-group. We can then be prone to seeking out and exaggerating the negative aspects of the other side, partly to feel better about ourselves and partly to feel more secure about our social identity.

Our brain's penchant for dividing the world into "us" and "them" doesn't mean social identity groups are inflexible, however. We can form new groups and do so with very little nudging.

Social psychologist Henri Tajfel demonstrated this through a series of studies with British schoolboys. When the boys arrived at Tajfel's psychology lab, they were shown a film with clusters of dots flashing across the screen and asked to estimate how many dots they'd seen. Once they'd turned in their answers, the researchers explained that some of the boys were "over-estimators" and others were "under-estimators," setting up an imaginary "us" and "them" divide. But the researchers didn't actually check the boys' counts against the films; they just assigned them to a group randomly, half to the over-estimators and half to the under-estimators. Once the boys had their new group identities, the researchers gave them some money and told them they had to dole it out to two other boys taking part in the experiment, who were only identified by number and their made-up group membership. Most gave their money to a member of their same group.[1]

In a poignant demonstration of this concept, in 1968 Iowa school-teacher Jane Elliott conducted an exercise to try to explain the assassination of the Rev. Martin Luther King Jr. to her third-grade all-White classroom. On day 1, she told her students that children with brown eyes were "superior" to children with blue eyes and that blue-eyed children were less intelligent and badly behaved. The students with brown eyes got to eat lunch first and enjoyed a longer recess. The students with blue eyes had to wear a collar around their necks so there would be no doubt of their lower status. The children didn't hesitate in embracing their roles, with the brown-eyed children lording it over the blue-eyed kids and the blue-eyed children becoming sad, withdrawn, and timid. On day 2, she switched the roles, and it played out again (though the blue-eyed children were slightly more understanding of what it felt like to be the "underdog").[2] This is the power of in-groups and out-groups.

You may be thinking that children must be more susceptible to social identity, and this surely explains why Tajfel and Elliott witnessed such dramatic in-group preferential behavior. But numerous social identity experiments have been conducted with adults and garnered the same sorts of results. It shouldn't be all that surprising, given that "belonging" is one of the eight basic human needs identified by psychologist Abraham Maslow; only biological survival and safety are more fundamental, and social groups help us meet those needs, too.[3] The studies of social identity also tally with lived experience. In the US, Black and White racial groups have for centuries served as a primary set of "us" and "them" categories. More recently, the Republican and Democratic political parties have had "us" and "them" social identity dynamics. Humans create "us" and "them" categories regularly. The challenge is to harness them to good end.

At one extreme, our tendency to form groups, exaggerate the differences between them, and attribute bad-faith motivations to out-group members can lead us to assume and hold tight to a position of moral superiority that can too easily slide into demonization or dehumanization of people on the other side of an issue. It's almost impossible to gain the trust of someone whose views you seem to hold in contempt. And without trust, it's extremely difficult to solve complex, contentious problems. It's in this context that we lose our capacity to live and govern well together.

Our tendency to form groups like our families and neighborhoods provides us with safety, connection, belonging, and meaning. It also facilitates cooperation—mostly with members of our own in-group. Fortunately, when people choose to take part in a collaborative problem-solving process, it's common, no matter their background or their differences, to see them embrace shared identities like the ones described in Chapter 6, "Relationships at the Core." Then they do something more unexpected: they push beyond these shared identities to the even greater feat of developing a new *group identity* as fellow problem-solvers. The emotionally, socially, and spiritually challenging process of building a complex, shared understanding of the issues and stakeholders leads people to become invested not only in finding solutions but in trusting and collaborating with one another.

So the key is to expand who is in our group so that we're able to extend our natural empathy and care to a wider circle of our fellow travelers. That means getting out of our bubbles of like-minded folks and building relationships with people who see the world differently than we do.

Management consultant Sabah Alam Hydari has seen the benefit of doing this in her work helping global companies integrate sprawling, diverse groups of employees into cohesive, successful teams that appreciate their different genders, religions, nationalities, and levels of experience. Step by step, she asks colleagues to explore:

1. **Their hidden identities**, to help them see the identities they share
2. **Narratives**, opening up about a moment of courage or vulnerability in their lives
3. **Otherness**, allowing space to share a story of a time when they felt they were in the out-group and then reflecting about a time when they themselves had treated someone as an out-group member (for example, making assumptions about a person joining the team before they'd even met them)
4. **A shared identity and goal**, around which they might center their team

After exploring these four dimensions together, "scores were much higher for feeling like a team, being willing to support one another, having a shared goal, and understanding the self."[4]

Hydari developed her approach—she calls it the *forging team inclusiveness loop*—shortly after terrorist attacks in London in 2017. In the wake of the attacks, she had suddenly felt shoved into an out-group, and under threat. "The racist slur 'Paki' was hurled at me regularly," she recalled, and "I found myself responding defensively during conversations with colleagues."[5] She realized she needed to find a way to bring together coworkers who might feel divided into in-groups and out-groups to form a connected, collaborative unit, even when they might be working in different cities or time zones.

With effort and commitment, we can use our tendency to form groups to facilitate community and stop reflexively viewing people unlike ourselves as the "other side" and instead see them as part of our problem-solving team.

MAKING CONTACT

It took decades for the government of Canada and the Inuit people to come to an agreement about how to carve out a land for the Inuit out of the vast Northwest Territories. Hundreds of pages of rights and benefits had to be discussed and decided. Who would own any subsurface resources? Where would the boundary be drawn between the Inuit land and land claimed by another First Nations people, the Dene? Governments and prime ministers were voted in and out of office as the discussions went on. So, in 1990, when the two sides seemed close to a final settlement, Inuit leaders invited Tom Siddon, then Canada's Minister of Indian Affairs, and his wife, Pat, to stay with them on their traditional lands, in their traditional way, in the hope that this would create a connection that would ensure the agreement was ratified.[6] "Pat and I were taken by dog sled across ice and snow to Igloolik on the western side of Hudson's Bay," Siddon told a Canadian reporter. "Our Inuit guide built an igloo and that night we slept in it on caribou skins. In the morning I woke with my back against a block of ice."[7]

During the trip Siddon was amazed at how well the guide could navigate across the snow blanketing the Arctic plains in every direction; he was more amazed when the guide explained that he navigated by observing "waves in the snow." There was clearly a deep connection between this Inuit man and his environment, and Siddon was moved by it. When Siddon later sat down to supper with the Inuit leaders he assured them that they would always have his support for the land claim. He strongly recommended the final agreement's ratification and the creation of the new territory of Nunavet to the prime minister in 1993. Bonds of mutual trust and respect had been forged on the sea ice.

The story of Nunavet mirrors our own experiences watching how people nurture and sustain mutually respectful and trusting relationships in collaborative problem-solving groups. It's also backed up by *contact theory*, an idea first developed in the 1950s by Harvard psychologist Gordon Allport and since tested, refined, and verified by scores of other researchers, as shown in a review of 500 distinct experiments conducted over 50 years.[8] Based on this evidence we can confidently say that, in appropriate conditions, interpersonal contact is one of the most effective ways to reduce prejudice between groups.

Of course, contact in and of itself doesn't produce greater trust. There are too many examples of contact provoking worse conflict, including war, and recall the old proverb that "familiarity breeds contempt," which certainly can be true. But in our experience, when interactions are governed by collaborative mindsets and structured for respectful exchange, familiarity more often than not breeds respect and even affection. People feel great relief when they have positive experiences related to the character and views of others, even as deep disagreements may persist. Indeed, researchers have identified conditions that strengthen the positive effects of contact, and one of the most powerful is working together toward a common goal, especially a goal that can only be attained if different factions work together.[9] This is the whole point of collaborative problem-solving.

There are many ways to nurture and sustain trust among stakeholders to help get them on the path to sharing a common goal around an issue. Several are particularly useful because they support other aspects of collaborative problem-solving:

- **Doing your homework.** The research and outreach you do to map the terrain of your problem is an opportunity to build trust with those who have different views and to reassure them that the process that you're organizing will be fair to all who participate. Interviewing stakeholders and asking them engaged questions helps to demonstrate that you're committed to solving the problem, willing to learn, and interested in their experiences and perspectives. It also shows that you respect their needs and concerns enough to include them in the eventual solution.
- **Breaking the ice.** Don't worry, we're not suggesting that you spend the night on the Arctic plains! Instead, consider adding more short refreshment breaks into any meetings—time before, during, and after hands-on problem-solving sessions. These unstructured icebreaker moments open the door for people to interact more casually and personally, planting seeds of trust that will likely grow and thrive even when discussions become more formal.
- **Breaking bread.** As described in Chapter 6, "Relationships at the Core," having meals together is surprisingly effective at sparking relationships between people from different walks of life. They're also good at nurturing trust, because people tend to fall into more personal conversations while relaxing over a meal. In one set of studies, researchers even found that strangers who were asked to wait in a room and have the same snack to eat trusted each other more, or cooperated with each other more later, depending on which task they were given.[10]

On the first full day of meetings for the Reentry Ready project to find ways to better prepare people who had been in prison to return to their community, there was understandable concern that the group might end up splitting into preconceived "us" and "them" groups—the people who were "tough on crime" and those who were advocating for "prison reform"; the people working in prisons and those working in prisoner rights. The tension in views and experiences, particularly between Marc Howard, who'd titled his book on prisons *Unusually Cruel*, and Daren Swenson, who'd spent 30 years working in prisons, was something the project managers were keeping a close eye on.

Both Marc and Daren are thoughtful in their choice of words and collaborative by nature, but when people feel strongly about an issue, they can step outside their usual bounds of behavior. Neither would be disrespectful or rude, not purposefully, but they didn't know each other yet, and there was concern about whether they'd form a relationship that could yield constructive results for the entire group. The project team hoped that having an open, engaged conversation early on would help to plant a seed of trust for future work. So Marc and Daren were seated next to each other at the dinner to cap off the first day.

When Marc saw the dinner arrangements, he couldn't believe that he was sitting next to someone from CoreCivic. "I had a very simplistic and negative opinion of, and strong distrust of, the private prison industry, period," he recalled. He texted his wife to share his dread. And then he sat down next to Daren. After a slow start, their conversation got warmer. They swapped stories about why they'd decided to take part in Reentry Ready. They talked about what they wanted for people being released from prison. And they discovered their ambitions were surprisingly similar. Both wanted people leaving prison to thrive and not get reengaged in the criminal justice system. Daren explained how his company was expanding its business to include more reentry programs, so that a significant source of income would come from helping people succeed in transitioning back to "normal" life.

"We had a great conversation," Marc said, "and I felt, in a way, that distrust gradually—I have to stress *gradually*, because it wasn't like some big eye-opening, lightbulb moment or anything—starting to melt away."

The seed of trust planted at that dinner has thrived, growing into a professional relationship that has continued for years after the Reentry Ready project published its solutions.[11]

SETTING GROUND RULES

It helps to develop agreements as a group about how you're going to interact with each other. Ground rules help everyone develop more trust in the process—including trust that all voices will be heard.

Ground rules might state that the dialogue, including individual participants' views, will be confidential and the outcome will become public only once all participants agree—so no social media! It might also call for participants to refrain from criticizing each other's motives.

Many scholars believe the ground rules set down for the Constitutional Convention were instrumental to founding the new national government. These included a rule of confidentiality to "prevent erroneous and mischievous reports"; speaking rules, where no delegate was allowed to address the convention for a second time "until everyone else who wanted a say had had their chance"; and attendance rules, where deliberations requiring full agreement would only take place when all of the delegates could take part. These rules were agreed before anyone presented any ideas for how the US government should be organized going forward.[12]

We urge you to take time to think about the ground rules in advance of getting participants into a room together because your ground rules will largely set the tone of the conversation. One of the participants in the Health Care Coverage for the Uninsured project was an advocate for low-income consumers. For years, the person said, they would regularly find themselves at odds with—and angry about—the positions espoused by one of the other participants who represented health insurance companies and other corporate interests in the field of medicine. They openly referred to this person as their "nemesis." The ground rules for the dialogue, which included confidentiality and listening without interrupting, brought down the temperature in the room so people could really get to know each other. Afterward, when they found themselves working together, even when they were at cross purposes, they started with: "How are you? How is your family? I can't quite fathom the latest positions your group has taken. Can you explain them to me so I can understand?" Good ground rules support a good exchange of ideas and help people form bonds that will often last long after your last group meeting.

Creating a list of ground rules may sound pedantic, but they're actually highly effective. It isn't so much that people don't know how to treat each other with respect. Rather, because we often feel threatened when we're in a conflict, our judgment and decision-making functions can get clouded. We're more prone to say or do things from a place of heightened emotion. Ground rules remind the group of the values and behaviors they already subscribe to. They *reground* them.

Try It Out

You can start with a proposed list of ground rules and ask the group to make additions and subtractions or have the group start from scratch. What's most important is to make sure that the group participates in creating, and buys into, the ground rules.

If you want to start with a list, our top suggestions to get your discussion of ground rules underway are:

- Listen to learn rather than to respond.
- Ask questions rather than assume.
- Accept what each person says as their sincere belief and don't question motives.
- Speak from the heart and to the heart of the matter. Share the why, not just the what.
- What we learn can be shared, but the names of the people and organizations who shared each part of the puzzle stay within the confidence of the room. This is a form of the Chatham House Rule.[13]

DEEPENING TRUST

Once you have the initial groundwork of trust—laid in place by doing your homework, setting ground rules, or other trust-building activities—the people you've invited to the problem-solving table will likely start to feel safe enough to make genuine and vulnerable disclosures about themselves and their perspectives. Disclosure deepens trust. Indeed, one of the most effective ways to nurture and sustain trust is to create well-facilitated, structured opportunities for people to be genuine and vulnerable with each other. This is because disclosing is risky. Disclosing sensitive things about yourself—for example, your fears, your faults, or your backstory—conveys that you have some trust in the people you're sharing with. Once you've extended trust, you're more likely to be trusted in return, because it's easier to get trust after you give it.

From this foundation, well-facilitated, structured dialogue is the path to eliciting self-disclosure. Well-structured dialogue of disclosure aims to:

- **Get to the why.** What's the story behind their position and perspectives?
- **Complexify people's understanding of each other.** Encourage people to see each other in a multidimensional way—not only a Republican but also a gameshow fan, or not only a Democrat but also a person of faith. It also reveals that each person is not just pro this or anti that but rather that each holds nuanced and sometimes conflicting views on issues.
- **Identify shared higher ground both on the issues and interpersonally.** Even the most strident partisans can often agree on some pieces of the puzzle around a given issue. For example, both pro-lifers and pro-choicers agree that babies who are born should be well cared for and unwanted pregnancies should be avoided. Identifying common values, goals, and life experiences also builds this trust.

This is an ongoing process. Trust isn't built once. It's less like the foundation stone of a hearth and more like the fire that needs to be regularly stoked. During the Reentry Ready project, as the only representative of a private prison facility company, Daren might easily have become defensive. He remembered sharing stories about his professional experience—such as the change in the company's culture when they moved from referring to people in prison as inmates to referring to them as residents—and being met with skepticism. Rather than disengaging from the group, he extended himself. "Some of the people at the table were saying things to the effect of, 'Well, you know I don't trust what you're saying.' My answer was, 'You tell me what facility you want to go see, and I'll meet you there. We'll tour it."

Marc said this made a lasting impression. "It was his actions more than his words. He just showed a commitment to the issues that we were all trying to solve."

Trust grows and thrives by developing a deeper and more nuanced understanding of each other, and each other's views, and by identifying shared values, goals, and identities.

CONNECTING QUESTIONS

Connecting questions are an excellent way to facilitate deeper disclosure. These are questions that lead individuals and groups to make meaningful connections quickly—in other words, to go deep fast. They help people find their shared values, identities, and goals.

A connecting question typically asks you to share a deeply held perspective or describe a formative life experience. You might be asked to talk about the issue at hand or what values you most cherish.

Usually, you're also asked to share why whatever you've chosen to share really matters to you—to elaborate your perspectives or experiences into a story. Research demonstrates the staying power of personal stories over facts and data. "People believe that facts are essential for earning the respect of political adversaries, but our research shows that this belief is wrong," the authors of a report reviewing 15 independently conducted experiments wrote. "In moral disagreements, subjective experiences seem truer (i.e., are doubted less) than objective facts."[14] Conservative political and cultural commentator David Brooks champions stories, too. "Storify whenever possible," he wrote in the *New York Times*. "I no longer ask people: What do you think about that? Instead, I ask: How did you come to believe that? People are much more revealing and personal when they are telling stories. And the conversation is going to be warmer and more fun."[15]

When conflict is intense or challenging, people may imagine that those on the other side do not share any of their values. This is rarely true. A connecting question that focuses on surfacing people's values can often be the most effective way to help people realize their shared values. Almost nothing else builds more trust than the recognition of shared values.

Try It Out

With practice, you'll find connecting questions can be effective with many different groups in many different situations. They're particularly useful to kick off meetings but can also be used to change the topic of conversation or to close a gathering.

How to do connecting questions:

- **Everyone gets a turn.** Instruct participants not to respond until every person in the group has answered the question.
- **Pose the question.** The prompt might be "Please share a formative life experience that shaped your views of this issue," or "What is the value that most guides you in your work on this issue, and why?" Generally, people should be asked to also share the "why" behind their answer.
- **Let people connect.** Follow the question with a discussion of the responses. What struck them about other people's answers? What surprised? What will stick with them?
- **Don't rush.** Give people plenty of time to answer the question and discuss the experience.

Structured contact and dialogue can produce an alchemy of trust, converting divided and dubious individuals into people who honor mutual dignity and difference when working with each other. It isn't always easy to generate trust, but in our experience, these methods work reliably.

Building trust usually takes time, but once this trust is built you have a firm foundation to support deeper exploration of your issue— and the promise of solutions. Renowned leadership expert Stephen Covey said, "Change happens at the speed of trust."[16] When it comes to trust, it's sometimes necessary to go slower at the start to eventually go further faster.

CHAPTER 10

Really Hear Everyone

Daren Swenson, vice president at the private prisons provider CoreCivic, and Marc Howard, professor of government and law at Georgetown University and an advocate for prison reform, spoke throughout the series of meetings put together as part of Convergence's Reentry Ready project. They took time to hear more about each other's experiences, focusing on the thing they both wanted: better support for people returning from corrections facilities to their community. Over time, Marc said, "I felt that he seemed committed . . . [and] that increased to the point where I felt, *You know, we're actually on the same page here. We agree.*"

When Daren had extended an open invitation to anyone interested in visiting a CoreCivic facility to see how the company looked after the residents, Marc took note. That was something he'd like to do, he thought. So as he planned a trip to Nashville to tour college campuses with his daughter, he got in touch with Daren. "Would it be possible to meet up and potentially visit a facility?" he asked. Daren happily arranged the tour, and he also later asked after Marc's daughter's college applications. They hadn't become close friends, but their mutual trust was growing and leading to an ongoing conversation.

Marc, with the vice dean of Georgetown's business school, had cofounded the Georgetown Pivot Program, a reentry program providing classes and work experience to formerly incarcerated people. After attending a suite of skills-focused, classroom-based courses, Pivot Fellows get hands-on experience as an intern with one of the program's partnering employers, then get support as they look for a permanent position or start up their own business. Fellows also have access to training in public speaking, business communications, career planning, personal finance, and conflict resolution. Marc wondered if the Fellows might like to hear Daren's perspective and his ideas for delivering reentry programs through CoreCivic. He wasn't sure how it would go, especially because one of the Fellows in the cohort had been a resident of a CoreCivic facility where Daren had previously worked. But the Fellows were all eager to hear what Daren had to say. Marc remembers how genuine and open Daren was with the Fellows. "I have a very strong detector for bullshit and Daren passed that with flying colors in terms of his sincerity."

Since the close of the Reentry Ready project, Daren and Marc have kept in touch, particularly when projects arise where they can learn from each other's deep but distinct wells of experience. One of those opportunities came up after Marc cofounded the Frederick Douglass Project for Justice, which organizes respectful conversations and meetings between prison residents and members of the communities they'll be returning to. One of CoreCivic's facilities became the very first site to host Douglass Project meetings.

"When Marc and I started talking about it, I know he was frustrated, because he was having to go through long approval processes from departments of corrections," Daren said. Daren knew one of the departments that CoreCivic had long provided services to was looking for ways to build more connections between residents and the neighboring community, so he brought Marc's idea to the department's leadership and gained permission to try it out. It was a great success. Daren takes quiet pride in having helped to cut through the red tape and further the Douglass Project's mission. "The value that we can add is that we can oftentimes be innovative and try something different," he said.

Marc hadn't expected that a private prison company would be so engaged in working with a criminal justice center. "Getting into that first program was huge," Marc said, "because it opened the door to showing correctional leaders in other places that it can be done in a way that's not unsafe." Daren has since talked with other prison directors to explain how the project works from his perspective as a corrections professional and to share the benefits he's seen among residents and staff. This outreach had helped to extend the Douglass Project into eight more states by the end of 2023.

Marc and Daren come to their work from very different life experiences. They have different lenses through which they see the world.

But they share a genuine interest in hearing others' ideas—not just hearing people out, but instead listening to understand and open the door to new possibilities.

THE WISDOM OF LISTENING FIRST

When you engage directly with stakeholders to find a path toward a set of shared solutions, you may be tempted to dig right into the facts—and if you do, you'll probably discover that for every relevant fact there's probably a competing and contradictory fact, each of which is deemed to be trustworthy by somebody in your collaborative problem-solving group. This is why, in the previous two chapters, we suggested building trust and an understanding of each other's perspectives before you start to sift through the facts that might inform the solutions you're considering.

Before we go any further, let us be very clear: We are *not* saying that knowledge and facts don't matter. We believe firmly that they do. What we are saying is that timing also matters. First build shared understanding of each other and each other's perspectives, and then explore the facts.

Human beings, every one of us, have a fundamental need to be heard. Unfortunately, our need to hear is not as strong. We're often not ready to hear new information that contradicts our views, and we're more ready to hear contradicting information when we feel that others have understood where we're coming from. Trust in experts and the institutions that produce knowledge—even in facts themselves—is lower now than in the past.[1] Many parties to a conflict will not be receptive to new facts until they feel understood by those who see the world differently from the way they do.

The good news is that, once people truly feel heard, in our experience they're usually happy to listen to others, too, including people with strongly opposing views. As participants grow more willing to consider information that contradicts their views, they become less entrenched in defending personal positions. They also tend to express themselves in more nuanced, complex ways, with fewer adversarial jabs and extreme statements. They stop thinking about who's winning the war of information and start engaging in a conversation to explore what they each bring to the table.

Even with the same information in front of them, different people develop different perspectives on the same problems and bring different pieces of the solution to the table. We each:

- Have more access to information about ourselves than about others
- Draw on different life experiences that shape how we process information
- Put different weights on different types of information
- Place greater weight on different values—for example, favoring self-determination and independence versus community and interdependence[2]

We can sometimes be quick to dismiss ideas that differ from our own by applying higher standards to others' views. In one remarkable experiment, people were given a set of logic problems and had to write a justification for the answer they chose. They were then asked to evaluate other people's arguments about the same problems. Unknown to the participants, some of them were presented with their own argument as if it was someone else's. *More than half* rejected the arguments that were in fact *their own!*[3] This is why cultivating curiosity and exercising deep listening are so useful. They can disrupt our tendency to dismiss ideas other than our own, plus they're energizing to a group's sense of community.

Fortunately, despite our division, most Americans express interest in learning from each other. The vast majority of people—75% of Americans—say it's possible to learn new things from people with political views different from their own. Even more, 79%, say they make an effort to understand where people with different views are "coming from."[4] In our experience, getting the order right—understanding first perspectives and then facts—helps people live up to these stated aspirations.

Even if the other sides' perspectives don't seem especially well reasoned, every person's story makes as much sense to them as yours does to you. There is a lot going on that is shaping others' perspectives that you likely can't see. Their story of the journey makes sense for them and is based upon the facts as they experienced them.

Regardless of whether or not you think others' facts are accurate, it will be very hard to solve a problem if you can't understand how other people's view of the situation makes sense to them. Hearing and understanding your perceived adversaries' stories can help to reduce any feelings of frustration simmering around an issue, making it easier to engage in constructive problem-solving with the full range of stakeholders you'll likely need.

In addition, the other stakeholders in your problem-solving group will probably be able to sense when you're skeptical about what they're saying, like Daren said he sometimes could in the early Reentry Ready meetings. They might even be able to read it on your face, because we sometimes "leak" flashes of emotional expressions without even knowing it.[5] If you've already closed down to others before you've grown to understand how and why they think a certain way, it will be very hard to learn from them and harvest the pearls of wisdom that they possess.

TAKE TURNS

Most of us recognize that longstanding, tough problems are complex; that's why they haven't yet been solved. Views on them are complex, too. You may yourself hold conflicting views. It can help to start the process of hearing others more effectively by taking stock of your own perspectives to see where you might be in conflict with yourself. Research shows that being aware of such contradictions within ourselves makes us more tolerant of people who are different than us.[6]

As a problem-solver you'll want to try to help stakeholders move beyond the existing and typically binary categories—I'm right and you're wrong, "us" and "them"—so that they might explore the complexities of the issue with you and everyone else. It's within the complexities of the issue that stakeholders can catch a glimpse of the sparkling subtleties in each other's motivations and needs and start to take into account aspects of the issue that you and they have not previously seen or understood. With new insight into each other's worlds, you'll together be better positioned to find mutually beneficial solutions and, ultimately, the higher ground that you're after.

In our experience, more effective problem-solvers start by listening to and understanding other people's stories before sharing their own. This conveys your intellectual and personal humility and will help make others much more receptive to hearing your story when it's your turn.

Try It Out

When it does come time to share your own story, there are ways of speaking that increase the likelihood that you'll be heard.

- **Hedge.** The issues and your views on them are complex. Recognize that you yourself may hold conflicting views. Avoid speaking in absolutes. Use words like "probably," "sometimes," or "maybe" rather than "always," "definitely," or "everyone." This shows that you're hearing the other side's views as equally valid and valuable as your own.
- **Affirm.** As humans we have much in common, but this can be hard to notice when you're focused on things about which you don't agree. Highlight areas of agreement, no matter how small or obvious, to show that you're paying close attention to the other person's or other side's views and can see commonalities.
- **Stay personal.** Speak from your own experience. Speak more about yourself—your own feelings, needs, values, and concerns—than about the other person or side, especially their faults.
- **Own missteps**. Acknowledge the excesses and mistakes you or your side have made.

DIALOGUE AND DEBATE

The best tool for building the complex understanding of complicated and contentious issues needed for wise and durable problem-solving is dialogue. The late Daniel Yankelovich, a well-known pollster and social scientist, described the power of this form of conversation in his book *The Magic of Dialogue*:

> When dialogue is done skillfully, the results can be extraordinary: long-standing stereotypes dissolved, mistrust overcome, mutual understanding achieved, visions shaped and grounded in shared purpose, people previously at odds with each other aligned on objectives and strategies, new common

ground discovered, new perspective and insights gained, new levels of creativity stimulated and bonds of community strengthened.[7]

These extraordinary benefits of dialogue may sound like wishful thinking, a process that's too good to be true. But our experiences, as well as those of many other collaborative problem-solving and conflict resolution practitioners over recent decades, validate Yankelovich's claim. People who thought they could never even talk to each other, let alone engage constructively over time, find there are ways to bridge their divisions, work for a higher, common purpose, and often strengthen their interpersonal bonds.

Unfortunately, we too often default to debate, a process in which people with different perspectives engage on an issue by focusing on winning arguments. We can get stuck in debate mode not only when we're tackling tough problems but also in many everyday interactions when things aren't going quite our way.

Lynn Schoch, a professor at Ivy Tech Community College in Bloomington, Indiana, has for many years taught a class on argument and rhetoric. He finds the tools of collaborative problem-solving—what he calls "the Convergence approach"—to be useful in helping students to be better informed and more skillful in their writing, because it really helps them better understand how other people think. Lynn tells his students he wants them to learn three things to carry with them into the world:

1. Your opponent is not your enemy.
2. Your opponent is not dumb.
3. Write or speak in a way that your opponent will want to listen. To do this, you first have to listen to your opponent, so you can understand what will interest them.

One student who took part in a session about the Convergence approach as part of Lynn's classes said, "I had to throw out pretty much everything I knew about how to handle an argument by around week three or four." This was a case of learning to turn off debate mode and engage in dialogue during disagreements.

Dialogue	Debate
Is collaborative—two or more sides working together toward common understanding	Is oppositional—two sides opposing each other and attempting to prove each other wrong
Aims to find common ground	Aims to win
Listens to understand	Listens to find flaws and counter-arguments
Reveals assumptions for reevaluation	Defends assumptions as truth
Causes introspection on your own position	Causes critique of others' positions
Surfaces new information	Relies on predictable points
Opens the possibility of reaching a better solution than any of the original solutions	Defends your own position as the best solution and excludes other ideas
Involves concerns for the other person or side	Involves countering the other position without concern for feelings or relationships
Assumes that many people have pieces of the answer and that they can put them into a workable solution	Assumes there is one right answer and that someone has it
Creates opportunities for transformation because people are encouraged to question the dominant discourse—that is, to identify and express fundamental needs that may not already be reflected and to explore new ways to define and resolve the problem	Limits opportunities for transformation because people stick to the constraints of the dominant discourse—that is, the existing definition of a problem and the options for resolving it are assumed to be the only possibilities and that everyone's fundamental needs are already clearly understood

Debate isn't bad. It can be a useful tool to surface different ways of analyzing and solving problems. However, debate can also be destructive when it becomes repetitive, entrenched, self-serving, or rhetorical.

It wouldn't have been surprising if the community conversations held in Falcon Heights, Minnesota, after the shooting of Philando Castile had descended into a debate—those opposed to the city's policing contract versus those in favor of revising it, or those who thought the city leadership was to blame versus those who blamed the police. Emotions were running high, and many people felt a strong connection to the issues. "People were driving thirty miles just to go to these community conversations and learn how we were going to resolve this," recalled Melanie Leehy, the co-chair of the inclusion and policing task force. The task force encouraged dialogue instead of debate. In conversation after conversation, they asked people about their values, the values they wanted to see in the community, and the values they wanted to see in the city's approach to policing. Hundreds of people weighed in, and all were encouraged to speak from the heart. "I wanted people to be comfortable to be who they are, because whenever we tell people they have to be like everybody else in the room, healing does not happen," Melanie said.

While debate can be useful in clarifying positions, where there is conflict, a collaborative approach—dialogue—is needed to secure the solutions that work for the most people.

MAKE THE CIRCLE

Any problem-solver can apply the principles and skills of dialogue in a range of settings, including during one-on-one interviews with stakeholders. Building shared understanding through dialogue can absolutely take place outside of a formal collaborative problem-solving process. (If you want more detail about setting up a formal process, you'll find it in Part IV, "Process.") As a committed problem-solver, you might bring stakeholders together and lead the group yourself, or you might consider engaging a professional facilitator or someone with natural facilitation skills.

Structured dialogue exercises have proved to be very effective in getting people to switch from a default debate mode into dialogue mode. Indeed, a few simple exercises have been shown to be highly effective in getting even entrenched partisans to make the switch.[8] Flipping this switch often puts former adversaries on a glide path to mutual understanding and mutual-gain solutions.

A technique that Mariah has used in almost every collaborative problem-solving process she's facilitated is called *the circle*. It has its roots in Native American and other Native Peoples' healing and problem-solving practices and has been adapted for use in a number of settings, including as an alternative to suspension and expulsion from school.[9]

In this version of the circle, the problem-solver or another facilitator has people sit in a circle, ideally without a table in the middle because this seating arrangement fosters more vulnerability. The space should feel warm and inviting; sometimes Mariah puts a plant or an object relevant to the topic of the conversation at the center of the circle.

Depending on the group, the facilitator may start by reading a few words of wisdom from a poem, a quote, or another source. Then they pose a well-crafted question to the circle. Like the connecting questions in Chapter 9, "Nurture Trust," the question posed to the circle is meant to prompt self-disclosure and vulnerability, to help everyone participating get underneath their stated positions and right to the heart of the matter, unearthing the complexities of the issue within themselves and around the room. However, because some trust has already been established, the question posed to the circle can often delve deeper. This moment is an opportunity to explore each other's views and feelings at length and give people a space to be personal, own missteps, and imagine a future where the problem is resolved.

Here are examples of some well-crafted questions:

- What's one aspect of _____ that you feel the other side misunderstands?
- What's oversimplified about _____?
- Where do you have mixed feelings, doubts, or uncertainties regarding _____?
- What's the question no one is asking?
- What do you and your supporters need to learn about the other side to understand them better?
- What will the world look like when _____ is addressed?

Each person around the circle takes a turn to answer. Most of the time it's best not to allow anyone to respond or even to ask questions. Go all the way around first. Then open it up for reflection.

These are some questions that usually lead to reflection:

- What themes did you notice?
- What surprised you?
- What are you taking away from this conversation?
- What had real meaning for you from what you just heard?
- What's taking shape? What are you hearing underneath the variety of opinions being expressed?

Finally, open up the circle for a direct group discussion of what's been shared. At this point, people in the circle may be invited to ask follow-up questions. You can also lead a discussion about where the group goes next from here.

The circle can be an intense exercise, which is why it's not usually appropriate to set this up until you and the other stakeholders have established more trust with one another. So although it may seem as though the connecting questions you've done earlier might cover the same ground, in our experience the circle and exercises like it will yield new insights once you've got some initial trust in place. Most people disclose in steps, revealing a bit more each time they share. Connecting questions plant the seeds of trust; the circle gives that trust space to root, grow, and flourish.

Evidence for practices like the circle comes not only from our own consistent success using them but also from research. Putting your feelings into words has been shown to increase "cognitive ease" and reduce the stress-provoked flight, flight, or freeze response.[10] When our brain isn't overwhelmed by a cascade of stress hormones, we can more easily access higher-order executive functioning skills such as managing emotions, perspective-taking, and analyzing competing claims— all of which are key elements in effective problem-solving. And as we saw in Chapter 9, "Nurture Trust," people build bonds through hearing each other's stories, not through throwing facts around. Dialogue, much more so than debate, supports collaborative problem-solving.

FIND FACTS TOGETHER

Because the complexity of issues makes us anxious, we may feel comforted by overly simplistic solutions offered by members on our own side. However, solutions to tough problems require the knowledge and insight of *all sides*. Improving our healthcare system requires both the public and the private sectors to play a role. Making our schools safe requires both more mental health services and more security measures. Effectively integrating the work of various business divisions currently working in silos often requires a comprehensive understanding of what each team does and how they do it.

With full understanding of all stakeholders' perspectives, you can turn to exploring the wider landscape of facts and figures around your issue and possible ways to address it. You have a few paths. Where trust remains high enough, it can be a straightforward process of identifying some things to read and some speakers to listen to as a group and then discussing them. In our experience, if you spend enough time on nurturing trust and really hearing each other, this approach to fact-finding is usually sufficient.

However, in some cases, even when substantial time has been spent on building trust and understanding, the stakeholders may still have trouble agreeing on what sources are credible. The lower the trust in the room, the harder it is to agree on facts, figures, and ways to forge ahead. If you've come together around a highly polarized public issue, you'll almost certainly face challenges here. When participants have been exposed to a lot of highly divergent interpretations of an issue, it can be hard to find agreement on the sources to draw upon. When they've been exposed to misinformation or conspiracy theories, it may prove harder.

That doesn't mean you won't be able to find a durable, shared solution that satisfies all sides if stakeholders don't see eye to eye on what appear to be key facts and figures. In some instances, agreements may be reached even if there is a persistent disagreement.

Where there are key facts that do need to be established, you may have to spend time agreeing as a group on the sources of information you'll use. It will be your first practical exercise of collaborating together.

One approach is to agree on a roughly equal number of sources from each side of the debate. Another is to set some criteria for sources, such as sources published in a reputable scientific journal, supported by evidence from a peer-reviewed study, agreed upon by most experts on the topic, or other metrics.

Numbers play an important role in decision-making but so too does the lived experience of individuals impacted by the issue. Groups can get stuck debating the relative value of these two types of information. They shouldn't. Both matter; they're just different. Knowing the decibel level of noise created by a new highway is important factual information; knowing how nearby residents experience the noise from the highway is important lived experience information. A city council deciding whether to invest in a noise-mitigating barrier would want to have access to both types of facts.

If you've been following the chapters in Part III, you've got your map, you've nurtured trust, and you've spent time getting to know all the stakeholders and finding facts together. It's now time to develop mutually beneficial solutions.

CHAPTER 11

Generate Options for Mutual Gain

When the delegates arrived in Philadelphia for the Constitutional Convention at the end of May 1787, quite a few came with firm views on how to reorganize the country's government.[1] The delegates from Virginia, led by James Madison, actually had a fully fleshed-out plan in hand, with just a few blanks to be filled in for details like the length of term of members in the new national legislature. The Virginia Plan proposed a strong federal government with the power to veto state-level laws. There would be two houses in the legislature, both with representation based on state population.[2]

Other delegations scrambled to find quill, ink, and parchment so they, too, could present plans to the convention. William Paterson introduced the New Jersey Plan two weeks later. It was designed to ensure that big states like Virginia didn't run roughshod over the smaller states by giving every state just one representative each in the new legislature. It embodied such small changes from the existing Articles of Confederation that many delegates threw up their hands in frustration, and a couple days later, it was voted down. Alexander Hamilton, representing New York, countered with a proposal—he was painstaking in avoiding the word "plan"—to return to the idea of a strong national government.[3] It got nowhere. The smaller states became louder in their protests. They weren't being heard.

Then, on July 2, a breakthrough came—a vote was held on the possibility of having equal representation of the states only in the Senate and keeping population-based representation in the House. The vote was tied. This opened the door to a deeper conversation about how exactly a dual system of representation might work. A subgroup of delegates was given the task of coming up with some practical ideas, and two weeks later they presented the "Great Compromise," which proposed the system of representation we use to this day. No country had ever before had a system like it.

POSITIONS VERSUS INTERESTS

Most of the time, most people approach problem-solving in the same way they negotiate. They go into a negotiation knowing what they want, try to get all they can, and then they try to split the difference with the person they're negotiating with once loggerheads are reached. You want to buy a house or make a business deal, and you offer a little less than you're willing to pay in the hope that the other party will meet you halfway *because* they've asked for a little more than they're willing to accept, expecting they'll have to compromise a bit. Or you go in knowing what parts of the solution you absolutely must get and what you're willing to "give away" to the other side. You've got your plan, and you're sticking to it, mindful that giving the other side something might make people more willing to agree to it.

Splitting the difference can work, in problem-solving as well as deal-making. However, when it comes to complex and contentious issues, it doesn't always lead to the wisest or most durable results. And having a firm plan in mind from the start can make it difficult to understand others' needs and goals and move beyond a win–lose conversation. Fortunately, there is another way, and it's really effective.

Roger Fisher and William Ury revolutionized conflict resolution with their 1981 book, *Getting to Yes: Negotiating Agreement Without Giving In*, in which they made a fundamental distinction—positions are not the same as interests.[4] A *position*, Fisher and Ury explained, is a specific, fixed solution that a person or group gets behind to address a particular problem. An *interest* is the goal or need that the person or group is trying to satisfy with a solution; it's the "why" behind the position. A position is taken to serve underlying interests but it's usually not the only way to serve them. Indeed, it's rarely the best option if you want the solution to last. There are often multiple ways you could serve your interests, and where other options also serve others' needs and goals, they're better.

Fisher and Ury also made clear that most of us start and end negotiations with fixed ideas for how to resolve an issue, and much of the time such positions are mutually exclusive. The Virginia Plan and the New Jersey Plan couldn't both be enacted because they called for very different setups for Congress. Only when the Constitutional Convention's delegates focused on their underlying interests—finding a way to ensure a that strong national government gave some balancing power to the smaller states—were they able to arrive at an agreement and hash out details like the length of senators' terms. The key to effective problem-solving, as Fisher and Ury saw, is moving from positions to interests and then integrating people's interests to reach a shared solution.

For example, let's say a city government wants to build a new trash incinerator in a neighborhood and residents of the neighborhood oppose it. The city's position is that the incinerator must be built in this neighborhood, which is close to where the trash is being picked up. The residents' position is that it can't be built in their neighborhood because of the impact it will have on themselves and their homes. Those positions are mutually exclusive. The incinerator can't be built *and* not be built in the neighborhood. Now the parties are stuck at an impasse.

In contrast, when you look at the problem in terms of interests, options start to emerge. The city's interests are to get rid of trash as economically and safely as possible. The neighborhood residents' interests are their health and safety and the value of their property. These interests aren't mutually exclusive. In fact, we can see that both sides are interested in safety and financial impacts. Given these shared interests, there's opportunity for a win–win agreement.

Interests can be a wide array of goals and desires, or they can be deeper, more basic human needs such as safety, security, belonging, significance, and purpose. It's a bit like unpeeling the layers of an onion: the outer layers are a person's or group's positions, the middle layers are their goals and desires, and the most inner layers are the core human needs that we all share. In almost any dispute, all three layers are present, even though we often spend most of our time talking about the outer layer.

In collaborative problem-solving, we peel back the layers. It's deeper down that you find the ingredients for satisfying solutions.

That's why the previous three building blocks are so key: they're the activities and tools that allow you to get underneath the top layer, closer to the heart of the matter.

IDENTIFY OPTIONS

Once you've engaged everyone with a stake in the issue to understand the full range of interests at play, you can turn to developing solutions that integrate the parties' most important needs—or at least some of them. This will often involve brainstorming and other creative thinking strategies where people are invited to imagine using a technique called OPTIONS to address the full range of stakeholder interests.

OPTIONS is an acronym to help you remember and apply the most important aspect of this approach. It stands for "Only Proposals That Include Others' Needs Succeed."

Let's consider the case of the city planning to build a new incinerator. To integrate both the city's and the residents' interests, the solution could include building the incinerator in the neighborhood but also beefing up air-quality protections; committing to regular air-quality testing and meetings with residents to discuss the test results; creating more local parks to improve air quality and boost property values; and providing residents with a tax credit on their property taxes for many years. Or the solution could be that the neighborhood agrees to support increased property taxes and fees to finance a city-wide recycling and composting program, which they predict, over time, will reduce waste to levels sufficient for processing trash at the existing incinerator outside town.

As these scenarios show, integrative solutions are not a panacea. They often still involve hard trade-offs, but they usually result in solutions that are wise and effective because they incorporate the interests, needs, and knowledge of a wider group of people, not just one "winning" side. They're usually more enduring, too, as stakeholders take part in developing the shared agreement. There's nearly always something in it for everyone.

One real-life example of how people can arrive at a shared agreement without compromising their principles comes from Convergence's project started in 2012 on financing long-term care for elderly people and people with disabilities. Leaders in the field of long-term services and supports asked Convergence to convene a collaborative project to find ways to pay for this care, which so many Americans can't afford.

The positions of the group's members started out far apart. Some in the room felt market solutions were best to pursue because the US already had a private insurance industry providing some long-term care coverage and it made more sense to expand and stabilize it rather than watch insurers leave the market. These advocates for market-based solutions pointed out that government-based solutions had been tried and failed.[5] A new government program might crowd out existing long-term care insurance; it would also add enormously to the government deficit. Others argued that the private sector was clearly failing to deliver long-term care coverage *because* insurers were leaving the market. In their view, it made no sense to try to expand the private sector market. Instead, it made more sense to build on the approach of popular programs like Social Security and Medicare, perhaps even adding a new component to one of those programs and slightly increasing payroll tax to cover the cost.

These starting positions gave way over time to a more nuanced view as the participants came to understand the scale of the challenges and one another's perspectives on the issue. At one stage in the project, which lasted more than three years, the group suspended work to await the results of a study they had helped to design on the efficacy of some of the long-term care financing options they were considering. Both sides had brought their own estimates of different long-term care proposals to the table, and these different numbers had led them to essentially talk past each other. As the dialogue continued, they'd recognized that one of the obstacles to reaching any agreement was that the official government estimates of the cost of financing long-term care were based on inadequate models. The only way to resolve which options were affordable and feasible was to help create a better estimating approach and then subject their rival ideas to that model.

That study, conducted by the Urban Institute and the actuarial firm Milliman, was published in 2016. It found that neither public nor private efforts alone would solve the problem.[6] The numbers forced all of the participants to rethink their approach to a solution.

Among the findings were that long-term care insurance providers were typically capping policies at five years because of the increasing costs of care. In many ways more important, the highly uncertain and potentially huge liabilities of people aging with severe chronic conditions like Alzheimer's disease, which could leave them in need of significant non-medical services and support for many years, were also looming. Some changes might be made to open up the market, but the Milliman and Urban Institute analytics showed that premiums would likely be expensive, in part because people who anticipated needing long-term care services—people with disabilities or chronic health problems—would go out and buy policies, while people who didn't already have health problems wouldn't.

Yet it was also obvious that expanding existing government programs wasn't likely to be feasible. Medicaid was already covering long-term care services for those who had exhausted all of their own resources paying for services and supports. This was starting to stretch Medicaid's capacity in several states. For this reason, the group came to the view that the private sector also had a major role to play alongside an expanded role for the government as a "stop gap" when private solutions weren't enough.

The group's final report was a blend of public and market solutions. It called for a universal public program to help cover the catastrophic costs some families face in paying for long-term care. The program would give relief to private insurers for the costs of services and support they covered and limit their insurance liability, making it possible for more insurers to be able to offer long-term care policies at affordable and predictable prices. The report also made recommendations intended to make it easier to increase the uptake of private insurance. It brought together public financing and private markets, finding the most promising solution not in one or the other but in both, together.[7]

INTEGRATE INTERESTS

As we saw in Chapter 10, "Really Hear Everyone," we've found that collaborative problem-solving works best when people take the time to build an understanding of each other's interests and needs. It's often useful to deploy the OPTIONS approach as you create an explicit list of all the interests and needs at stake.

In a more formal process, a facilitator or convener might give a short training on interests and needs before working with the problem-solving group to create this list. However, it can also be done more simply.

We suggest first explaining the concept of positions being different from interests. Then get people thinking and talking. The prompt for conversation can be very broad: "Based on everything we've learned about each other and the issue, let's make a list of the interests and needs of all of the stakeholders." With these interests and needs visible to everyone, ask them to identify shared solutions. You may want to post the OPTIONS acronym and what it stands for on the wall to remind people to avoid win–lose solutions and instead think of more creative, integrative ones.

Even where the stakeholders are not gathered together in a room (real or virtual), you or another facilitator can develop a list of all the interests and needs that are at play by meeting with the stakeholders individually. Then look through a combined list of all interests and needs to generate OPTIONS-based approaches that are more likely to result in effective and enduring solutions.

Finally, the group selects a solution or set of solutions from the OPTIONS-based list that has been generated. More often than not, this happens organically. During the process of generating OPTIONS-based solutions, where everyone is keeping in mind that only proposals that include others' needs succeed, the wisest and most durable solution often becomes obvious. If this doesn't happen, there are several ways to reach agreement on an integrative solution. One is to review all of the options and create a shortlist of those that meet the most needs, then work together to improve each of these options until the group reaches agreement. If a solution still hasn't emerged, a very effective approach is to select a "strawman" set of options and have participants who aren't yet satisfied offer improvements to it until everyone feels their key needs and interests are being met.

Try It Out

Think about the issue you selected in the "Try It Out" in Chapter 2, "How to Reach Convergence." Create a list of all the interests and needs you can think of for everyone who has a stake in the issue. Take extra time and effort to consider the interests and needs of stakeholders with whom you disagree. Could you be missing anything?

Now, look at the full list and try to generate an OPTIONS-based solution, one that incorporates as many of the interests and needs from your list as possible.

NEGOTIATING *THE TREATY OF TRAVERSE DES SIOUX*

Capitol buildings are important spaces. They house the seat of government and serve as a symbol of community and authority. Often they also contain a lot of history—documents, furnishings, paintings, and statues that reflect key moments and people, as well as the community being served. And they don't get renovated very often. So it was a big deal when the Minnesota State Capitol Building underwent its first-ever restoration starting in 2013.

During the restoration, Minnesotans started discussing the paintings and statues in the Capitol. Almost no art had been added since the Capitol was erected in 1905. The images or stories of many Minnesotans weren't included or were depicted in ways that were upsetting to some groups. In particular, there were two paintings depicting Native Minnesotans in the Governor's Reception Room, where bill signings, press conferences, and other important state business take place, that drew people's attention. Neither were inspiring to many members of the 11 federally recognized tribal nations living within the borders of Minnesota. One especially felt like an insult.

The painting *The Treaty of Traverse des Sioux* depicts the signing, under duress, of the treaty under which the Dakota ceded 24 million acres of land in what is now Minnesota, Iowa, and South Dakota to the US government. In exchange for this land, the US promised to give the Dakota people a reservation as well as payment in money, goods, and access to education. Most of these promises went unfulfilled.[8] Without access to the land upon which they had hunted for generations, the Dakota would have to rely on treaty payments for their survival, but these didn't materialize: Before the treaties were formally ratified, the US Senate removed the provision for a permanent reservation. Instead, the Dakota could live on land previously set aside for them but only until it was needed for non-Native settlement, and they would only get a sliver of the money they were expecting. By 1862, stripped of their land and left without the food and money promised them, the Dakota were starving. These conditions played a direct role in the US–Dakota War of 1862, which left 358 White settlers, 77 US Army soldiers, and an unknown number of Dakota dead. It culminated in the largest one-day mass execution in American history in which 38 Dakota fighters were hanged.[9]

Because of its position in the Governor's Reception Room, *The Treaty of Traverse des Sioux* was the backdrop for many government events, and many people wanted to have it removed entirely from the restored Capitol. The painting and treaty are both part of Minnesota history, however, and a number of voices, including prominent historians, argued for the painting to remain. Recognizing the range of positions and interests involved, Minnesota's governor, Mark Dayton, chair of the group entrusted with overseeing the Capitol restoration, convened a committee to discuss how all of the art in the Capitol would be handled. Fifteen Minnesotans were chosen for their expertise in art, history, American Indian and Minnesota culture, and architecture. Representatives from all three branches of the Minnesota state government were also included.[10]

One of the committee members was professor, artist, and author Gwen Westerman, who is an enrolled member of the Sisseton Wahpeton Dakota Oyate. Each member was asked to provide a statement on their views of art in the Capitol. "Just how are Dakota people depicted in the art of the State Capitol?" she asked rhetorically. "They are shown through a constructed myth of the primitive savage in direct conflict with advancing 'civilization.'" Gwen was troubled that *The Treaty of Traverse des Sioux* was "more often than not viewed by visitors without the aid of adequate interpretative text that explains what they are seeing—half-Naked Indians in feathers, animal skins, and blankets from the distant past before Minnesota was a state." The painting and its placement, she wrote, "tacitly endorse the belief that Native peoples in Minnesota failed to adapt to so-called progress and are barely relevant to the development of the state." A strong-voiced woman who is used to standing up for herself from her years working in the corporate world, Gwen's position came across loud and clear. But she also conveyed her interests: giving visitors much more information about the painting's context and legacy, so they could become aware of the history of the treaty and the contributions of Native peoples to the state of Minnesota and the country.

With a project like the Capitol restoration, the community of stakeholders is much larger than the membership of a committee, or even the employees who go to work each day in the building; it's the entire public. So, the committee members made a concerted effort to understand and integrate the full range of perspectives in the state. The committee chairs and the governor formally consulted with leaders of 9 of the 11 tribal nations. Eleven public input meetings were held across the state, and a survey was completed by more than 3,500 Minnesotans. Experts in art, architecture, and history gave presentations.

Out of this learning the committee drafted a vision statement to guide their work:

> The purpose of art in the Minnesota State Capitol is to tell Minnesota stories. Works of art in the Capitol should engage people to:
> - Reflect on Minnesota history
> - Understand Minnesota government
> - Recognize the contributions of Minnesota's diverse peoples
> - Inspire citizen engagement
> - Appreciate the varied landscapes of Minnesota[11]

There was also a strong consensus that art in the Capitol should be unifying and affirming. "All Minnesotans," they agreed, "should be able to relate to the art in the Capitol and thereby feel connected to their state government and the art that is displayed."[12] At the same time, they said, the art should grapple with the difficult issues that are a part of Minnesotans' stories. When an artwork depicted difficult subjects, it should be put in context, including a range of perspectives and describing how perspectives have changed over time. The Capitol was a public space, and it was fitting to engage the public in understanding the state's history within its corridors.

When their meetings came to a close, the committee members concurred that much of the art in the Capitol needed more robust interpretation. Art that tells stories that unify Minnesotans would be displayed in the parts of the Capitol that are seen by the most visitors; art that tells more difficult stories would be placed in areas that had room to mount more extensive interpretative materials and that were more conducive spaces for reflection. *The Treaty of Traverse des Sioux* was moved from its spot in the Governor's Reception Room as the backdrop for press conferences to a newly refurbished room. In-depth information about the history of the painting and the treaty was hung alongside it. In addition, the state commissioned a series of elegant panels featuring a range of Minnesotans' portraits and their perspectives on the painting. The room also hosts a summary of how the committee came to the decision to recommend the painting's relocation and new display, with the values and interests they attempted to integrate spelled out.

Committee co-chair Paul Anderson, a former Minnesota Supreme Court justice, was one of the people who had at first resisted moving *The Treaty of Traverse des Sioux*. He felt a "significant connection" to the history of the treaty, because his ancestors were among the first wave of European settlers to make a home in Minnesota because of the treaty's signing. His appointment to be chief judge of the Court of Appeals in Minnesota had been announced with the painting as the backdrop. He'd attended many important sessions in the Governor's Reception Room and had many opportunities to consider the painting and its legacy. He knew that the painting had been specially commissioned to hang at the west end of the room and that the artist, Francis David Millet, had taken great efforts to make it "accurate and realistic" by researching witnesses' accounts and building and weathering a replica of the canopy under which the treaty was signed before he started painting. Judge Anderson also appreciated the painting's value as a work of art, because Millet had been one of the finest artists of the period.

By the end, he said, his thinking about the painting had evolved. Now, having a wider understanding of the painting's meaning to other groups and individuals, he felt it "should no longer have the 'privilege of place' behind the governor and other state officials when they conduct our state's most important business." When someone suggested that the painting might remain in the Governor's Reception Room with a curtain lowered to cover it during important meetings, he realized this would not serve many stakeholders' interests. More people would be satisfied if the painting wasn't hidden from view when it might offend but instead was moved, displayed openly, and explained.[13]

Engaging the public and encouraging first-time and repeat visitors became a key part of the committee's recommendations for the Capitol's artworks. To increase visitor engagement, the group recommended adding art that portrayed broader and more recent depictions of Minnesota's history, accomplishments, and achievements, bringing the story of Minnesota forward, from 1905 to the current day. In 2018, the state legislature codified the committee's work in law, establishing a permanent committee charged with advising and making recommendations for art exhibits that are displayed in special spaces set aside in the Capitol. All art selected must satisfy the integrative criteria laid out in the committee's vision statement, a testament to its enduring wisdom.

Fittingly, one of Gwen's poems, "Give-Away Song," speaks to the power of really understanding each other's values, experiences, and emotions around issues as you seek options for mutual gain:

> share from the heart
> in a world where words can be
> meaningless when they come
> only from the head.[14]

CHAPTER 12

Take Your Time

At this point we hope we've convinced you that collaborative problem-solving has immense benefits. Spoiler alert: Speed is not necessarily one of them! While it may save you time in the long run, finding wise, durable solutions built on higher ground often requires patience and fortitude.

It's probably also clear that the building blocks of collaborative problem-solving laid out in Part III are not a light lift. Ensuring that the full range of views are represented, nurturing trust, developing a shared understanding of the complexity of the issues, identifying the underlying interests of the parties, and creating new identities based on a shared commitment to solving the problem—all of these things take time. However, as a very smart, wiry-haired man once said, "Time is relative."

COLLABORATING SAVES TIME IN THE LONG RUN

Reflect back again on the issue that you selected in the "Try It Out" in Chapter 2, "How to Reach Convergence," or consider another divisive or challenging issue in your workplace, school, place of worship, or community. How long have people been fighting about it? How about an unresolved, contentious issue in the state where you live? How long have people been fighting about that? Probably for quite a while.

Yet polls show that Americans are not as divided as we think, even when it comes to some of the most divisive issues in the country. For example, less than 1 in 10 Americans, across political parties, support cuts to Medicare.[1] On border security, more than 8 in 10

Americans, across political parties, believe that those who enter the country illegally should be "treated humanely" and "processed quickly and fairly."[2] Similarly, nearly 9 in 10 Americans support having police officers receive training on how to de-escalate tense situations to avoid the use of force.[3] Despite the strong consensus around these issues, for how long have Americans longed for systems in healthcare, immigration, and law enforcement that work better? Longer than most anyone would like.

Compared to the amount of time it takes to fight, collaborative problem-solving is usually more efficient, because it usually leads to fewer challenges from any "losing" sides because the goal is that there are no losing sides. When people or groups feel defeated, they're less likely to accept the solutions agreed to by the "winners." Instead of working to support the solutions, they often put their energy into electing different politicians or changing the rules. Each time power shifts, the answers to the issue get undone and redone, and this can go on repeatedly.

That's what happened for more than a decade around Minnesota child custody law. It was only after the governor told the state legislature that he wouldn't sign a bill into law unless it was the product of collaborative problem-solving that the different factions finally came together and realized they agreed on overhauling the laws to center on children's needs rather than parents' preferences. Sweeping new laws with wide support were passed within a couple of years. "We had been in some real extended battles," recalled Brian Ulrich, a volunteer for the Center for Parental Responsibility. "We tended to be so interested in getting our own point across, both sides of this collaborative effort, that we never really did a good job of listening to where there were some common shared values, and this process allowed that to come out."[4]

Indeed, because of all the ways that one-sided victories can be stymied and contested, collaborative solutions are often downright speedy in comparison. In addition, a collaborative approach can usher in better communication and increased cooperation over the long haul, leading to an even better rate of return on everyone's investment of time.

With all that said, problem-solvers do need to be prepared to put a meaningful amount of time into assembling and maintaining the building blocks. Just how long you spend nurturing trust among stakeholders depends a lot on the complexity and scale of the issue you're addressing, the motivations and commitment of the stakeholders, and other factors. While there are no hard and fast timeframes that apply to this work, from our experience it might take a few weeks or months to implement building blocks to support problem-solving around an issue within an organization such as a religious congregation or a business, including the time you take to map the terrain with stakeholders; some groups might come to solutions within days, however. For a state-level policy issue, especially if contentious, it may take half a year to a year to develop solutions. For a national policy issue, it often takes longer, and it can take longer still to implement solutions because of how slow it can be to make institutional change. Being aware of, and communicating from the start, the amount of time that you and other stakeholders may need to dedicate to collaborative problem-solving will help to set the expectations of participants and any groups they represent. A quick win or immediate resolution is not always in the cards.

It seems like such a small thing, but we've been struck again and again by how people's investment of a good amount of time can be a huge factor in unsticking a previously stuck issue. We have each worked on many issues where past attempts at problem-solving failed in large part not because of how contentious they were but because no one was dedicating enough focused time to problem-solving.

SHORT ON TIME

There are times when investing in these building blocks leads to relatively rapid breakthroughs. This was the case in Minnesota when, facing a firm deadline, a group came together to work out the terms for how to distribute the state's share of the billions of dollars due to be paid out by opioid makers to deliver public and private health services to people who became addicted to overprescribed drugs.

Much of the pressure was due to the terms of the settlement that was negotiated between the various state attorneys general and the Big Pharma companies: it included a schedule where the state as a whole would receive a smaller payout from the settlement fund if any municipality declined to sign on to an agreement about how to distribute funds by a particular date. The drug makers had insisted on this provision because they wanted to avoid getting hit by additional lawsuits from individual cities, counties, or other government entities. But the clause meant that some county, city, and tribal representatives felt under pressure to accept terms that didn't necessarily reflect the impact of opioid addiction in their community.

Julie Ring, executive director of the Association of Minnesota Counties, also couldn't shake the memory of how the previous major settlement with Big Tobacco had ended with most of the money flowing into state coffers and getting used for general purposes during the 2008 global financial crisis rather than it going to projects to directly prevent and mitigate tobacco use and harms. Though she had training in conflict resolution, she kept catching herself losing trust in other stakeholders, and at one point she was convinced they wouldn't make the deadline. The different government reps and the AG's office just weren't coming to the table. Everyone was frustrated, and the deadline was barreling down on them. "You had this pressure, that we had to have the signature, you had to have these signers by certain dates," she recalled.

A curveball came her way when State Representative Dave Baker, one of Minnesota's most vocal advocates for opioid settlement funds and addiction services, seemed to expect that most of the money should be distributed to the state government's commission on responding to the opioid epidemic rather than shared more fully with local governments dealing directly with the problem. This was exactly what Julie dreaded—a repeat of missteps that she'd watched unfold after the tobacco settlement. Yet, at the same time, she knew he wouldn't be seeking to funnel funds in this way for political reasons. Instead, if he wanted the funds to go to the commission, it was because he'd put his heart and soul into the commission after his son died as a result of opioid addiction. Dave considered the commission his most important legacy.

Dave's concern about how the money would be distributed was actually different than what Julie had gleaned. He was mostly concerned about how small-population, rural counties, like the one he and his family called home, would fare. They didn't have the sort of bureaucratic infrastructure that the big counties did and were more likely to need help from the state commission to be able to deliver the services that county residents needed. He didn't care exactly how much money the drug makers forked over. His main concern was having assurance that no one else's son or daughter would die because of unbridled greed.

The deadline could have squeezed out the space that people from across the state needed to build trust and really hear each other, but according to both Julie and Dave, it helped that many of the people around the table knew each other from previous settlements and government projects. Because they could draw on existing relationships and a reservoir of trust, it was as though they'd been meeting for two years when they'd only been meeting for a few months. They didn't always agree, but they all reminded themselves that they wanted the same thing: to maximize what they could do for everyone in each of their communities. That shared vision, that shared belief in doing the right thing by the people of the state and reaching higher ground, "that's what brings people together at the end of the day," Julie said. Before the deadline, all of Minnesota's jurisdictions signed on to the agreement, ensuring the state received the maximum settlement.

PROCESS IS POWERFUL

Most of the stories we've been sharing describe the experience of people who've taken part in a formal collaborative problem-solving process like Education Reimagined, Reentry Ready, the Minnesota Capitol restoration project, and the Convergence dialogue on guns and suicide. We've featured these stories because one of us has been in the room while stakeholders were getting to know each other and solving the problem at hand; usually we were also part of mapping the terrain of the problem and planting some of the seeds of trust between participants. However, the building blocks are tools that can be used in any problem-solving setting. They require a commitment of time and energy, but that time and energy can be your own.

In Part IV, "Process," we walk you through the steps of establishing a formal collaborative problem-solving process. These formal processes can be scaled up for public issues—from your local community up to the national government—or kept smaller to fit the size of your organization. If you have constraints on your time, budget, or other resources, you can still apply the collaborative mindsets and building blocks and get positive results.

If, however, you can engage in a formal collaborative problem-solving process, this increases your chances for success, whether your process is big or small, long or short. This is because using a formal process:

- **Generates greater gravitas.** Stakeholders are often more aware that a process is taking place and can track developments.
- **Creates clarity.** Participants have formally committed to taking part in a clearly defined problem-solving process with a regular schedule of meetings.
- **Increases resources.** The people taking part are likely to contribute more time, energy, and other resources to a formal process than to something that feels ad hoc, because they can see there's some institutional commitment to having an outcome.
- **Ensures thoroughness.** A formal process helps to ensure that enough time and attention are given to each building block because they're embedded in the process itself.

On top of these benefits, we've also found there's something a little special about a full-blown collaborative problem-solving process. Maybe it's some drive to succeed that develops within participants because they've formally committed to taking part; maybe it's an unconscious expectation across the group that solving problems is the logical outcome of a problem-solving process; or maybe it's simply that all the building blocks and steps put together in this constellation are more than the sum of their parts.

Whatever it is, engaging in a formal collaborative problem-solving process, no matter the scale, is likely to be worth the time and lead to powerful, enduring outcomes.

IV

Process

Up until now, we've focused on the why and what of collaborative problem-solving. We now turn to the crucial missing piece—*how* to effectively and successfully engage with others to resolve problems in a step-by-step process.

In this part of the book, we bring together the mindsets in Part II and the building blocks in Part III and add to them a set of steps that, in combination, can be far greater than the sum of the parts. In conversations around complex, thorny issues like healthcare policy and police–community relations, we've been surprised and gratified to see how thinking, doing, and organizing often come together powerfully. So often, in our experience, the collaborative problem-solving process unwinds the knot of a seemingly intractable conflict and unspools a positive path forward.

For complex public issues, you'll likely find it very productive to thoroughly follow all of the process steps with care. For smaller, simpler issues, perhaps issues at the level of a community of worship or a workplace, it's still best to consider all of these steps, but some may not be necessary, or could be executed with less rigor and formality. As with the mindsets and building blocks, it's also not necessary to employ the full suite of steps. Any steps that you undertake are likely to be a boon to problem-solving. In the chapters we explain how you'd implement all the process steps and offer some lower-intensity versions, too. The steps are:

- Discovery and Design
- Dialogue and Destinations
- Achieving Consensus and Impact

We've laid out the steps in a series of three chapters, but in reality the elements of a collaborative problem-solving process aren't strictly linear. Every process evolves in an organic manner. It's common to revisit aspects of earlier steps as you go along.

We've not attempted to include every detail of a complete collaborative problem-solving process. We've distilled the process to the key steps needed to give many more people access to the benefits of collaborative problem-solving without having to become full-time specialists. In addition, we want to give everyone who takes part in a full process, no matter their role, an understanding of the steps that lead to success. For those who want to dive in deeper, we highly recommend *The Consensus Building Handbook: A Comprehensive Guide to Reaching Agreement*, edited by Lawrence Susskind, Sarah McKearnan, and Jennifer Thomas-Larmer of the Consensus Building Institute in Cambridge, Massachusetts.

You won't always want or need to convene a full collaborative problem-solving process, but where you do, we strongly encourage you to take all the steps outlined in the next three chapters. Doing so will make success more likely. In nearly every process in which we've taken part, we've felt the rich rewards far outweighed the effort.

CHAPTER 13

Discovery and Design

The first steps in a full collaborative problem-solving process involve discovery and design. During this phase, problem-solvers learn about the issue and the players involved (discovery) and then lay out how the collaborative problem-solving process will be organized (design).

The discovery steps are fundamental to collaborative problem-solving—so fundamental that we made them one of our building blocks: Chapter 8, "Map the Terrain." Before inviting anyone to join a group for problem-solving, you'll want to learn the full range of perspectives around the issue and identify the stakeholders. You'll then be in a position to ensure you're convening participants who reflect the complete spectrum of needs, concerns, and views in play, and who collectively have the authority or influence to move solutions forward.

The design portion of discovery and design is the extra element that comes into play during a formal problem-solving process and may not be much needed in informal processes. During design, the person or team leading this first stage of the process will chart the course ahead, recommending a timeline for meetings, the optimal location and frequency of meetings, and a possible gameplan of what might be achieved over the course of the various meetings:

RIPE AND RIGHT FOR COLLABORATION

Sometimes groups like Convergence seek to identify issues that would benefit from a collaborative problem-solving approach and initiate a process as an "outside" group, but that's rare. Ordinarily the seed for a collaborative problem-solving project is planted when someone gets interested in solving a tough problem that affects them or their work and which appears to be at an impasse. For the most part, identifying the issue is easy. It's the frustrating problem that's keeping you up at night.

Take the case of the Minnesota Security Hospital, which in 2015 and 2016 took part in a problem-solving process designed by the state of Minnesota's Office of Collaboration and Dispute Resolution. The hospital is the only facility in the state set up to assess and treat people with severe mental health issues who are also considered dangerous. All hospital patients have been civilly committed by the courts as mentally ill and dangerous; most have multiple health conditions—schizophrenia or another serious mental health issue coupled with chemical dependency, brain injury, trauma, developmental disabilities, behavior disorders, or a combination of these. Many have also committed serious crimes, including violent crimes like assault and murder. They can be emotionally volatile and physically aggressive. It's tough to be a patient or an employee there. "Direct-care staff were getting hurt in the line of duty," recalled Scott Melby, now chief operations officer at the Forensics Mental Health Program (the new name of the hospital).

Scott understands the stress that comes from working directly with hospital patients, day in and day out. His mother had been a nurse for years on the mental healthcare campus in St. Peter that includes the facility. In fact, his mom was the person who suggested that he apply for a job in Minnesota's mental healthcare system when he graduated from college with a degree in business in 1986. For his first 14 years he'd been direct-care staff, starting in a position that was then called "human services technician." He found he enjoyed the work, so he made it a career, rising up at other facilities in St. Peter.

Several years before Scott became a manager at the Minnesota Security Hospital, some families had sued another Minnesota state hospital for overusing restraints and seclusion. As part of the legal settlement, hospitals across the state were ordered to reduce the use of these practices.[1] However, restraints and seclusion were often still being overused. In one case, a patient at the Minnesota Security Hospital had been secluded for 25 days on a cement slab with no mattress. By 2011, authorities had told the hospital management that if such practices weren't significantly curtailed, the facility would lose its license to operate. The management had introduced a "positive behavioral supports" approach to addressing violent behavior as required by the settlement.

The shift to positive behavioral supports wasn't sticking. Most of the direct-care staff were accustomed to a security-focused approach; they didn't have a background or training in social services or other psychiatric counseling skills. Many felt unequipped to ensure people's safety, including their own, under the new approach. Citing their lack of understanding about how to use the behavioral approach and their lack of clear authority to restrain patients, no matter the threat of harm, staff had allowed a patient to repeatedly bang his head against a wall for three hours, until he needed to go to the emergency room for medical attention.

One special challenge the hospital faced was out-of-date facilities that caused safety challenges, such as too many blind corners. When the building was constructed in 1982, it was "touted as being the best in the nation," Minnesota State Representative Jack Considine, a former behavior specialist at the hospital, told the *MinnPost*.[2] Thirty years later, the building's design was failing patients and staff alike. Scott could give a tour of the corridors and stairways pointing out the places where assaults were most likely to happen, because they were out of the sight of cameras or distant from staff hubs. The rooms were dark and drab, adding to the sense of danger and discomfort. Little about the space conveyed safety or security.

Just as troubling, the hospital had too few psychiatrists and psychologists. In 2012 the entire professional psychiatric staff had resigned in protest of the previous director's management approach, and it had proved difficult to refill these roles. All in all, the hospital lacked the essential infrastructure for positive behavioral supports and interventions.

As a result, the number of serious injuries on campus had gone up. Between 2013 and 2017, there were 370 patient assaults on staff members that required medical treatment; in 2016 alone, there had been 51 injuries caused by patients assaulting other patients. The constant threat of injury exacerbated issues with improving patient care. The union representing direct-care staff and the hospital's management were at a point of crisis. Union reps were adamant that their members weren't safe and asserting that management didn't care. Leaders like Scott felt the staff had lost trust in them. Direct-care staff were starting to leave in greater numbers, too.

Minnesota's governor, Mark Dayton, called for a collaborative problem-solving process to address the problems. This was an institution where *everybody* felt things were at an impasse and something had to be done, but they couldn't agree on what to do. Governor Dayton asked the Office of Collaboration and Dispute Resolution, which Mariah ran, to design a process involving all of the stakeholders—the hospital management team, labor unions, patients' families, mental health advocates, and the Minnesota Department of Human Services leadership.

"We obviously needed to do something different, because it was pretty clear what we were doing wasn't working, and I was willing to give it a shot," said Scott, who at the time of the process was program manager at the hospital. "I wanted to be an effective manager and create a workplace that was better for our staff and our patients." Scott also had a sense that a full collaborative problem-solving process could help to reset the conversations between management and direct-care staff by bringing an "outside set of eyes" to the issues they were having.

Because the governor called for the Office of Collaboration and Dispute Resolution to design a formal collaborative problem-solving process for the Minnesota Security Hospital, it was obvious this needed to be done. But in other circumstances, it isn't always so clear. You can consider a number of criteria and questions to help you decide whether to commit to designing a formal process.

Criterion	Questions to Ask
Impasse	Does the problem feel "stuck"?
	Does it feel like the people who should be working together on solutions aren't?
	Is there hostility between groups or some other thing keeping them from working together?
	If they were able to agree on some solutions, would that "unstick" the issue?

Criterion	Questions to Ask
Impact	Is the issue important enough to warrant a collaborative problem-solving process or could it be solved through compromise or by an authority making a decision?
Influence	Does there appear to be a path to implementing the solutions that arise out of the group, either because the person or organization convening the problem-solving process is committed to it, or because the stakeholders who are likely to take part have the collective authority or influence to make things happen?
Balance	Does it appear that representatives of all perspectives on the issue would be willing to come to the table?
	Is it likely that a table with balanced representation from stakeholder groups can be built?
Means	Are there enough time and resources to conduct a full collaborative problem-solving process?
Value-add	Would a collaborative problem-solving process add value? Or would it duplicate and potentially compete with other work in the issue area?

Fully exploring the questions for each of these criteria can help you determine whether a formal collaborative problem-solving process might be useful or necessary for resolving your issue.

FRAME THE ISSUE

Once you've decided that a formal collaborative problem-solving process is a good fit for an issue, you need to find a way to bring everyone to the table. This involves framing the issue in terms that can't be misunderstood to suggest that one side holds all the truth about how to see the issue or to imply any particular solution. The framing needs to be open to everyone's perspectives, building on what you've learned from and about stakeholders in the discovery phase. It needs to be inviting to people of divergent views.

In interviews to learn about the Minnesota Security Hospital process, some stakeholders talked about improving patient care. Their view was that too many patients were still being restrained and secluded, and that there were not enough mental health professionals on staff. Other stakeholders framed the issue as being about staff safety. In their view, too many staff were being injured by patients. They felt they had lost the tools to keep themselves safe and that there weren't enough security staff members. With some exploration, it became clear that patients who received high-quality treatment and who were supported by appropriate physical and personal infrastructure would be far less likely to hurt others. So in the collaborative problem-solving process, the issue was framed as being about quality care leading to mutual well-being and safety, for both patients and employees.

In another situation, when Convergence worked on the design of the project on healthcare coverage in which Carla Willis of the American Medical Association took part, the team quickly learned that talking about a goal of "universal healthcare coverage" was a barrier to bringing several important stakeholder groups to the table; the stakeholders read this term as code for imposing a system run by the government, like a mega-sized Medicare, or the National Health Service in the UK. The frame eventually came together around the goal of increasing healthcare coverage as quickly as possible for as many people as possible—Health Care Coverage for the Uninsured. This frame didn't in and of itself rule out reaching universal healthcare coverage but avoided using a term that some stakeholders saw as divisive.

The Difficult Conversations Lab at Columbia University has explored the impact of framing on people's interest in working with others. Researchers asked people on opposite sides of the abortion debate to have a brief conversation about the issue with one other person and then consider writing and signing a joint statement about their shared views. Before the discussion, however, they read one of two versions of an article on a different issue: guns. In the first version of the article, the gun issue was presented as a war between two camps; in the second, it was framed as a complex issue that could be seen through many lenses, mentioning that there are plenty of conservatives who favor universal background checks for gun ownership and plenty of liberals who support the right to bear arms. Everyone in the groups that read the complex frame was willing to work together and sign a statement, compared with only 46% of those who read the war frame.[3] That's the power of thoughtful framing.

Even with less contentious issues, it pays to think about your framing. For example, during the coronavirus pandemic, many companies had their employees work from home if they could. When employers started thinking about having employees return to working in-office one or two years later, they sometimes met resistance. Many people had become used to balancing work and life from home and liked not having a daily commute. Managers, for their part, wanted the benefits of more in-person collaboration and use of office equipment and other resources. In cases we looked at, employers who invited employees into a collaborative discussion were more likely to get participation and genuine engagement when they framed the issue as being about "future workplace and space planning" rather than "returning to the office." One financial services provider framed the conversation even more broadly, as "future ways of working," with employees invited to experiment over a six-month period with different patterns of coming into the office to help them feed different experiences into the company's stakeholder interviews.

Here are some tips for successful issue framing:

- **Connecting.** Aim to unify all sides' views by using connecting words such as "and"—for example, gun rights *and* safety.

- **Needs.** Include core needs that are at stake, particularly where people already appear to be converging on a need—for example, safety at the Minnesota Security Hospital.
- **Widening.** Use expansive language that doesn't suggest you've already decided on one way forward—for example, "workspace planning" rather than "returning to the office."
- **Solutions.** Focus on the goal of finding solutions—for example, "developing solutions to the issue of housing affordability" rather than "understanding our broken housing system."

Try It Out

Using the tips above, frame the issue you chose to address in the "Try It Out" in Chapter 2, "How to Reach Convergence," in a way that you think all sides would agree is a fair, accurate, and balanced description of the problem. Now check it against our tips—does it check one or more of the boxes of Connecting, Needs, Widening, or Solutions? If it doesn't, is there a way to reframe the issue to make the most of one of these inclusive ways to approach framing?

ROLES AND RESPONSIBILITIES

Regardless of the scale or scope of your issue, if you've decided to set up a more formal collaborative problem-solving process, you'll need to find people to fill key roles: the convener, the facilitator, and participants.

The Convener

A convener is a respected leader or institution that has the credibility to bring diverse people together to work on a common problem and motivate them to do the hard work of building consensus and finding higher ground. Conveners champion collaborative problem-solving while also, in most situations, either staying neutral on the outcome or committing to honor any consensus that emerges. Some conveners take part in both oversight of the overall project and implementation of the group's recommendations.

The convener might be a government body or an elected official; a CEO, division manager, or other business leader; a not-for-profit organization, philanthropy, or labor union; the dean or head of a school; or a community leader such as a PTA president, neighborhood association chair, or head of a student organization or club. The convener could also be an individual such as an ombuds or professional mediator engaged by an organization to advance a collaborative problem-solving process. In the Minnesota Security Hospital process, the convener was Governor Dayton, who was deeply committed to the facility being safe for patients and staff but remained neutral on whether that outcome would be optimally accomplished through more staffing, different staffing, different programs, changes to the facility, or other options.

The Facilitator

A facilitator is an impartial person who ensures effective process design and day-to-day management of conversations. This person provides a credible, welcoming space for open dialogue and problem-solving. The facilitator you choose needs to be a skilled and respectful listener who can keep discussions on track, help to defuse tensions that arise, and summarize how the discussion is progressing. It often helps to have a highly trained facilitator, but in some instances, and especially if the discussion is not too highly charged, someone with natural abilities to listen, reflect back others' points of view, and generate trust can handle the role. In the Minnesota Security Hospital process, the facilitator was Mariah, representing the Office of Collaboration and Dispute Resolution. In Convergence projects, we always utilize a highly skilled facilitator.

Other project management activities, such as the logistics of finding places and dates to meet and informal contact with stakeholders outside of the formal problem-solving sessions, may be handled by the convener, the facilitator, or both. The decision about how to divvy up this work will depend on people's skills, resources, and capacity.

Both the convener and facilitator roles need to be fulfilled in a full process, but they can be fulfilled in different ways. For example, a university center might serve as both the convener and the facilitator for a process to address student concerns on campus; the head of a business division might serve as the convener and also handle project management but bring an external facilitator on board.

Participants

In Part III, "Building Blocks," we described how identifying everyone who has a stake in the problem affects the likelihood that the group will find effective and enduring options and solutions. Participants are representatives from each of the stakeholder groups that you've identified who then take an active part in the dialogue process run by the facilitator. The table of participants needs to be balanced to ensure there's someone to voice every major need, concern, and point of view around the issue. This widest range of voices is what makes it possible to find optimal solutions. In the Minnesota Security Hospital process, more than a hundred stakeholders—including representatives from the staff, labor unions, patient families, mental health advocates, the hospital administration, and the Minnesota Department of Human Services leadership—were interviewed, and then about 30 people were invited to be core participants.

IDENTIFY THE RIGHT PEOPLE FOR THE ROLES

It's essential that the convener and facilitator be trusted by the participants and the wider community of stakeholders.

Perhaps the most important factor in securing trust in the convener is that the person is both deeply committed to solving the problem and simultaneously neutral or at least open to various approaches to how that is accomplished, as Governor Dayton made clear when he convened the collaborative problem-solving process for the Minnesota Security Hospital. Another way that a convener can garner trust is by demonstrating their commitment to do everything they can to see the group's consensus solutions implemented and then also having the means to follow through. Unfortunately, too many of us have had the experience of serving on some sort of committee or task force only to see recommendations gather dust on some leader's shelf. Again, Governor Dayton had both the authority and the commitment to ensure that the hospital group's collaborative work would be put into action.

Sometimes it's not possible to find a single convener that all participants and stakeholders can trust. In this case, it works well to have a pair of conveners who, together, engender trust because they come to the problem from differing, if not divergent, perspectives.

Participants must also trust the facilitator. Like the convener, the facilitator must be committed to the problem-solving process but stay neutral on the outcome. The facilitator's skills in and of themselves garner participants' trust. As Ellie Bertani, who was director of HR Strategy and Innovation at Walmart US when she participated in Convergence's Working Up project on improving economic mobility for lower-wage workers, recalled, "the facilitation of the workshops was designed to build an incredibly safe space for people to feel protected and heard and come together around some aligned values and interests." The facilitator creates the trusted space in which relationships and shared solutions can germinate, develop, and thrive.

When selecting a facilitator, we've found certain qualities, experiences, and backgrounds help to support participant and stakeholder trust and engagement:

- High-quality mediation training, facilitation training, or other relevant education (possibly including certification in psychology, coaching, or leadership training)
- Ability to remain neutral on the issue at hand while demonstrating empathy and care for the participants
- Perceived as fair-minded and respected by all participants
- Successful track record of facilitating processes like the one you're setting up

The International Association of Facilitators is one of several resources to help problem-solvers find and vet professional facilitators.[4]

Try It Out

For the issue you choose in the "Try It Out" in Chapter 2, who might fulfill each of the key roles—convener, facilitator, and participants?

Who has the trust of stakeholders and can effectively convene them? Does that person or organization also have the authority to implement changes, which would add to their attractiveness as a convener? Do you need to have a pair of conveners to obtain the trust of all stakeholders?

Who might serve as a trusted and skilled facilitator or could help you to identify a good choice?

From among the stakeholders you've identified, who would be great representatives of their group's perspectives and needs at the dialogue table? Are there some groups or individuals who would be indispensable or uniquely valuable participants?

CHART THE COURSE AHEAD

Near the end of the discovery and design phase of the process, it can be helpful to consolidate all of this work into a written document that summarizes everything the problem-solvers have developed so far, including a plan for how the collaborative problem-solving process will be run. This is the gameplan and timeline for your process. It's often called a *group charter*, because it charts the course ahead for the group's problem-solving work.

The group charter helps to ensure that all participants have a shared understanding of the work they're undertaking together and how they'll get that work done. It might include:

- How you've framed the issue, including a summary of the full range of views on the issue that led you to this issue frame
- Initial ideas about pieces of the problem that might be addressed individually, and the order in which it might make sense to tackle them based on your interviews with stakeholders
- The individuals or organizations who've agreed to serve as convener and facilitator, or a list of candidates if you're still thinking about these roles
- A list of the types of stakeholders who should participate in the process, including the names of any specific individuals who have agreed to be participants
- A timeline for the process, including anticipated meeting frequency and duration

- What will happen with the group's final product—for example, if the convener has the authority to implement it, or if they need to submit it for approval to another body

The group charter may also cover guidelines for how participants will work together. It could describe how final decisions are expected to be made—for example, by full consensus, super majority vote, majority vote, or some other method—where these have been chosen by the convener or determined by the contours of the problem. The spirit of collaborative problem-solving is to find shared agreement, or consensus, around an issue, but not all problems need 100% agreement to be agreeable to most, and perhaps even all, stakeholders.

Often, group charters will also include ground rules like those outlined in Chapter 9, "Nurture Trust," as well as other rules of engagement, such as the role of social or traditional media.

Now that you've set the table for conversation, so to speak, you're ready to begin engaging participants in a formal problem-solving dialogue.

CHAPTER 14

Dialogue and Destinations

In the next steps of a full process, the problem-solving participants begin their facilitated dialogue and start to consider possible destinations—where they're trying to go, together. This involves generating criteria to guide their group decision-making and developing creative options—what most people think of when they imagine a collaborative problem-solving process. From the first meeting until the last, you and the participants will benefit from drawing upon Part III, "Building Blocks." In particular, in early meetings the focus will be on building trusting relationships and a shared understanding of the issues. In our experience, you'll find the skills and tools shared in Chapter 9, "Nurture Trust," and Chapter 10, "Really Hear Everyone," especially useful in supporting dialogue in the midst of divergent views and disputed facts.

The process facilitator is key to supporting respectful and productive dialogue. Much of the success of the Constitutional Convention was credited to naming George Washington to preside over the proceedings. As the retired commander-in-chief of the American forces in the Revolution, Washington's stature was unrivaled among the delegates. He also remained neutral throughout the deliberations, speaking only once about the substance of the nation's new constitution. He made it his mission to keep things calm and orderly, ensuring all sides had opportunities to speak.[1]

The facilitator also keeps the conversation rolling. Ellie Bertani from Walmart recalled that Convergence's Working Up project on economic mobility was successful in large part due to the facilitator's skill, particularly "his ability to architect a series of activities, exercises, and conversations to move things forward and keep everyone . . . on topic."

We've found that it helps to structure ongoing conversations around challenging issues by:

- Summarizing and synthesizing
- Reframing for productive conversation
- Finding a shared goal
- Forming principles of agreement and a vision for the future
- Brainstorming

SUMMARIZING AND SYNTHESIZING

At times in a collaborative problem-solving process, the dialogue may feel unfocused, as though *too many* competing needs are being thrown on the table. Participants can start to lose trust in the process to deliver solutions, and then they disengage. When the conversation shifts like this, it often helps if the facilitator recaps what's being said and weaves together the strands of conversation, identifying the important underlying needs that participants are expressing. This is *summarizing and synthesizing*.

Synthesizing is a skill that you'll want your facilitator to have. It can help participants get clarity when ideas or information are complex and potentially divergent. It can also help them to see how each idea connects to the whole and discover areas of agreement they may be missing. Most important, synthesizing helps people to feel heard and understood. When people's needs are explicitly named, as they are in a good synthesis, the recognition builds belief that *all* needs matter and that they can coexist symbiotically. This recognition generates progress by helping participants start to identify solutions that meet multiple needs.

How to Synthesize	Issue	Synthesis
Link disparate interests.	Affordable housing	So we're looking for options that both create more affordable housing *and* protect the value of existing homes. Who has ideas?

How to Synthesize	Issue	Synthesis
State areas of common ground.	Police–community issues	I'm hearing that it's important to this group that all members of the community, including our young men of color and our peace officers, feel safe.
Describe the issue as a shared problem rather than individual positions.	Water quality	A healthy environment that includes clean water and a secure food supply is important to everyone in this room.
Boil down each side's perspective to their core needs—what's most important to them.	Trash incinerator	We're seeking ways to remove trash from our community safely and cost effectively.
Tie together solution options that address the concerns of two or more stakeholders.	Community park	It sounds like one option could be designing a park with lots of natural features that children can play in.

If you're playing the role of facilitator in your process, or you need to fill a gap in facilitation, it's handy to have a few synthesizing phrases at the ready:

- Here's what I've heard so far . . .
- The common thread seems to be . . .
- Here's how I see the connection between all that has been said . . .
- What's really important seems to be . . .

After synthesizing, the facilitator often checks with the group to see if any part of the synthesis is inaccurate or missing something important. Typically, however, participants will let the facilitator know if they feel as though the synthesis doesn't feel right, either in the group setting or one on one. For this reason, synthesizing is an ongoing dynamic. It's not a step in the process so much as a tool that gets deployed during meetings when needed.

REFRAMING FOR PRODUCTIVE CONVERSATION

Many stakeholders have passionate views born out of frustrating or painful experiences related to an issue. This may lead them to make statements that are unproductive—being unclear, demanding, threatening, or even potentially toxic. Underneath the pain and frustration, people usually want a constructive response to their statements; they don't actually want to end their dialogue. Unproductive statements can be transformed into productive statements through *reframing*.

Every strong statement contains some underlying interest or concern. People often switch to more constructive communication when they believe their needs or concerns are being heard and addressed. Reframing is a tool for demonstrating that the listener hears and is willing to engage with the speaker's needs or concerns. It gets dialogue back on track by transforming arguing into problem-solving. The facilitator, as the person in the room who's neutral about the issues, will usually take the lead in reframing, but anyone can reframe to great effect.

It's important to understand that reframing isn't a quick exercise, like a game of Mad Libs where you insert new nouns and adjectives into a sentence and move on. It can take some time to understand what lies underneath problematic language. You have to listen for the true heart of the message to identify the underlying interests, needs, and concerns that are driving people's strong emotions. Once this is done, it's possible to remove unproductive language and reframe using productive language that's more likely to feel true to the individual—but this is still not a guarantee. Any time a facilitator reframes, they'll want to ask the speaker if they've got it right. If the person says "no," it's time to ask for more information and try reframing again.

Unproductive Statement

Affordable housing will bring in people who don't contribute to the tax base and will be a big drain on our community. This city is going to go broke.

How to Reframe	Productive Reframing
Eliminate toxic language, blame, and fault, replacing these with neutral words.	It sounds like you want to build a community in which all members contribute to where they live.
Shift language from positions to interests.	It sounds like you're seeking a solution that will protect property values.
Define issues jointly rather than from one participant's perspective.	We're looking for ways to make our community affordable and to do it in a way that fosters the growth that we all benefit from.

Unproductive Statement

If you don't agree to add 500 affordable housing units, it will be clear that you don't care about people who have less. You're heartless and just looking out for yourself.

How to Reframe	Productive Reframing
Shift from non-negotiable values or feelings to negotiable options.	It sounds like the change won't seem like a meaningful commitment to you unless the number of affordable housing units is substantial.
Move from judgments of character to behaviors.	It's important to you that our community is welcoming to those who have fewer resources as well as those who are already established here.
Seek common solutions rather than a fight.	We're all here tonight to try to find ways to make our community affordable and prosperous.

"Both" Statements

How to Reframe	Productive Reframing
Emphasize commonality of interests, removing either/or framing.	Despite our differences, I hear everyone tonight saying they're here because they want our community and community members to thrive, including through having housing that is affordable and preserving property values.

FINDING A SHARED GOAL

Dialogue works best where there is a common goal, even if it is somewhat general in nature. It could be a desire to improve economic mobility among lower-income workers, the need to create the right balance between growth and environmental protection in a community, or the desire to have an immigration system that protects the economic and physical security of those already living in the US while being appropriately humanitarian for this country of immigrants. What's important is that those participating have the same destination even if they are drawn toward different paths to getting there.

So, at some point early in the process, it helps to identify your shared goal. Sometimes a shared goal is obvious and can be included in your initial framing of the problem being solved. More often, it emerges from the process of building trust and understanding among participants.

In the Minnesota Security Hospital process, different stakeholder groups cohered around the idea that high-quality patient treatment and conditions would lead to safety for both patients and staff. This began to take shape in a goal to build new hospital infrastructure that would support better care and provide a better environment for everyone. A bright, open floor plan would get rid of blind corners. A staff office with a wide, unobstructed view of common areas and patient rooms would help, too. Smaller groupings of resident rooms would make it easier for staff to monitor if patients were passing around items that might be used to harm themselves or others. The ideas here extended beyond renovating the hospital's buildings. Extra training for direct-care staff would help them to transition from security-focused interventions to behavior- and treatment-focused approaches with patients. Finding ways to reduce the need for staff to take on extra shifts would help to reduce overwork and stress.

However, the most important aspect of the goal of better hospital infrastructure was the sense that this goal was shared. It wasn't imposed by one side or the other. "The collaborative problem-solving process I feel helped us collaborate and repair imperative communication, which is utterly necessary to function within the Minnesota Security Hospital," said Tim Headlee, president of AFSCME Local 404, who participated in the process as a representative of unionized direct-care providers. "Ensuring healthy communication, I feel, helped the direct-care teams recognize limitations, build trust, and raise employee morale, in turn creating a healthy work environment that will benefit all."[2]

It may not be possible to use dialogue to resolve deep issues of moral and religious principle. However, with some imagination it may still be possible to convene stakeholders on opposite sides of a charged issue and find shared goals. For example, starting in the late 1990s, two organizations dedicated to dialogue—the Public Conversations Project (now Essential Partners) and Search for Common Ground— each undertook projects to bring together opposing sides on the issue of abortion.[3] This came at a time when there had recently been multiple violent incidents at abortion clinics around the country, including ones where people were killed.

It was taken as a given that people would not change their minds on the fundamental issue of the morality or legality of abortion. Yet both dialogues uncovered that people with strong moral and religious beliefs could understand the views of people on the other side of the issue; they could build trust and respect with one another and engage in positive conversation. Despite their fundamental differences on abortion, one of these process groups agreed on a suite of shared goals, including preventing teenage pregnancy and improving foster care and adoption policies. This opened the door to working together and continuing dialogue.

Shared goals often incorporate moral values such as opportunity, dignity, fairness, care, security, and unity because our morals underpin why and how humans are prompted to support each other in activities from feeding a community to caring for children to avoiding spreading diseases. They're what have got us working well together across the ages. However, it's important to remember the work on moral foundations we discussed in Chapter 7, "Seek Higher Ground": while all humans seem to share a broad set of moral values, we sometimes prioritize those values differently. In addition, some people are naturally more attuned to avoiding risk and protecting against threats, while others are attracted to what is new and different (which inherently carries more risk because it's unknown to them). Both sets of priorities are essential for successful problem-solving. Without individuals who pay attention to threats, we'd find our communities more often in danger; without individuals who are drawn to the new and different, we'd find our communities stagnating more often.

A number of conflict resolution experts have found success in the practice of "moral reframing," which involves presenting your needs in a way that is consistent with others' moral values.[4] People who are more attuned to defending against threats tend to be more culturally and politically conservative. People who are more drawn to the new and different tend to be more culturally and politically liberal. Both conservatives and liberals prioritize the values of caring and fairness.[5] That's where shared goals can often be found. For example, a liberal person might talk about how a living wage fosters self-sufficiency and family stability and a conservative individual might talk about how a strong military helps America foster liberty and human rights for people around the world.

An initial framing of Convergence's Working Up project around "economic inequality" caused some participants to hesitate, even as they acknowledged inequality to be a problem. For them, inequality was conflated with an unwelcome notion of redistribution of income, which felt counter to their moral value of fairness. Increased "economic mobility," or opportunity, became a framing that could work across the spectrum. The Working Up project name reflected this.

The themes of opportunity and dignity come up again and again in our work because they're goals that integrate a range of moral values. The most powerful shared goals include the salient moral values of all stakeholders.

Try It Out

Identify a goal for the issue you identified in the "Try It Out" in Chapter 2, "How to Reach Convergence." Now apply moral reframing to it while keeping others' values in mind.

Think about the moral values of caring and fairness, which tend to be shared across divergent worldviews and beliefs. Can your goal be put in terms of either of these widely held values?

Be honest about both your needs and the other side's. Is the goal that you've identified really one that meets the needs of a wide range of people?

FORMING PRINCIPLES OF AGREEMENT AND A VISION FOR THE FUTURE

Especially in the earlier stages of a process, while participants are still building trust and getting to know one another's concerns and needs, it may be difficult to reach agreement on specific options for solutions. Indeed, in some dialogues, like the one on abortion, this may not be possible. So before you start to sift and sort through options, it can be incredibly useful, and at times essential, to first agree on principles that will guide the group's work going into the future. A well-defined statement setting out *principles of agreement* is a yardstick against which the group can measure future ideas. It also helps to build group trust in the process and provides a sense of shared purpose among participants.

For example, in the Working Up project, the participants—including stakeholders from businesses like Walmart, IBM, Microsoft, and McDonald's; the US Chamber of Commerce; unions; and advocates, left and right—all agreed to seek a shared answer to the question: "How can work become a stronger engine of economic mobility for lower-income workers?" This led them to agree on a set of principles linking work with economic mobility, including:

- **Working with dignity for a decent income** is central to a good life in our society. . . . Therefore, all Americans should have the opportunity to work to their full potential.

- **Participation in the workforce** should provide all workers with substantial opportunities for increasing their skills, capacities, income, and assets over time to facilitate upward mobility.
- **Work, supplemented by supports and benefits,** should provide sufficient income, economic security, and stability for workers and their families to live in dignity.
- **Responsibilities related to work and returns from work** should be shared appropriately among workers, employers, government, and society.[6]

The group chose its principles of agreement well before digging into a specific discussion of options for making work a more effective engine of economic mobility. Vitally, the principles of agreement left open the important debate over who should pay for what—for instance, on the principle of assuring sufficient income for a life of dignity, whether it should be employers paying through wages or the government paying through tax changes or other supports, or some combination. All stakeholders could agree to the principles without feeling that they might be ceding ground. And this allowed for a moment of genuine breakthrough, according to project director Russell Krumnow. As he recalled, employers and worker advocates had both been trying to find ways to support people on lower wages, but they "were butting heads all the time." They'd been viewing each other as part of the problem rather than part of the solution. Finding principles of agreement got them aligned on working together toward a shared goal.

Sometimes, principles of agreement are combined with *visioning*, a process of creating a description of a preferred future that pushes beyond the idea of a shared goal. Groups can create a shared vision by asking, *What will our organization, or our community, or our world, look like when this issue has been resolved?*

The specific ideas about what a future Minnesota Security Hospital facility might look like transformed a shared goal into a vision. But an effective vision doesn't have to be as tangible as an architect's sketch of a new building. In the wake of the shooting of Philando Castille in Falcon Heights, Minnesota, Melanie Leehy and other city residents developed a shared vision for the future by defining seven values to guide their shared community. One of these values was mutual safety for residents and police: "We value safety, including protecting residents and guests from personal harm and protecting groups from prejudice, discrimination, and hostility. Respect for life and minimizing harm to all are our highest priorities in public safety and policing. We believe that mutual safety is built through mutual trust."[7] When it came time to consider which proposals to submit to the mayor and city council, the task force reviewed ideas against the full set of community values to see which would serve their vision for Falcon Heights' future.

Try It Out

Think back again to the issue you chose in the "Try It Out" in Chapter 2 and the list of stakeholders you'd need to include in any effort to solve the problems you're working on. Keeping their perspectives in mind, come up with a few principles of agreement that you think would be shared by the widest range of stakeholders.

Now look at your draft principles of agreement and consider if it might be a foundation for finding shared recommendations.

If you're not sure they would, revisit your principles of agreement. Is there anything else that might be added to, changed, or removed from your list?

BRAINSTORMING

Once the group has built trust and forged a shared understanding of the issues, a shared vision, and some principles of agreement, they're ready to begin developing solution sets. Chapter 11, "Generate Options for Mutual Gain," provides several useful approaches for doing this. A good place to start is with the familiar activity of *brainstorming*.

Many of us have had bad experiences with brainstorming—for example, being asked by a manager at work to take part in a brainstorming session where we've been told that all ideas are welcome, only to have our colleagues or our manager critique almost every idea that's subsequently offered. So it's worth stepping back and considering the purpose of brainstorming so your group can really engage with it.

Brainstorming was the brainstorm of BBDO advertising executive Alex Osborn, who first wrote at length about it in his 1942 book *How to "Think Up."* "You can think up better if you team up with others," he wrote. "Two heads are better than one, and five are better than two, but only if their owners will honestly make them work for the good of the group. Too often members of a group will either let their imagination idle or will apply their minds to purposes other than the ideas for which the group is shooting."[8] Osborn said the most successful brainstorming sessions he hosted were after a nice meal, when everyone felt more relaxed, and some ground rules were set down: "all are equal," "every idea, 'crackpot' or 'crackerjack,' is recorded," and "not until the next day are [the ideas] scrutinized for merit."[9] He swore by the effectiveness of brainstorming sessions to foster out-of-the-box, creative thinking in business and other realms of life.

Since Osborn first described the brainstorming process, it's become a regular feature of business strategy, evolving into offshoots like "blue sky thinking," where only the sky's the limit. This sort of unedited, creative thinking session is a great way to get a group of people with different views on a problem talking and sharing their ideas for solutions. It can be as simple as providing the group with a set of ground rules, setting a timer for 15, 30, or 60 minutes, and then writing down every idea conceivable in that timeframe on flip chart paper. Sample ground rules could be:

- Generate as many ideas as possible.
- Wild ideas are encouraged.
- Suspend judgment—say whatever comes to your head.
- Build upon each other's ideas.
- Evaluate ideas later—either later today or at the next meeting.

It's often useful to remind participants a few times during the session that suspending judgment does *not* imply agreement, even with their own ideas. The group is generating creative ideas to narrow down later, using the OPTIONS ("Only Proposals That Include Others' Needs Succeed") threshold, the group's shared principles of agreement, or other criteria. Right now, the goal is to come up with as many possible destinations as possible.

In the next chapter, which describes the final process steps, they'll decide on their path forward.

CHAPTER 15

Achieving Consensus and Impact

After participants have agreed on fundamental principles that will guide their final recommendations and brainstormed possible solutions, you can turn to the final steps of collaborative problem-solving: building agreement on a set of higher-ground solutions that satisfy the widest range of stakeholders and then developing a plan to move these ideas forward.

Sometimes areas of likely agreement emerge during brainstorming, with a few clear winners, quite a few "maybes," and perhaps some ideas that that aren't attracting much enthusiasm. If you've got some clear winners and some promising "maybes," you may have a leg up in the process of finalizing solutions that the entire group can support. On contentious issues of some complexity, the group will almost always need to review their potential solutions with care. While doing so, it's helpful to use the OPTIONS ("Only Proposals That Include Others' Needs Succeed") technique that was described in Chapter 11, "Generate Options for Mutual Gain."

Skillful facilitation can make all the difference here as the group engages the potential solutions, either alone or in combination with each other, and discusses how they meet—or don't meet—the needs of various stakeholder interests. The facilitator's job is to draw out the views of everyone affected to ensure that participants fully understand where people stand, but it also helps enormously if each participant continues to be invested in listening to and understanding others' views. Objections and concerns should be addressed rather than side-stepped, only to gum up the works later.

Much of the time, the group will accept some solutions as they were originally conceived, tweak or refine others to answer people's needs and concerns, and reject some as being unrealistic or too limited in meeting the needs in the room. They may also use some of the brainstormed solutions as a springboard to lift ideas to a higher level—the higher ground that is so often gained through collaboration.

The most essential element in creating impactful solutions is developing a set of solutions that meets the most needs of the most participants, or said another way, that maximizes mutual gain. To achieve solutions that meet this bar, we've found it pays to:

- Break the problem into parts.
- Define "consensus."
- Determine if there's actionable agreement.
- Choose paths for impact.
- Make a plan of action.

So how does a group go from a list of options to a package of mutual-gains solutions that all participants support and work to implement? The good news is that if you've followed some or all of the approach laid out in Part II, "Mindsets," and Part III, "Building Blocks," you'll have already laid a foundation on which higher-ground solutions can be built.

BREAK THE PROBLEM INTO PARTS

When no obvious or widely supported higher-ground solutions have emerged from the group's brainstorming, there are a few techniques that can help participants engage more deeply on various aspects of the issue. One valuable practice is to identify component parts of the issue and break up into workgroups to delve more deeply into each individual component.

This step is often necessary when trying to come up with solutions for a complex, tough problem because it can be difficult for everyone in the room to understand the entire problem in depth. Breaking down the problem and coming up with solutions for the various parts of it allows participants to focus on learning everything they can about a smaller area of substance.

It's also the case that getting agreement on specific solutions is harder in a large group setting. Even with a group as small as 15 to

20 participants, you'll probably find that solution generation is more effective when you break into workgroups—though, like Goldilocks, workgroups can't be too big or too small, they have to be just right in size; 5 to 10 participants often works well, although sometimes an even smaller number can be utilized if they can resolve the major tensions at hand. It's also best to include participants who represent the full range of views on the issue in each workgroup. Doing so helps to ensure that the solutions developed by the workgroup will be endorsed by the full roster of participants in the collaborative problem-solving process.

To begin, workgroups often spend time learning about their area of focus through dialogue with each other and consultation with outside sources or experts. This gives them the extra information they need before brainstorming possible solutions that push beyond any solutions previously generated by the full process group. The workgroups usually operate under the same ground rules as the full group, for example, maintaining Chatham House rules where individuals can speak freely and then, when the workgroup's recommendations are presented, no one's name is attached to any specific proposal. They also measure their ideas against the overall group's principles of agreement or vision. Once they have agreed upon their solution sets, each workgroup shares their agreement with the full group, and the group as a whole works to synthesize the various workgroup solutions into one set of solutions for the problem.

Workgroups have a long history of helping people solve problems that seem stuck. As plan after plan for organizing the government was presented by various groups at the Constitutional Convention, votes were taken to test the support for each approach. None were gaining enough ground to win a supermajority of delegates. Then, after the idea to have representation in the House based on state population and in the Senate to be equal for each state reached a tied vote, a special workgroup—the "Grand Committee"—was set up to come up with the language for how this would operate. In working through specifics, the committee added an idea suggested by Benjamin Franklin that all spending matters would need to be first passed in the House before being considered by the Senate.[1]

During the Minnesota Security Hospital process, it soon became clear that building new infrastructure to support the move to behavioral, treatment-based care could be broken down into four discrete problem parts. So the larger group created four workgroups to tackle these individual pieces:

1. The positive behavioral supports and staff safety workgroup looked at ways to improve understanding of the changes in approach to patient care that had been put in place to reduce use of isolation and restraints. This workgroup's solutions were aimed at building the staff's capacity and comfort employing the new interventions.
2. The resident appropriateness workgroup considered challenges stemming from the placement of people at the facility who didn't belong there, such as individuals with developmental disabilities. It suggested legislative changes to ensure that those patients whom the facility couldn't serve well would not be placed there, and having additional resources to serve particularly complex patients.
3. The staffing workgroup addressed ongoing staff shortages and built consensus on the balance of security-oriented and treatment-oriented staff needed. Eventually, it would also look at how a different system for assigning shifts could reduce the amount of overtime required from direct-care staff.
4. The organizational wellness and communication workgroup was dedicated to improving workplace conditions and communication between managers and service staff. This group's vision for the future had helped them start to see the pieces of the problem they were solving with greater resolution.

The workgroups allowed the process participants to delve deeper into various problems and find solutions that would be more enduring than simply building state-of-the-art facilities while brushing staff shortages and communication problems under the rug.

You may find there are process participants who say they cannot live with the solution set being generated either through full group dialogue or workgroups. If that's the case, the group should explore ways to get more of what they need in the areas they care about most into the solutions being discussed. Ask them to propose changes that meet more of their needs in a way that doesn't reduce the ability of the solution set to address the needs of others. Sometimes getting those most important needs met is what will enable them to accept the parts of the solution they care less about and move the group toward full agreement.

If the group is still stuck it can be helpful to try to apply fair standards to all of the solutions being discussed. Ask the group:

- What would other interested stakeholders, including individuals and groups not participating in the process itself, perceive to be fair and honorable?
- What might a fair and neutral third party recommend?
- Is there a precedent that might be followed?

DEFINE "CONSENSUS"

A lot of the time people assume that consensus is really hard or impossible to reach. We've found that achieving consensus is not as hard as it sounds. One of the keys is in defining what the group means by "consensus." Consensus does *not* mean that everyone gets exactly what they want. The most important element is integrating everyone's perspectives and needs into higher-ground solutions.

You'll probably want to include an agreed-upon definition of consensus in your group's ground rules, but this definition will only be put to the test later in the process, once there's a better understanding of the likely terrain for a solution set. One of our favorite definitions goes like this:

We will agree that the group has reached consensus when we can all honestly say:

- I have listened and believe I understand the perspectives of all involved.
- I believe I have been heard and that others understand my perspective.
- I believe that the proposal before us is the best available option at this time.

It can also be useful to set a threshold for achieving consensus. Sometimes the nature of the decisions being made by the group will mean that the threshold must be high; the group as a whole needs to be strongly supportive of the solution set. In other cases, a low threshold can work well, meaning that so long as everyone is at least neutral on a proposed solution, the group will go ahead with it. Even if not every idea thrills every participant, the key to a satisfying consensus is for the group as a whole to be enthusiastic about the package of ideas and willing to invest in moving them forward.

A tool that we've found useful for assessing the level of consensus is Fist to Five, where the group identifies where more consensus still needs to be built. The facilitator asks everyone to start with a closed fist and then show how they're feeling about a solution by a show of fingers on a hand.

Number of Fingers	Strength of Support
Fist	I block this proposal.
1	I have many concerns about this proposal
2	I have some meaningful concerns about this proposal.
3	I am neutral on this proposal.
4	I support this proposal.
5	I strongly support this proposal.

In the Minnesota Security Hospital process, participants used Fist to Five to assess possible solutions, setting a threshold of moving forward with those proposals that polled with three fingers or more from everyone. The threshold could be set higher, at four or five.

When this poll is taken, it's not a pure yea-or-nay vote. Instead, it's a way to get the temperature of the room and stoke dialogue where people have misgivings. Ask anyone who has held up a number of fingers below the group's agreed threshold for consensus to offer ideas for improving the proposal in a way that makes it more appealing to them without making it less appealing to others. You'll often find there's a lot of room to build consensus when people are showing two to three fingers. There may even be room where participants say they'll block an idea or have many concerns—or if not, there's room to hear why they can't support it and consider this when creating the final solution set.

Different projects will naturally lead to different thresholds for consensus. A process convened by leaders of a business or not-for-profit may start with a goal of complete agreement, but it's the convener's prerogative to decide how important it is to get dissenters on board. The leaders may decide that having conducted a process that's been widely inclusive of differing points of view gives them what they need to make a good decision without complete support from participants. The lingering question might be how, if you do take a solution forward without the consensus you agreed at the start, this might affect morale and your ability to implement solutions.

DETERMINE IF THERE'S ACTIONABLE AGREEMENT

As your collaborative problem-solving process comes to a close, it's likely that the group will arrive at a set of specific solutions and have a good sense for whether there's enough heft in their agreement to justify working jointly to implement them. That's not always the case, of course. In some processes, the group may come to feel that they've had a wonderful conversation, found areas of common ground, and built trusting relationships but didn't achieve a critical mass of agreement to warrant issuing a set of recommendations and advocating for change together.

In our experience, however, most efforts do yield collective action even where some key issues don't get resolved. In Convergence's Working Up project on economic mobility, for example, there was spirited conversation about whether to recommend a higher national minimum wage. Some participants believed this would help lower-income workers achieve greater economic stability and put them on a stronger path to upward mobility over time; others balked, pointing to regional differences in the cost of living and how hard it would be for businesses, particularly small businesses, to face a big increase in staffing costs. As you may recall from Chapter 14, "Dialogue and Destinations," the project's participants had agreed to the principle that all people working full time should be able to achieve incomes that enabled them to live with dignity; they just disagreed on how much of that goal should be met by wages and how much by other means, such as tax credits.

Interestingly, this shared principle put many people in the room into unfamiliar positions. Some of the more liberal participants, who normally gravitated to having the government do more, found themselves favoring a greater role for the private sector in lieu of the group agreeing to a higher federally mandated wage. These participants saw employers paying a "living wage" as an important complement to public policy. Likewise, some corporate representatives, who were often or usually in the corner of less government and more free market solutions, resisted a higher federal minimum wage but showed openness to other public investments, like greater support for workforce training programs.

The Working Up group ultimately did not resolve their disagreement on the minimum wage. Nonetheless, they were able to agree on a series of other ideas concerning the quality of jobs, pathways to help workers on lower wages find better jobs, and tools to help people build savings and wealth over time.[2] And they were able to make an impact relatively quickly because several proposals were then adopted by key stakeholder groups. Walmart and McDonald's both made changes that increased access to higher education and career advancement initiatives and made shift scheduling more predictable. Walmart, in particular, drew upon the Working Up framework to guide its own internal "Opportunity Agenda." This led to stronger career ladders for associate advancement; more input from associates on when they worked (a major factor in achieving upward mobility); and a generous tuition assistance program allowing associates to achieve language skills, degrees, high school diplomas, college degrees, and other credentials at no cost. The country's largest private-sector workforce was deeply impacted by the Working Up group's collaborative problem-solving efforts.

The goal of most collaborative problem-solving processes is to gain enthusiastic support for the final set of proposals from a wide range of stakeholders, and to gain stakeholders' active involvement in moving ideas forward. Because participants often want to carefully consider how the entire package of solutions meets their needs, some groups adopt this rule: *No agreements are final until all agreements are final.* This gives people more space for dialogue around the solution set, free from any feeling that they might be giving assent prematurely to a particular proposal, particularly if they need to get agreement from their home base before signing on. To be effective and durable, stakeholder support for the package of recommendations should be thoroughly considered and genuine.

Especially where participants don't have full authority to commit to the solution set, such as in processes around public issues that need to be put forward to officials in local, state, or national government, it's important to allow the participants sitting at the table to communicate back to their organizations to get approval and buy-in as the process moves along. Those not at the table won't have had the transformative experience of building relationships and trust with others who see the world differently but will often be critical actors in coming to an agreement on solutions and seeing them realized. The convener or facilitator can help support this by brainstorming strategies with individuals or the full group that might help process participants to translate their experience to their home base. This should not be left until the very end, when consensus has already been reached, but instead be done regularly throughout the process, to seed ideas and surface concerns.

CHOOSE PATHS FOR IMPACT

In Chapter 8, "Map the Terrain," we described the importance of power mapping, where you identify who has the authority to implement the solutions recommended by the group. As part of the group's consensus, they should also be clear about what they want to achieve, and how.

As we've noted, if the convener has the authority to implement the solution set, as in the case of a CEO or university dean, then the path to implementation is straightforward. It's simply a matter of deciding whether and when to take on board the solutions that came out of the collaborative problem-solving process. Impacts here might be changes in business practices, internal policies, or the culture of the organization or institution.

Alternatively, to the extent that a project focuses on a public policy problem like affordable housing or healthcare for uninsured Americans, it's crucial to involve people who can directly or indirectly move ideas forward in the public domain. In some instances, an issue may require multiple fronts, both public and private, to fulfill the promise of the solutions recommended by the group, as in the case of the

Working Up project on economic mobility. This ordinarily will require a team effort among stakeholders and potentially outside endorsers to convince those with various types of responsibility to consider and adopt ideas. Similarly, if the shared goal of a project is to transform public understanding on a community or national issue, then it will be important to involve individuals and organizations, both those at the table and others who join subsequently, who have the experience and means to get things done.

In the case of the Falcon Heights, Minnesota, project on improving policing and inclusion in the community, the recommended solutions were a mix of things that could be implemented by the city leadership, community leaders, and individual residents. Changing the policing contract and terms could only be implemented by the city council. Holding events to foster an inclusive community required involvement from both the city, as the official sponsor, and community members, who would need to be part of organizing activities and getting people to turn up. Individuals who attended meetings were asked to commit to taking specific actions to make the community more inclusive.

Impact goals can range widely, including:

- Achieving changes in public policy at the local, state, regional, or national level
- Educating the public or key constituencies about key issues
- Changing business practices
- Effecting culture change in organizations, institutions, or the public at large
- Improving the quality of dialogue and building relationships between stakeholders in the issue space, which often lead to joint work over time
- Generating increased and ongoing collaboration in the issue space
- Creating radiating impacts of people working together more effectively over time

In the case of the Minnesota Security Hospital, the group developed a set of solutions covering all of these categories of impact. Together they worked to secure passage of legislation that substantially increased staffing to bring the organization into alignment with similar facilities. This extra staffing meant the hospital could set up behavior teams to assist staff in caring for and working with the most challenging patients, a solution that came out of more than one of the process workgroups. Money raised through the sale of bonds was appropriated to making improvements to the buildings, including the creation of smaller units and common spaces with better sightlines. Members of the hospital management felt that the collaborative problem-solving process was instrumental in persuading the state legislature to invest money in improving the facilities at a time when the hospital's license was still conditional.

Many of the recommendations for organizational culture and policies put forward by the organizational wellness and communications group were also implemented. One significant change was that the union representing many of the direct-care staff agreed to change the working title of this frontline position from Security Counselor to Forensic Support Specialist. This better reflected the new therapeutic focus of the facility, the expertise required in the position, and the direct-care staff's commitment to the new behavioral supports approach.

The process allowed the group to rewrite the narrative about what was causing the escalation of violence from staff blaming each other and the behavioral supports approach to structural issues, such as inadequate training, inadequate facilities, and lack of staff. This change in the frame opened the vista of potential solutions that they could agree on and implement together. It also led them to work together in the public arena to shift the broader narratives about the facility and mental health in general.

"I think that the process we went through demonstrated to me that everyone's heart is in the right place, and it's hard to see all perspectives without really listening and gaining understanding," said Carol Olson, executive director of the Minnesota Security Hospital during the process. "It's easy to overlook the complications of each other's job, to forget what it's like to work 24/7 directly with patients. Listening fully isn't a given, nor is it easy. You have to start with establishing trust that all coming to the table will do that."[3] Most important, the set of solutions that they agreed upon has led to fewer injuries at the hospital.

MAKE A PLAN OF ACTION

In the course of any group's deliberations, even before final agreements are made, it can be very useful to inventory the capacity of each participant and key stakeholder to help move ideas forward into action. You'll be building here on what you learned from power mapping, but your plan of action will be more detailed and nuanced.

This often calls for an "all hands on deck" spirit to getting things done. To this end, it can be very useful to garner specific commitments from most or all participants as to what they can do, and when. While each will vary in what they can do, they'll all usually have a strong interest in having their hard work to forge shared solutions take effect in the real world. At the very least, they can be ambassadors for the solutions that have been developed. In many instances, conveners, participants, and other stakeholders can help enlist others to endorse the recommended solutions.

Participants might also make appearances together, especially if they are "strange bedfellows," on an issue, underscoring how people who ordinarily disagree have come together to make progress. For example, a stakeholder could invite a participant from the "other side" to jointly give a briefing to their own constituency as a way of demonstrating to skeptics that there's wide support for the solutions being put forward.

Try It Out

Think about the issue that you identified in the "Try It Out" in Chapter 2, "How to Reach Convergence." How would you answer the following questions?

- **Commitments.** What kinds of commitments could you seek to move agreed solutions forward? Would it be asking stakeholders to shift priorities in the work they already do to incorporate relevant proposals from the solution set? Would it be asking them to deploy communications or lobbying capacities? Could they reach out for endorsements from individuals or groups who can add momentum to implementation efforts?

- **Champions.** Who's a good candidate to convene stakeholders and endorsers after the formal process comes to a close? Who's a good candidate to coordinate group efforts going forward? These individuals or organizations may not be the same as the convener of your process. For example, Convergence sometimes convenes processes where implementation is handed over to another group, while in other cases, Convergence continues to facilitate efforts to coordinate implementation.

Finally, in creating a path forward to your higher ground, it's essential to be clear about who's taking responsibility for which aspects of the plan. When the participants around the table have authority to make particular changes, roles and responsibilities might be straightforward, but much of the time, people come to the collaborative problem-solving process with different levels of authority and different expectations about their involvement in implementing the outcome. Especially where disparate stakeholders need to work together over time to bring a solution set to life, you may need to set up periodic check-in and strategy meetings to keep implementation activities on track. The convening organization may take responsibility for organizing such meetings, or other participants can take up the task. Key will be that those convening the group in the future are trusted by a wide range of stakeholders to stay true to the spirit and substance of what has been agreed.

The relationships forged between participants over the course of the process are the secret ingredient in your recipe for radiating impacts over the longer term. Alongside Ellie Bertani of Walmart, Judy Conti, director of Government Affairs for the National Employment Law Project (NELP), participated in the Working Up project on economic mobility. Judy came into the project thinking of the US Chamber of Commerce as her bugbear—a consistent, dug-in opponent of the policy solutions for workers that she and NELP were advocating for. She was surprised and gratified to discover they had many more goals in common than she'd imagined, many of which came together in the Working Up group's recommendations.

But the benefits of the process didn't end when the final report was published. Judy remembers how, when Ellie invited a group from Working Up to attend Walmart's annual general meeting of shareholders, "it gave all of us a lot more opportunity to sit and, in a more informal way, continue to build our relationships and discuss our issues across lines of difference, and to hear from more people who were trying to do the same kind of work."

Through the representative from the Chamber of Commerce who took part in Working Up, Judy was introduced to her counterpart on employment policy at the Chamber. The two of them talk often—about ways to support workers as well as their favorite football team, the New York Giants—and have grown to be colleagues and friends. "We're not just opposing each other all the time. We're actively looking for places where we can find commonality and work together in the future."

Judy helped to facilitate an introduction between the Chamber and the National Women's Law Center, which was looking for other organizations that might be interested in developing legislation to protect the rights of workers during and after pregnancy. Judy feels the wide-ranging alliance that came together around the Pregnant Workers' Fairness Act, which was signed into law in December 2022, "came together more quickly and more easily than it could have otherwise because I had a level of trust that the folks at the Chamber of Commerce were willing to be honest brokers." Having spent three years together in a collaborative problem-solving community, the participating organizations grew to respect, trust, and vouch for each other.

The work you've done to nurture trust and build bonds between people is how you'll continue to make an impact long after the process draws to an end. There's no higher ground than that.

Conclusion: We All Can Be Collaborative Leaders

Veteran conflict resolution pro Tom Dunne's commitment to collaborative problem-solving long predates his involvement with Convergence as a charter member of its board and leadership council. He often shares his formative experiences serving in Vietnam. He was part of a group of US Marines who approached a village that they'd been told was friendly to Americans, only to find the local residents greeting them with gunfire. It would have been easy to defend themselves, but Tom and others in the group quickly realized that none of the shots were landing on them; the villagers were purposefully shooting above their heads. They were friendly, but they were scared, because only a couple days before they'd been bombed by US planes. This was one of many moments during the war that inspired Tom to spend the rest of his life seeking ways to resolve conflicts collaboratively rather than by brute force of word or deed.

After returning to civilian life, Tom began his long and successful career in conflict resolution. Among his early jobs was organizational development specialist at the US Postal Service. One day he received a call from the postmaster of a large office in the South. The postmaster had a problem. When Tom asked what he need help with, the postmaster answered, "Well, some of the old boys drove by my house last night and blasted it with a shotgun."

Tom had imagined handling disputes between managers and frontline workers, but not violence like this. What was going on?

The postmaster explained that, over the past few years, a variety of issues had been festering in his district. Most recently, the unions representing the mail carriers had demanded that a portable toilet be installed on every Jeep. Management had issued a swift "absolutely not" in response. That had raised the temperature a lot more than they'd expected, culminating in the previous night's shooting. Yet the postmaster said he believed this dire situation might actually be an opportunity to improve the conversation.

Together, Tom and the postmaster came up with a plan to invite 20 representatives of the unions and management to a two-day problem-solving session, which the postmaster would convene and then turn over to Tom to facilitate. They'd be charged with the task of working together to identify issues that were causing conflict and come up with proposed solutions, which they'd present to the postmaster at the end of the second day. All of the participants would have to agree to attend both days and work to find solutions that everyone could support.

Even before the formal session kicked off, the upcoming collaborative problem-solving process brought dividends. When Tom arrived before the group meeting, the postmaster greeted him by saying, "Ever since I put out the word about this meeting, things have calmed down! The unions have not presented me with a single grievance!" Tom reflected based on his experience over the years, "In some sense, the improvement usually begins the moment that the leaders state their commitment to working together towards a mutual solution."[1]

When the participants had assembled, the postmaster told them that Tom's assignment was to help them succeed in working together to solve their shared problems. He assured them of his confidence in them, and then said he would get out of their way so they could get the job done.

After the postmaster left, the managers and union leaders began to eye each other skeptically. Some voiced recriminations about past events and challenged whether the other side was undertaking the meeting in good faith. Tom gently moved the conversation to a place of wary readiness to listen to each other and work together.

For much of the rest of the day, the union groups and the managers worked separately to list what they saw as the sources of the strife between them. They came up with a list 50 problems long. Everyone then walked around the room and marked the problems that they felt were priorities, eventually sorting their issues into three categories:

1. Things that we can fix right here, during tomorrow's session
2. Things that we can fix over the next several weeks or months if we set up joint workgroups
3. Things that will take care of themselves if we deal with the first two categories

The next morning, several joint union–management teams were formed to begin working on "category 1" items. Naturally the portable toilet issue was one of the first to be brought up. Initially, it was a fairly heated exchange. The managers were angry that such an absurd proposal was still being raised. If a portable toilet were installed in each Jeep, they argued, there would be no room for the mail! The union reps were equally angry. They'd been complaining for years that the mail carriers, especially those with rural routes, were often many miles away from proper toilet facilities and management had been utterly unwilling to address the issue. They were tired of being stonewalled and had been reduced to making the proposal out of desperation. And it had worked! Asking for portable toilets had finally gotten the issue on the table for discussion.

Tom could see the opportunities for problem-solving opening up. Now that the two sides' mutually exclusive positions—Jeep toilets or no Jeep toilets—had been distinguished from their underlying interests—accessible toilet facilities for mail carriers and routes that were as efficient as possible—the process group could brainstorm solutions that integrated everyone's interests. For example, it might be possible to arrange with gas stations for the carriers to use their toilets, or to look at redrawing routes so that a public toilet was available every few miles or so.

At the end of the second day the postmaster returned. A senior manager and a union president gave a joint presentation on what had transpired, and the various workgroups presented their recommendations for the specific issues they had dealt with. The postmaster approved whatever recommendations he could on the spot as well as the problem-solving group's proposed process for dealing with issues that remained unresolved. He also asked the group to write a joint report to the whole office describing their accomplishments and plans. The report was distributed a few days later with a cover letter from the postmaster.

A week later, Tom received his copy of the report. The concluding sentence of the postmaster's cover letter was the most gratifying element of all: "These remarkable agreements to improve our organization were possible because we approached the effort as a team. If we can continue with the teamwork that marked these two days, we will be able to deal with any problems that come up in the future."

OUR ROLES AS LEADERS

Tom's story illustrates the immediate and longer-term benefits of taking a collaborative problem-solving approach even in situations where passions run very high. It's a way of shifting the culture of conflict away from confrontation toward a sense of community, shared ownership, and mutual benefit. Choosing to be a collaborative problem-solver is a powerful way to lead.

One of our great hopes for this book is to help readers choose what kind of leader you personally want to be (whether you're a current leader or might be one in the future), what kinds of leaders you want to associate and work with, and even what kind of leaders you want to entrust with your vote. In her book *Lead Like It Matters...Because It Does!* former university administrator and executive coach Roxi Bahar Hewertson has set out tenets of effective leadership. "Leading is all about relationships," she writes.[2] We agree. In our view, people with the skills to connect with others—to listen, stay open to others' ideas and views, engage them without defensiveness, and develop higher-ground solutions—have crucial capacities for effective, and at times transformative, leadership.

Yet sometimes people in positions of influence and authority resist taking a collaborative approach. This might be because, in the short term, it can be easier to make decisions on your own. Or it might be that you imagine collaboration involves too much compromise or too much superficial camaraderie. As we've said, we know it takes hard work, but collaborative problem-solving typically yields more effective and more enduring solutions specifically because it's not about compromise or just feeling good about each other.

We asked Roxi about the experience of collaborative problem-solving among the leaders she's worked with. "Creating a collaborative culture takes courage, intention, and commitment. It isn't about 'making nice' or death by consensus. Nor is it about avoiding or ignoring conflicts," she said. "It is about bringing the right people together and creating a safe place for every person in the room, on the screen, in the hallway, or on the phone . . . to grow trust in one another, to be able to speak their truths and opinions without fear, and to do so in ways that are productive versus destructive. This may sound like a tall order, but the reality is no business, team, family, community, or country can be successful without a sincere willingness to collaborate with other people, in life and in work, and who will, at times, be at odds. When we admit that we all bring wisdom and perspective into every relationship, being curious to learn from each other becomes the foundation of every productive collaboration, relationship, and culture. After all, we have always needed to collaborate with each other to survive. To thrive, having a deep commitment to collaboration is a game changer."[3]

We hope that a wide range of readers can see themselves in this book and find value in applying the lessons. Indeed, collaborative problem-solving has a proven track record in all sorts of settings, and in our communities, organizations, and societies at large, we've only just begun to tap the potential of what could be achieved through it.

Let's take a look at some of the ways you or your leaders could tackle problems.

Community Leaders

PTA presidents, members of neighborhood associations, and others who stand up, formally or informally, in their community are often working with people who have a wide range of views on issues. That includes religious institutions, where you might think there's a lot of agreement around moral values—but they're not immune from internal conflict either! Being able to forge strong bonds across divergent views and find solutions that integrate people's needs and concerns is the bread and butter of serving the *whole* community—the gold standard. Guided, productive conversations like the ones held in the city of Falcon Heights, Minnesota, can help to bring a community together to address a difficult event or conflict.

Public Officials

Because many government leaders have the authority to make decisions on matters of public concern, they have strong convening power to assemble the disparate stakeholders affected by an issue. Especially on politically sensitive or intractable issues, public officials like governors, state legislators, mayors, county and city officials, and school board members can use collaborative approaches to find better solutions while also strengthening connections among people who have previously been at odds. And since the government officials themselves, or their representatives, can also be participants in collaborative problem-solving processes, they can support the use of this approach without fear that they will need to swallow solutions that are at odds with their beliefs and principles. As appropriate or necessary, they also can make clear that while they intend to honor any consensus reached by the group because it will reflect agreement among all the key voices to the conflict, they still hold the final decision-making authority.

Especially at the national level, our society would benefit from a more collaborative way of governing. Beyond supporting politicians who have a collaborative mindset and approach to doing the people's work, there are a number of initiatives trying to improve the way the nation works. For example, Governor Spencer Cox (R-UT) and Governor Jared Polis (D-CO), respectively the chair and vice-chair of the National Governors Association, in 2023 put forward a plan called "Disagree Better: Healthy Conflict for Better Policy" to highlight the benefits of having political leaders who take a collaborative approach. "Americans need to disagree better. And by that we don't mean that we need to be nicer to each other, although that's helpful," the mission statement reads. "We need to learn to disagree in a way that allows us to find solutions and solve problems instead of endlessly bickering. . . . We know that conflict resolution takes work and involves difficult conversations. It's much easier to sow division than to persuade or find solutions. . . . Through healthy conflict, we're confident that we can find common ground and improve our families, our communities and our nation. Together, we can disagree better."[4] We need more leaders committed to the hard work of creative problem-solving with those across the aisle.

Business and Organizational Leaders

Executives and senior managers in both for-profit companies and not-for-profit organizations can usefully apply collaborative problem-solving to issues, whether they're internal to their organization or involve the local community or general public. If an organization needs to establish a new strategic plan, it can benefit from mapping the terrain of the issues and stakeholders involved. Skillfully framing issues to be addressed and inclusively gathering stakeholders whose collective knowledge and experience can generate the best possible solutions is also invaluable for long-term planning and breaking down silos. The ultimate decisions for a new strategic direction will rest with the C-suite or board of directors, but by taking a collaborative approach, leaders will gain access to more broadly informed solutions and get more widespread buy-in.

Many businesses are facing increasing pressure from stakeholder groups—for example, customers who disagree with decisions around policies or products, or employees who want to be heard on issues of importance to them in the workplace. A collaborative approach can help them navigate competing stakeholder demands, at a minimum helping them to better understand how decisions will play out and potentially generating win–win options before a boycott or walkout hits the bottom line. As Neil Bradley, executive vice president and chief policy officer of the US Chamber of Commerce told us, we all work and operate in "a world in which the risk factors for any particular business decision, investment, or new line of business—really any decision—are more numerous and more complicated than ever before. Leaders need to think about the best risk management strategy, particularly when there are strong differences of opinion and the potential for backlash. The collaborative approach is an important tool in the business leader's toolbox."[5]

In the not-for-profit space, philanthropies can employ collaborative problem-solving to maximize the impact of the groups they're funding, for example, by convening their grantees and asking them to identify and work toward shared goals rather than operating in silos. This may help to reconcile potentially counterproductive conflicts between approaches being taken by different organizations.

Of course, not every issue that arises can or should be addressed collaboratively. Sometimes leaders do just need to make decisions without going through the process of gaining input from a wide range of stakeholders. Rob spent 35 years as a leader of not-for-profit organizations, and while his leadership style is inclusive and collaborative, he regularly had to remind people that the organizations he led were not democracies. In the interests of conserving time and resources, many if not most decisions just need to be made based upon the best judgment of those who have been entrusted with authority. In these instances, being clear about whom the decision-making process will involve and communicating openly about it will help people accept those decisions with less resistance. In other words, collaborative mindsets can help to make a top-down decision easier for others to understand.

Educational Institutions

Collaborative problem-solving has been used successfully in higher education to get faculty and students to work better together, particularly when there's been a major challenge on campus. More broadly, a range of educators are employing collaborative skills to help improve students' critical thinking and problem-solving skills. "Fair consideration of others' ideas and experiences is a foundational skill for successful critical thinking, and it leads to an environment in which diversity is not only tolerated, it's seen as a powerful force for innovation and creative problem-solving," said Annie Gray, dean of the School of Arts, Science and Education at Ivy Tech Community College in Bloomington, Indiana. "The Convergence method has the ability to improve student mastery of important communication and problem-solving skills which will set them up for success in an academic environment and beyond."

Some educators also argue that practicing key elements of this approach—such as respectful listening, staying curious, and giving others the benefit of the doubt—also prepares students to be better citizens and help fulfill the American ideal: *E pluribus unum*—"Out of many, one."

BUILDING A BETTER WORLD THROUGH COLLABORATION

There are countless problems that need solving in our daily lives, our places of work and worship, our communities, our country, and our world. These problems are worth fighting about. But we need to fight the good fight in a good way—a way that doesn't damage but instead creates and sustains the interpersonal relationships that are essential to problem-solving as well as living peacefully and respectfully together.

The founders of the US recognized from the start that we must find ways to accommodate differing views and factions. Collaborative problem-solving is a tried and tested method for doing so. Disagreement is a normal and healthy part of life; it's also key to the American experiment. In his book *Love Your Enemies*, Arthur Brooks, the former president of the American Enterprise Institute, noted how America emerged out of "the cultural innovation of embracing competition in economics and politics," and that, as in sports, competition fosters and sustains excellence. "Tolerance and civility are too low a standard," he writes. "You need to be grateful for the other side, just as you should be grateful for having more than one team in your favorite sports league."[6] We need more tools to ensure we're having a healthy competition of ideas, thankful for the challenge of the other side's passion and expertise, and not stoking contempt based upon an incomplete or inaccurate understanding of why other people think and act the way they do. This is why it's so vital that we embrace collaborative approaches to living, working, and solving problems together.

We don't seek or envision a world free of conflict—that would be unrealistic, unproductive, and, as we've said, boring. But we do believe that in a far wider range of circumstances than currently recognized, we as a society can turn conflict into convergence and create a virtuous cycle of sustained collaboration over time. We all can develop skills to argue well and even passionately while honoring the dignity of our opposites and our shared humanity. The mindsets, building blocks, and skills in this book are useful not only for collaborative problem-solving but also for disagreeing well. Fighting only to prevail or defeat others may win the argument but cause us to lose each other. And sustained anger and resentment toward others often has a corrosive effect on people's well-being, including our own.

We've found that the collaborative mindsets help to support better conversations in many situations beyond the need to address tough issues. More grandly, we also believe that more widespread practice of collaborative problem-solving around issues, big and small, would greatly help our often troubled world. We need more people seeking higher ground. We need to support a cultural shift away from heightened confrontation and divisiveness toward more collaboration and more effective problem-solving. We hope you're persuaded by the power of this approach, to try it out, and then take it out into the world with you.

It requires commitment and practice to exercise these new mental muscles, and especially for those not yet grounded in the idea of collaborative problem-solving, we urge you to take it one step at a time. As we've said before, you don't need to employ all of the mindsets, building blocks, and process steps for these ideas to make a real difference in how you manage and improve conflict and communication. Try them on for size as life and work allow.

As you gain confidence in how to apply them to different situations and start to see the results they can produce, you'll naturally gravitate toward deepening and perfecting your practice of them. Becoming an effective collaborative problem-solver is about gradually learning how to pay attention to what you're thinking, what you're learning, and how you're interacting with other people. It comes through regular use. The more you invest in being curious, in truly understanding the life experiences and perspectives of others, and in looking for mutual gains, the greater the potential for effective, durable, and wise solutions to the problems you're facing, and the more likely that you'll form surprisingly positive relationships in the process.

As Becky Pringle, president of the National Education Association, told us, "The heart of it is the quality of relationships. If you work on building the quality of relationships, then you will increase the quality of the conversations that you have. If you increase the quality of the conversations that you have, then you'll increase the quality of the collective thinking that you will have. And ultimately that will increase the quality of the results." In this handful of words, Becky has captured the essence of collaborative problem-solving writ large.

Together, all of the mindsets, building blocks, and process steps in this book can create distinctly better conversations among people, including those who see the world very differently. It's through the quality of these conversations, steeped in trust and understanding, that collaborative problem-solving dialogue does its magic, pushing people's thinking to a higher ground, generating breakthrough ideas, and forging unlikely alliances for action and bonds of community that people previously never thought likely.

Our hope is that the stories and lessons we've shared will inspire you to apply collaborative problem-solving in your life, in whatever way is most appropriate and helpful to you in the various roles you play. If taken to scale, we believe collaborative problem-solving will contribute not only to better solutions to specific problems but also to a shift in our culture toward a more cohesive, pluralistic, and effective society.

Pocket Guide for Collaborative Problem-Solving

I. **Mindsets—the essential starting place for effective collaboration**
   - **Conflict Can Be Constructive.** See conflict as an opportunity to learn and push thinking to a new level. When conflict starts to feel threatening, try to stay present, breathe, and refocus on your body.
   - **Everyone Gets the Benefit of the Doubt.** Remember that negative intentions are rare and seek to understand who people are—their experiences, their values, and why they think the way they do—before passing judgment on them or their viewpoints. Ask yourself, *Why do I think they're saying this?*
   - **Curiosity Is the Cure.** Especially when you hear things that you disagree with or don't fully understand, cultivate curiosity and keep asking questions to learn more rather than just react. Ask yourself, "What am I missing?" Ask the other person, "Can you tell me more about that?" Then briefly summarize what you think you've heard and ask, "Did I get that right?" and "Is there more you can share about that?" Remind yourself that no one person or group holds all of the answers on complex issues.
   - **Relationships at the Core.** Stay focused on building quality relationships as a key to solving challenging problems. Spend time breaking bread and getting to know each other more deeply. Seek your shared goals, values, identities, and life experiences and focus on them. The stronger the relationships built, the more likely mutual benefit solutions can be found.
   - **Seek Higher Ground.** Strive to develop solutions that integrate the perspectives and meet the competing needs of everyone who has a stake in your problem. This enables you to develop solutions that don't require anyone to relinquish their fundamental

principles. Drop the "win-lose" paradigm and instead hold on to the belief that you and others can find answers of mutual benefit and that you both want to solve a problem or make things better.

II. Building Blocks—fundamental concepts for effective collaborative problem-solving

- **Map the Terrain.** Before engaging on any issues, it's critically important to develop a full understanding of the issue you are trying to solve and what stakeholders you need to include to ensure that the full range of perspectives is represented. Determine which people have the individual or collective leverage to implement any solutions the group devises and include them as possible in your process. Stakeholder mapping, power mapping, research, and interviews help you understand the issue landscape.

- **Nurture Trust.** Trust is the essential lubricant for successful problem-solving. Finding shared values and identities, as well as understanding why people think the way they do are keys to achieving trust. Use connecting questions like "Please share a formative life experience that shaped your views of this issue," or "What is the value that most guides you in your work on this issue, and why?"

- **Really Hear Everyone.** When people listen well to one another, the odds of finding higher ground go up. Hearing directly from people about their views, values, and life experiences is likely to produce understanding and empathy that goes beyond other efforts to understand each other, like doing research through reading, where there is no interaction or deep communication involved. Listen first, then when it's your time to share, hedge by avoiding absolutes like "always" or "everyone," affirm areas of agreement, stay personal, and own any missteps (leave it to others to raise their own faults).

- **Generate Options for Mutual Gain.** Splitting the difference often leaves parties' needs unrequited. By focusing on each other's underlying interests (rather than people's positions) and avoiding a forced compromise on issues of deep principle, participants are more likely to find effective solutions, work together to implement them, and end up working together over time. To achieve higher ground, try the OPTIONS technique: "Only Proposals That Include Others' Needs Succeed."

- **Take Your Time.** While everyone faces time pressures, it takes time to build trusting relationships and to fully understand the complexity of differing points of view. Taking time to do this right from the beginning will save time and money down the road as participants find durable answers to the problems they are resolving.

III. Process—key steps for building consensus solutions

- **Discovery and Design.** The first step in setting up an effective collaborative problem-solving process is to ascertain how to frame the issue in a way that will bring all the key players to the table by using language that connects the views and includes the needs of all involved. This framing should be goal/solution oriented. The discovery process also helps collaborative problem-solvers identify who can fill the key roles of convener, facilitator, and participants as well as providing a basis for key design elements such as the location, duration, and flow of meetings.

- **Dialogue and Destinations.** The largest of amount of time in a collaborative problem-solving process is spent on this stage, in which participants engage in dialogue or deliberation to develop shared high-level goals, guiding principles, and a shared vision of a better future, and to brainstorm solutions for mutual gain. Several tasks usually performed by a facilitator are particularly useful: synthesizing disparate needs and views of participants helps them to identify solutions that meet multiple needs; reframing helps translate unproductive, unclear, or toxic statements that sometimes arise during difficult discussions into ones that participants can engage with constructively; and skillfully summarizing discussions can help ensure that conversations are on track, that views are accurately reflected. and that areas of both common ground and remaining differences are captured.

- **Higher-Ground Consensus and Impact.** In the final stage of collaborative problem-solving, participants refine the options they have brainstormed to ensure they meet their principles of agreement and maximize mutual gain. The Fist to Five technique can help a group identify where they have consensus and where they need to do more exploration of stakeholder needs. Once higher ground solutions are agreed to, participants often summarize their solutions in a report and then engage in strategies to implement their ideas, such as presenting the report to the leader of a convening organization, engaging in education or advocacy efforts, or seeking changes to national, state, or local laws. Finally, most groups benefit from developing a plan that clarifies who is willing to take on what responsibilities for implementing their strategies, including any ongoing need for collaboration among the participants.

Glossary of Key Terms

Active Listening/Deep Listening   Listening closely and attentively to others with the intention of developing a better understanding of the speaker's views and needs. Often takes practice to cultivate.

Amygdala Hijacking   A process initiated when you encounter stress and treat it as a physical threat. Inside your brain, your amygdala shuts down your prefrontal cortex, which is responsible for decision-making and problem-solving. This makes it difficult to address conflict calmly and rationally.

Catastrophize   Unconsciously and continuously believing that a situation is worse than it really is and even believing that only the worst possible outcome will occur.

Collaborative-Problem-Solving   An approach to addressing conflict that brings together people with the collective knowledge, experience, and influence needed to solve a problem, including those who are in disagreement. This approach calls for engaging them in a dialogue designed to build trust, elicit rich and respectful exchanges on the issues at hand, and generate solutions that integrate the needs of the range of stakeholders involved.

Confirmation Bias   The tendency to seek out and readily recall information that confirms our beliefs and to discount information that challenges our viewpoints.

Contact Theory   The idea that interpersonal contact under the right conditions is one of the most effective ways to reduce prejudice between groups. First put forth by Gordon Allport in the 1950s, it has since been tested, refined, and verified.

Framing   Scoping and naming the issues for collaborative problem-solving in a way that is inclusive of the interests of all of the stakeholders. For example, using single-payer healthcare systems as a frame to discuss extending healthcare coverage focuses on only one of many possible approaches to the issue, while framing the issue as providing healthcare coverage for the uninsured is inclusive of many possible ways to achieve that shared goal.

Fundamental Attribution Error   The tendency to view our own actions as a reflection of the situation we're in, and thus more charitably, but to view other people's actions as a reflection of their character. For example, thinking a colleague is behind schedule because he is selfish rather than because there are too many demands on his time.

Higher-Ground Solutions   These are solutions that go beyond compromise or "split the difference" approaches. Instead, by focusing on interests, these solutions reflect creative ways to meet the most important needs and interests of the most stakeholders. Unlike positions, these needs and interests are rarely mutually exclusive, which is why these types of solutions are also referred to as "mutual gains solutions." Higher-ground solutions are important for issues where stakeholders have deeply held beliefs and where compromise of principle is neither possible nor wise.

Moral Foundations   A concept developed by Jonathan Haidt and Jesse Graham to explain common moral themes across diverse cultures *and* to explain differences in political perspectives. The framework identified at least five universal moral foundations: Care, Fairness, Loyalty, Authority, and Sanctity. These foundations form the basis for our principles and guide our decision-making. However, different individuals and groups prioritize these foundations differently, which explains some of our different perspectives on political issues. In conflict, it is helpful to seek to understand the moral foundation that is shaping your perceived adversary's views.

Negativity Bias   The tendency to be more attuned to and affected by negative experiences than positive ones, because negative events and situations are threatening to our predisposition to protect ourselves from harm.

Outrage   The escalating cycle of blame, rumination, and expanding fury for revenge that is built up when anger, a healthy and potentially constructive emotion that can motivate needed change, is not expressed, and issues are left unresolved.

Pluralism   The recognition of the existence and value of diverse points of view.

Positions versus Interests   Positions are statements about where a person or organization stands on a particular issue and rarely provide insight into underlying motivations, values, or needs. Positions are often rigid and in opposition with other stakeholders' positions. Positions are the "what." Interests are a person or organization's underlying motivations, values, or needs. Interests are the "why" behind a certain position. In contrast to positions, there are often many ways to satisfy the interests of all the parties to a dispute. The concept was popularized by Roger Fisher and William Ury in their seminal book *Getting to Yes: Negotiating Agreement Without Giving In*.

Power Mapping   The process of identifying who has the influence and leverage to enact change around your issue. While collaborative problem-solving need not limit its participants to those with power, it is useful to know whose involvement can most readily lead to change.

Reframing   Translating a toxic, positional, threatening, or unclear statement into one that others can engage with productively by restating it, removing the problematic language, and replacing it with the listener's understanding of the speaker's core concerns and needs. Doing so helps both the speaker to feel heard and the listeners to respond more constructively, ultimately moving the conversation forward.

Stakeholder Mapping   The process of identifying key individuals involved in the problem you are addressing to ensure that problem-solvers understand the wide range of players who have a stake in the issue at hand. This mapping helps to guide good choices as to who should be involved in any collaborative problem-solving convening.

Synthesizing   The skill of recapping what has been said in a conversation and weaving various strands together so that participants can more clearly understand the state of play in any conversation. An effective synthesis generates progress by making participants feel heard and understood and by demonstrating that seemingly competing points of view can be integrated.

Notes

PART I. THE PATH TO HIGHER GROUND

1. Committee for a Responsible Federal Budget, "FixUS-Ipsos: America's Values, Goals, and Aspirations," accessed October 4, 2023 (FixUS-Ipsos poll conducted September 2020), https://fixusnow.org/americas-values-poll.

CHAPTER 1. WHY SOLVE PROBLEMS TOGETHER?

1. This included the description of the project by Ron Pollack, executive director at Families USA, during the Health Care Coverage for the Uninsured press conference, January 18, 2007.
2. Stuart Butler, correspondence with the authors, August 1, 2023.
3. In 2006, 30% of private sector workers were employed by organizations that didn't offer healthcare coverage, and another 20% had decided not to sign up for their employer's plan. Sharon A. DeVaney and Sophia T. Anong, "The Likelihood of Having Employer-Sponsored Health Insurance," US Bureau of Labor Statistics, November 30, 2007, https://www.bls.gov/opub/mlr/cwc/the-likelihood-of-having-employer-sponsored-health-insurance.pdf.
4. David U. Himmelstein, Deborah Thorne, Elizabeth Warren, and Steffie Woolhandler, "Medical bankruptcy in the United States, 2007: Results of a National Study," *American Journal of Medicine* 122, no. 8 (August 2009): 741–46.
5. US Institute of Medicine Committee on the Consequences of Uninsurance, *Care Without Coverage: Too Little, Too Late* (Washington, DC: National Academies Press, 2002), https://doi.org/10.17226/10367.
6. Donald J. Palmisano, David W. Emmons, and Gregory D. Wozniak, "Expanding Insurance Coverage Through Tax Credits, Consumer Choice, and Market Enhancements: The American Medical Association Proposal for Health Insurance Reform," *Journal of the American Medical Association* 291, no. 18 (May 12, 2004): 2237–42, https://jamanetwork.com/journals/jama/article-abstract/198729.

7. Werner Reis, "Letter: The AMA Health Insurance Proposal," *Journal of the American Medical Association* 292, no. 10 (September 8, 2004): 1173, https://jamanetwork.com/journals/jama/article-abstract/199379.

8. Health Coverage Coalition for the Uninsured, "Expanding Health Care Coverage in the United States: A Historic Agreement," January 18, 2007; William A. Dolan, "Report on the Council on Medical Service: No Child Left Uninsured," March 2007, https://www.ama-assn.org/sites/ama-assn.org/files/corp/media-browser/public/about-ama/councils/Council%20Reports/council-on-medical-service/a07-cms-report-1-no-child-uninsured.pdf.

9. Norman Z. McLeod, *Horse Feathers* (Paramount Pictures, 1932).

10. Quoted in Ralph Keyes, *The Quote Verifier: Who Said What, Where, and When* (New York: St. Martin's Press, 2007).

11. See, for example: Jonathan Haidt, *The Righteous Mind: Why Good People Are Divided by Politics and Religion* (New York: Vintage, 2013); Ezra Klein, *Why We're Polarized* (New York: Simon & Schuster, 2020); and Ben Sasse, *Them: Why We Hate Each Other—and How to Heal* (New York: St. Martin's Press, 2018).

12. Samara Klar, Yanna Krupnikov, and John Barry Ryan, "Is America Hopelessly Polarized, or Just Allergic to Politics?" *New York Times*, April 12, 2019, https://www.nytimes.com/2019/04/12/opinion/polarization-politics-democrats-republicans.html.

13. Victoria Balara, "Fox News Poll: 9 in 10 Voters Worried about Inflation, America's Future," Fox News, May 21, 2023, https://www.foxnews.com/official-polls/fox-news-poll-9-in-10-voters-worried-about-inflation-americas-future.

14. Dante Chinni, "Both Parties Think the Other Will Destroy America, NBC News Poll Finds," NBC News, October 23, 2022, https://www.nbcnews.com/meet-the-press/both-parties-think-other-will-destroy-america-nbc-news-poll-n1300111.

15. Jacob Liedke and Jeffrey Gottfried, "US Adults Under 30 Now Trust Information from Social Media Almost as Much as from National News Outlets," Pew Research Center, October 27, 2022, https://www.pewresearch.org/short-reads/2022/10/27/u-s-adults-under-30-now-trust-information-from-social-media-almost-as-much-as-from-national-news-outlets.

16. Ron Elving, "In a Time of National Division, Polarizing Primaries Are Part of the Problem," NPR, June 18, 2022, https://www.npr.org/2022/06/18/1105927483/in-a-time-of-national-division-polarizing-primaries-are-part-of-the-problem.

17. Jeffrey M. Jones, "Confidence in US Institutions Down; Average at New Low," Gallup, July 5, 2022, https://news.gallup.com/poll/394283/confidence-institutions-down-average-new-low.aspx.

18. Yanfeng Gu and Zhongyuan Wang, "Income Inequality and Global Political Polarization: The Economic Origin of Political Polarization in the World," *Journal of Chinese Political Science* 27, no. 2 (June 2022): 375–98, https://doi.org/10.1007/s11366-021-09772-1.

19. Amina Dunn, "Few Trump or Biden Supporters Have Close Friends Who Back the Opposing Candidate," Pew Research Center, September 18, 2020, https://www.pewresearch.org/short-reads/2020/09/18/few-trump-or-biden-supporters-have-close-friends-who-back-the-opposing-candidate.

20. Making Caring Common Project, "Do Americans Really Care for Each Other?" Harvard Graduate School of Education, December 8, 2021, https://www.gse.harvard.edu/ideas/news/21/12/do-americans-really-care-each-other.

21. PRRI Staff, "Competing Visions of America: An Evolving Identity or a Culture Under Attack? Findings from the 2021 American Values Survey," PRRI (Public Religion Research Institute), November 1, 2021, https://www.prri.org/research/competing-visions-of-america-an-evolving-identity-or-a-culture-under-attack.

22. David Klepper, "Democrats and Republicans Share Core Values But Still Distrust Each Other," AP, June 14, 2023, https://apnews.com/article/poll-democrats-republicans-values-polarization-trust-misinformation-7704ad7b024a7f2324453fecfffaf6f3.

23. Ibid.

24. Making Caring Common Project, "Do Americans Really Care for Each Other?" Harvard Graduate School of Education, December 8, 2021, https://www.gse.harvard.edu/ideas/news/21/12/do-americans-really-care-each-other.

CHAPTER 2. HOW TO REACH CONVERGENCE

1. Shamil Idriss and Rachel Kleinfeld, "No One Is Right in the Debate for and Against Philanthropic Pluralism," Chronicle of Philanthropy, June 15, 2023, https://www.philanthropy.com/article/no-one-is-right-in-the-debate-for-and-against-philanthropic-pluralism.

2. Ibid.

3. Kristen Cambell, "Which Comes First: The Equity or the Pluralism?" LinkedIn, June 27, 2023, https://www.linkedin.com/pulse/which-comes-first-equity-pluralism.

PART II. MINDSETS

1. Carol S. Dweck, *Mindset: The New Psychology of Success* (New York: Random House, 2007).

CHAPTER 3. CONFLICT CAN BE CONSTRUCTIVE

1. Carrie Menkel-Meadow, "Negotiating the American Constitution (1787–1789): Coalitions, Process Rules, and Compromises," in Emmanual Vivet, ed., *Landmark Negotiations from Around the World: Lessons for Modern Diplomacy* (Cambridge, UK: Intersentia, 2019), pp. 151–62.
2. Joseph J. Ellis, *The Quartet: Orchestrating the Second American Revolution, 1783–89* (New York: Vintage, 2016).
3. James Madison, *The Debates on the Adoption of the Federal Convention* 5 (1827), https://oll.libertyfund.org/title/elliot-the-debates-on-the-adoption-of-the-federal-constitution-vol-5.
4. Roy F. Baumeister, Ellen Bratslavsky, and Kathleen D. Vohs, "Bad Is Stronger than Good," *Review of General Psychology* 5, no. 4 (2001): 323–70, https://doi.org/10.1037/1089-2680.5.4.323.
5. Robert M. Sapolsky, *Why Zebras Don't Get Ulcers*, 3rd ed. (New York: Holt Paperbacks, 2004); Daniel J. Siegel, *Mindsight: The New Science of Personal Transformation* (New York: Bantam, 2010).
6. Daniel Goleman, *Emotional Intelligence: Why It Can Matter More Than IQ* (New York: Bantam, 1996).
7. John M. Gottman and Robert W. Levenson, "Marital Processes Predictive of Later Dissolution: Behavior, Physiology, and Health," *Journal of Personality and Social Psychology* 63, no. 2 (August 1992): 221–33, https://bpl.berkeley.edu/docs/41-Marital%20Processes92.pdf.
8. Gisèle Huff, *Force of Nature: The Remarkable True Story of One Holocaust Survivor's Resilience, Tenacity, and Purpose* (San Francisco: Simonet Press, 2022).
9. Ibid.
10. Convergence Center for Policy Resolution, "Reimagining Education: How Unlikely Allies Are Transforming Education for the Twenty-first Century" (January 2019), https://convergencepolicy.org/wp-content/uploads/2023/01/Education-Reimagined-Final-Report.pdf.
11. Huff, *Force of Nature*.

CHAPTER 4. EVERYONE GETS THE BENEFIT
OF THE DOUBT

1. Moshe ben Maimon ("Maimonides"), *Sefer Hamitzvot*, trans. by Berel Bell (Brooklyn, NY: Moznaim, 2006).

2. Kenneth Seeskin, "Maimonides," *Stanford Encyclopedia of Philosophy*, ed. by Edward N. Zalga, February 4, 2021, https://plato.stanford.edu/archives/spr2021/entries/maimonides.

3. Lee Ross, "The Intuitive Psychologist and His Shortcomings: Distortions in the Attribution Process," in Leonard Berkowitz, ed., *Advances in Experimental Social Psychology*, vol. 10 (New York: Academic Press, 1977), pp. 173–220.

4. Albert Ellis, *Reason and Emotion in Psychotherapy* (Oxford: Lyle Stuart, 1962).

5. Teresa M. Amabile and Ann H. Glazebrook, "A Negativity Bias in Interpersonal Evaluation," *Journal of Experimental Social Psychology* 18, no. 1 (January 1982): 1–22, https://doi.org/10.1016/0022-1031(82)90078-6.

6. David Rozado, Ruth Hughes, and Jamin Halberstadt, "Longitudinal Analysis of Sentiment and Emotion in News Media Headlines Using Automated Labelling with Transformer Language Models," *PLoS One* 17, no. 10 (October 18, 2022): e0276367, https://doi.org/10.1371/journal.pone.0276367.

7. J. Kiley Hamlin, "The Origins of Human Morality: Complex Socio-Moral Evaluations by Preverbal Infants," in Jean Decety and Yves Christen, eds., *New Frontiers in Social Neuroscience* (New York: Springer, 2014), pp. 165–88, https://link.springer.com/chapter/10.1007/978-3-319-02904-7_10.

8. Stanley Wechkin, Jules H. Masserman, and William Terris, "'Altruistic' Behavior in Rhesus Monkeys," *American Journal of Psychiatry* 121, no. 6 (December 1964): 584–85, https://doi.org/10.1176/ajp.121.6.584; Stanley Wechkin, Jules H. Masserman, and William Terris, "Shock to a Conspecifc as an Aversive Stimulus," *Psychonomic Science* 1, no. 12 (March 2014): 47–48, https://doi.org/10.3758/BF03342783.

9. Leslie Henderson, "Why Our Brains See the World as 'Us' versus 'Them,'" *Scientific American*, June 22, 2018, https://www.scientificamerican.com/article/why-our-brains-see-the-world-as-us-versus-them.

10. Robert M. Sapolsky, "Peace Among Primates," Greater Good Science Center, September 1, 2007, https://greatergood.berkeley.edu/article/item/peace_among_primates; Stephanie D. Preston, *The Altruistic Urge: Why We're Driven to Help Others* (New York: Columbia University Press, 2022).

11 "Our President," National Education Association, accessed July 25, 2023, https://www.nea.org/about-nea/leaders/president.

12 "Chairman of the Board and CEO Michael Sodini," Walk the Talk America, accessed November 21, 2023, https://walkthetalkamerica.org/michael-sodini.

13. Kathryn Worley, "Why We Support Walk the Talk America," AlphaTech Inc. (December 2022), https://atimfg.com/blog.

14. Lesie M. Carson, Suzanne M. Marsh, Margaret M. Brown, Katherine L. Elkins, and Hope M. Tiesman, "An Analysis of Suicides among First Responders: Findings from the National Violent Death Reporting System, 2015–2017," *Journal of Safety Research* 85 (June 2023): 361–70, https://www.sciencedirect.com/science/article/abs/pii/S0022437523000415.

15. Michael Sodini, "A Letter from Our Founder," Walk the Talk America, accessed November 21, 2023, https://walkthetalkamerica.org/why-we-were-founded.

16. James H. Fowler and Nicholas A. Christakis, "Cooperative Behavior Cascades in Human Social Networks," *PNAS* 107, no. 12 (March 8, 2010): 5334–38, https://doi.org/10.1073/pnas.0913149107.

CHAPTER 5. CURIOSITY IS THE CURE

1. Mónica Guzmán, *I Never Thought of It That Way: How to Have Fearlessly Curious Conversations in Dangerously Divided Times* (Dallas: BenBella Books, 2002), pp. xix–xx.

2. Raymond S. Nickerson, "Confirmation Bias: A Ubiquitous Phenomenon in Many Guises," *Review of General Psychology* 2, no. 2 (June 1998): 175–220, https://doi.org/10.1037/1089-2680.2.2.1.

3. Guzmán, *I Never Thought of It That Way*, p. xx.

4. Ibid, p. xxiii.

5. Ibid, p. 48.

6. Albert Mehrabian and Morton Wiener, "Decoding of Inconsistent Communications," *Journal of Personality and Social Psychology* 6, no. 1 (1967): 109–14, https://doi.org/10.1037/h0024532.

7. Harry Weger, Jr., Gina Castle Bell, Elizabeth M. Minei, and Melissa C. Robinson, "The Relative Effectiveness of Active Listening in Initial Interactions," *International Journal of Listening* 28, no. 1 (January 2014): 13–31, https://doi.org/10.1080/10904018.2013.813234.

8. Danielle DeSimone, "Concerns Rise Over Military Suicide Rates: Here's How the USO Is Trying to Help," USO Warrior and Family Centers, September 6, 2023, https://www.uso.org/stories/2664-military-suicide-rates-are-at-an-all-time-high-heres-how-were-trying-to-help.

9. Katherine W. Phillips, Katie A. Liljenquist, and Margaret A. Neale, "Is the Pain Worth the Gain? The Advantages and Liabilities of Agreeing with Socially Distinct Newcomers," *Personality and Social Psychology Bulletin* 35, no. 3 (March 2009): 336–50, https://doi.org/10.1177/0146167208328062.

10. Todd B. Kashdan, Ryne A. Sherman, Jessica Yarbro, and David C. Funder, "How Are Curious People Viewed and How Do They Behave in Social Situations? From the Perspectives of Self, Friends, Parents, and Unacquainted Observers," *Journal of Personality* 81, no. 2 (2013): 142–54, https://doi.org/10.1111/j.1467-6494.2012.00796.x.

CHAPTER 6. RELATIONSHIPS AT THE CORE

1. Quoted in "City of Falcon Heights Task Force on Inclusion and Policing," Minnesota Department of Administration, accessed November 21, 2023, https://mn.gov/admin/government/ocdr/projects/falcon-heights.

2. Abraham Lincoln, First Inaugural Address, March 4, 1861, available at the Avalon Project, Yale Law School, https://avalon.law.yale.edu/19th_century/lincoln1.asp.

3. Greater Good Science Center, "Shared Identity: How to Encourage Generosity by Finding Commonalities Between People," Greater Good in Action, https://ggia.berkeley.edu/practice/shared_identity.

4. Florence Fabricant, "'Breaking Bread' Showcases the A-Sham Food Festival in Israel," *New York Times*, January 31, 2022, https://www.nytimes.com/2022/01/31/dining/breaking-bread-documentary.html.

5. Yitzhak Bronstein, "Food Festival a Big Draw in Haifa," *Tablet*, December 10, 2015, https://www.tabletmag.com/sections/news/articles/arab-food-festival-a-big-draw-in-haifa.

6. Michael Kardas, Amit Kumar, and Nicholas Epley, "Overly Shallow? Miscalibrated Expectations Create Barriers to Deeper Conversation," *Journal of Personality and Social Psychology* 122, no. 3 (March 2022): 367–98, https://doi.org/10.1037/pspa0000281.

7. Mark Grabowski, "Both Sides Win: Why Using Mediation Would Improve Pro Sports," *Harvard Journal of Sports & Entertainment* 5, no. 2 (Spring 2014): 210, https://journals.law.harvard.edu/jsel/wp-content/uploads/sites/78/2014/11/Grabowski.pdf.

8. Mike Halford, "Former NFL Labor Mediator on NHL Lockout: 'I'd Volunteer to Do It for Free,'" NBC Sports, November 15, 2012, quoted in Mark Grabowski, "Both Sides Win: Why Using Mediation Would Improve Pro Sports," *Harvard Journal of Sports & Entertainment* 5, no. 2 (Spring

2014): 210, https://journals.law.harvard.edu/jsel/wp-content/uploads/sites/78/2014/11/Grabowski.pdf.

9. Tyler LeBouef, Zachary Yaker, and Lacey Whited, "Physiology, Autonomic Nervous System," *StatPearls*, May 1, 2023, https://www.ncbi.nlm.nih.gov/books/NBK538516.

10. Debra Umberson and Jennifer Karas Montez, "Social Relationships and Health: A Flashpoint for Health Policy," *Journal of Health and Social Behavior* 51, no. 1 (March 2010): S54–66, https://doi.org/10.1177/0022146510383501.

11. John M. Gottman and Robert W. Levenson, "Marital Processes Predictive of Later Dissolution: Behavior, Physiology, and Health," *Journal of Personality and Social Psychology* 63, no. 2 (August 1992): 221–33, https://bpl.berkeley.edu/docs/41-Marital%20Processes92.pdf.

CHAPTER 7. SEEK HIGHER GROUND

1. Stephen R. Covey, *The Seven Habits of Highly Effective People* (New York: Fireside, 1989), p. 207.

2. Dawna Markova and Angie McCarthur, *Collaborative Intelligence: Thinking with People Who Think Differently* (New York: Spiegel & Grau, 2015).

3. Jonathan Haidt, *The Righteous Mind: Why Good People Are Divided by Politics and Religion* (New York: Pantheon, 2012).

4. Kelly D. Brownell, "Thinking Forward: The Quicksand of Appeasing the Food Industry," *PLoS Medicine* 9, no. 7 (July 3, 2012): e1001254, https://doi.org/10.1371/journal.pmed.1001254.

5. Steve Pinker, *The Better Angels of Our Nature: Why Violence Has Declined* (New York: Viking, 2011), p. xxv.

CHAPTER 8. MAP THE TERRAIN

1. E. Ann Carson, "Prisoners in 2021 – Statistical Tables," US Department of Justice, Office of Justice Programs, Bureau of Justice Statistics, December 2022, https://bjs.ojp.gov/sites/g/files/xyckuh236/files/media/document/p21st.pdf.

2. Office of the Assistant Secretary for Planning and Evaluation, "Incarceration & Reentry," US Department of Health and Human Services, accessed November 22, 2023, https://aspe.hhs.gov/topics/human-services/incarceration-reentry-0.

3. William R. Kelly, *From Retribution to Public Safety: Disruptive Innovation of American Criminal Justice* (Lanham, MD: Rowman & Littlefield, 2017).
4. Katie Shonk, "Conflict Negotiation Skills for Ending Partnerships Peacefully," Harvard Law School Program on Negotiation, October 5, 2020, https://www.pon.harvard.edu/daily/conflict-resolution/conflict-negotiation-skills-for-ending-partnerships-peacefully; Julie Zauzmer, "One Goal of Methodists' Plan to Split the Church over Same-Sex Marriage and Clergy: Avoid Lawsuits," *Washington Post*, January 9, 2020, https://www.washingtonpost.com/religion/2020/01/09/united-methodists-separation-lawsuits.

CHAPTER 9. NURTURE TRUST

1. Henri Tajfel, "Experiments in Intergroup Discrimination," *Scientific American* 223, no. 5 (November 1970): 96–103, https://www.jstor.org/stable/24927662.
2. Karina Bland, "Blue Eyes, Brown Eyes: What Jane Elliott's Famous Experiment Says About Race 50 Years On," November 17, 2017, https://eu.azcentral.com/story/news/local/karinabland/2017/11/17/blue-eyes-brown-eyes-jane-elliotts-exercise-race-50-years-later/860287001.
3. Abraham H. Maslow, "A Theory of Human Motivation," *Psychological Review* 50, no. 4 (1943): 370–96, https://doi.org/10.1037/h0054346.
4. Sabah Alam Hydari, "Countering Otherness: Fostering Integration Within Teams," *McKinsey Quarterly*, January 12, 2021, https://www.mckinsey.com/capabilities/people-and-organizational-performance/our-insights/countering-otherness-fostering-integration-within-teams.
5. Ibid.
6. Terry Fenge and Paul Quassa, "Negotiating and Implementing the Nunavut Land Claims Agreement," *Policy Options/Options Politiques*, July 1, 2009, https://policyoptions.irpp.org/fr/magazines/canadas-water-challenges/negotiating-and-implementing-the-nunavut-land-claims-agreement.
7. Art Martens, "Good Politics Is Never About Personal Honor," *Similkameen Spotlight*, January 20, 2016, p. 7, https://issuu.com/blackpress/docs/i20160120044833299.
8. Gordon W. Allport, *The Nature of Prejudice* (Cambridge, MA: Perseus, 1954); Thomas F. Pettigrew and Linda R. Tropp, "A Meta-analytic Test of Intergroup Contact Theory," *Journal of Personality and Social Psychology* 90, no. 5 (2006): 751–83, https://doi.org/10.1037/0022-3514.90.5.751.
9. Muzafer Sherif, O. J. Harvey, B. Jack White, William R. Hood, and Carolyn W. Sherif, *Intergroup Conflict and Cooperation: The Robbers Cave*

Experiment (Middletown, CT: Wesleyan University Press, 1988); Thomas F. Pettigrew, Linda R. Tropp, Ulrich Wagner, and Oliver Christ, "Recent Advances in Intergroup Contact Theory," *International Journal of Intercultural Relations* 35, no. 3 (May 2011): 271–80, https://doi.org/10.1016/j.ijintrel.2011.03.001.

10. Kaitlin Woolley and Ayelet Fishbach, "A Recipe for Friendship: Similar Food Consumption Promotes Trust and Cooperation," *Journal of Consumer Psychology* 27, no. 1 (2017): 1–10, https://doi.org/10.1016/j.jcps.2016.06.003.

11. Convergence Center for Policy Resolution, "Reentry Ready: Improving Incarceration's Contribution to Successful Reentry" (2019), https://reentryready.convergencepolicy.org/wp-content/uploads/2019/06/Reentry-Ready-Full-Report_FINAL.pdf.

12. Carrie Menkel-Meadow, "Negotiating the American Constitution (1787–1789): Coalitions, Process Rules, and Compromises," in Emmanual Vivet, ed., *Landmark Negotiations from Around the World: Lessons for Modern Diplomacy* (Cambridge, UK: Intersentia, 2019), pp. 151–62.

13. Chatham House, "The Chatham House Rule," accessed October 26, 2023, https://www.chathamhouse.org/about-us/chatham-house-rule.

14. Emily Kubin, Curtis Puryear, Chelsea Schein, and Kurt Gray, "Personal Experiences Bridge Moral and Political Divides Better than Facts," *PNAS* 118, no. 6 (January 25, 2021): e2008389118, https://doi.org/10.1073/pnas.2008389118.

15. David Brooks, "The Essential Skills for Being a Human," *New York Times*, October 19, 2023, https://www.nytimes.com/2023/10/19/opinion/social-skills-connection.html.

16. Stephen R. Covey, *The Seven Habits of Highly Effective People* (New York: Fireside, 1989).

CHAPTER 10. REALLY HEAR EVERYONE

1. John Gramlich, "What Makes a News Story Trustworthy? Americans Point to the Outlet That Publishes It, Sources Cited," Pew Research Center, June 9, 2021, https://www.pewresearch.org/short-reads/2021/06/09/what-makes-a-news-story-trustworthy-americans-point-to-the-outlet-that-publishes-it-sources-cited.

2. Jonathan Haidt, *The Righteous Mind: Why Good People Are Divided by Politics and Religion* (New York: Pantheon, 2012).

3. Emmanuel Trouche, Petter Johansson, Lars Hall, and Hugo Mercier, "The Selective Laziness of Reasoning," *Cognitive Science* 40, no. 8 (November 2016): 2122–36, https://onlinelibrary.wiley.com/doi/full/10.1111/cogs.12303.

4. Rebecca Silliman and David Schleifer, "Eager to Build Bridges: Religious and Spiritual Americans' Desire to Connect Across Partisan Divides," Hidden Common Ground Report, Public Agenda (November 2022), https://publicagenda.org/wp-content/uploads/Religion-and-Spirituality-Report_FNL_HighRes.pdf.

5. Paul Ekman, *Emotions Revealed: Recognizing Faces and Feelings to Improve Communication and Emotional Life* (New York: Henry Holt, 2003).

6. Sonia Roccas and Marilynn B. Brewer, "Social Identity Complexity," *Personality and Social Psychology Review* 6, no. 2 (May 2002): 88–106, https://doi.org/10.1207/S15327957PSPR0602_01, cited in Peter T. Coleman, "Tired of Feeling Divided? What Americans Can Do to De-Polarize Our Nation," *Psychology Today*, November 9, 2017, https://www.psychologytoday.com/gb/blog/the-five-percent/201711/tired-feeling-divided.

7. Daniel Yankelovich, *The Magic of Dialogue: Transforming Conflict into Cooperation* (New York: Simon & Schuster, 1999), p. 16.

8. See, for example, Sam Kaner, *Facilitator's Guide to Participatory Decision-Making* (Hoboken, NJ: Jossey-Bass, 2014); Ron Kraybill and Evelyn Wright, *The Little Book of Cool Tools for Hot Topics: Group Tools to Facilitate Meetings When Things Are Hot* (New York: Good Books, 2006).

9. Mary Ellen Flannery, "How Restorative Practices Work for Students and Educators," *NEAToday*, June 13, 2019, https://www.nea.org/nea-today/all-news-articles/how-restorative-practices-work-students-and-educators.

10. Matthew D. Lieberman, Naomi I. Eisenberger, Molly J. Crockett, et al., "Putting Feelings into Words: Affect Labeling Disrupts Amygdala Activity in Response to Affective Stimuli," *Psychological Science* 18, no. 5 (May 2007): 421–28, https://doi.1111/j.1467-9280.2007.01916.x.

CHAPTER 11. GENERATE OPTIONS FOR MUTUAL GAIN

1. Carrie Menkel-Meadow, "Negotiating the American Constitution (1787–1789): Coalitions, Process Rules, and Compromises," in Emmanual Vivet, ed., *Landmark Negotiations from Around the World: Lessons for Modern Diplomacy* (Cambridge, UK: Intersentia, 2019), pp. 151–62.

2. Senate Historical Office, "The Virginia Plan," accessed October 27, 2023, https://www.senate.gov/civics/common/generic/Virginia_Plan_item.htm.

3 "Plans Presented to the U.S. Constitutional Convention," Quill Project, accessed October 27, 2023, https://www.quillproject.net/resources/resource_item/54.

4. Roger Fisher and William Ury, *Getting to Yes: Negotiating Agreement Without Giving In* (Boston: Houghton Mifflin, 1981).

5. Joanne Kenen, "The CLASS Act," *HealthAffairs*, May 12, 2011, https://www.healthaffairs.org/do/10.1377/hpb20110512.840200.

6. Christopher J. Giese and Allen J. Schmitz, *Premium Estimates for Policy Options to Finance Long-Term Services and Supports* (Brookfield, WI: Milliman, 2015), https://www.thescanfoundation.org/sites/default/files/milliman_report_-_premium_estimates_for_policy_options_to_finance_ltss.pdf; Melissa M. Favreault and Richard W. Johnson, "Microsimulation Analysis of Financing Options for Long-Term Services and Supports," Urban Institute, November 2015, https://www.thescanfoundation.org/media/2019/10/nov_20_revised_final_microsimulation_analysis_of_ltss_report.pdf.

7. Convergence Center for Policy Resolution, "A Consensus Framework for Long-Term Care Financing Reform," February 2016, https://convergencepolicy.org/wp-content/uploads/2022/11/LTCFC-FINAL-REPORT-Feb-2016.pdf.

8. Gwen Westerman and Bruce White, *Mni Sota Makoce: The Land of the Dakota* (Saint Paul: Minnesota Historical Society Press, 2012).

9. Minnesota Historical Society, "Traverse Des Sioux: Learn," accessed November 24, 2023, https://www.mnhs.org/traversedessioux/learn.

10. Subcommittee on Capitol Art, "Final Report to the Minnesota State Capitol Preservation Committee," August 15, 2016, https://mn.gov/admin/assets/2016-08-15-art-subcommittee-final-report_tcm36-252309.pdf.

11. Ibid, p. 8.

12. Ibid, p. 45.

13. Justice Paul H. Anderson, "Keep an Open Mind," accessed December 1, 2023, https://mn.gov/admin/assets/Anderson-keep-an-open-mind-8-3-2016_tcm36-251401.pdf.

14. Gwen Nell Westerman, "Give-Up Song," published by the Academy of American Poets as part of Poem-a-Day, July 26, 2021, https://poets.org/poem/give-away-song. Used by permission of the author. Copyright © 2021 by Gwen Nell Westerman.

CHAPTER 12. TAKE YOUR TIME

1. David Schleifer, Will Friedman, and Antonio Diep, "Where Americans See Eye to Eye on Health Care," Public Agenda, 2018, https://publicagenda.org/wp-content/uploads/PublicAgenda_HiddenCommonGround_HealthCare_2018.pdf.

2. David Schleifer and Will Friedman, "Where Americans Stand on Immigration," Public Agenda, August 2020, https://publicagenda.org/wp-content/uploads/Public-Agenda-Immigration-Report_FINAL.pdf.
3. Public Agenda, "America's Hidden Common Ground on Police Reform and Racism in the United States," June 29, 2020, https://publicagenda.org/wp-content/uploads/HCG-Race-and-Police-Reform-Memo-Topline.pdf.
4. Minnesota Office of Collaboration and Dispute Resolution, "See How Collaborative Problem Solving Works," August 26, 2019, https://mn.gov/admin/government/ocdr.

CHAPTER 13. DISCOVERY AND DESIGN

1. Minnesota Department of Human Services, "Person-Centered Practices, Positive Supports, and the Jensen Settlement," October 12, 2023, https://mn.gov/dhs/general-public/featured-programs-initiatives/jensen-settlement.
2. Briana Bierschbach, "Critical Condition: Can Mark Dayton Fix One of Minnesota's Most Problem-Plagued Institutions?" *MinnPost*, March 22, 2016, https://www.minnpost.com/politics-policy/2016/03/critical-condition-can-mark-dayton-fix-one-minnesotas-most-problem-plagued-i.
3. Katharine G. Kugler and Peter T. Coleman, "Get Complicated: The Effects of Complexity on Conversations over Potentially Intractable Moral Conflicts," *Negotiation and Conflict Management Research* 13, no. 3 (August 2020): 211–30, https://doi.org/10.1111/ncmr.12192.
4. International Association of Facilitators, https://www.iaf-world.org/site.

CHAPTER 14. DIALOGUE AND DESTINATIONS

1. Carrie Menkel-Meadow, "Negotiating the American Constitution (1787–1789): Coalitions, Process Rules, and Compromises," in Emmanual Vivet, ed., *Landmark Negotiations from Around the World: Lessons for Modern Diplomacy* (Cambridge, UK: Intersentia, 2019), pp. 151–62.
2. Quoted in Minnesota Department of Administration, "Minnesota Security Hospital," accessed November 24, 2023, https://mn.gov/admin/government/ocdr/projects/msh.
3. Barbara Brotman, "Two Sides in Abortion Debate Find Common Ground in Chasm Between Them," *Chicago Tribune*, January 25, 1998, https://www.chicagotribune.com/news/ct-xpm-1998-01-25-9801250343-story.html.

4. Matthew Feinberg, "Moral Reframing: A Technique for Effective and Persuasive Communication Across Political Divides," *Social and Personality Psychology Compass* 13, no. 12 (December 2019): https://doi.org/10.1111/spc3.12501.

5. Jonathan Haidt, *The Righteous Mind: Why Good People Are Divided by Politics and Religion* (New York: Pantheon, 2012).

6. Convergence Center for Policy Resolution, "Working Up: A Convergence Dialogue for Action to Increase Economic Mobility," final report, October 2018, https://workingup.convergencepolicy.org/#WorkingUpDialogue.

7. City of Falcon Heights Inclusion and Policing Task Force, "Overview of Recommendations," accessed November 24, 2023, https://mn.gov/admin/assets/Falcon%20Heights%20Final%20Recommendations_tcm36-392008.pdf.

8. Alex Osborn, *How to "Think Up"* (New York: McGraw Hill, 1942), p. 25.

9. Ibid, p. 29.

CHAPTER 15. ACHIEVING CONSENSUS AND IMPACT

1. US Senate, "About the Senate and the US Constitution: Equal State Representation," accessed December 2, 2023, https://www.senate.gov/about/origins-foundations/senate-and-constitution/equal-state-representation.htm.

2. Convergence Center for Policy Resolution, "Working Up: A Convergence Dialogue for Action to Increase Economic Mobility," final report, October 2018, https://workingup.convergencepolicy.org/#WorkingUpDialogue.

3. Quoted in Minnesota Department of Administration, "Minnesota Security Hospital," accessed November 24, 2023, https://mn.gov/admin/government/ocdr/projects/msh.

CONCLUSION: WE ALL CAN BE COLLABORATIVE LEADERS

1. Peter Coleman of the Difficult Conversations Lab wrote, "Research has shown that when people believe that others can change, they tend to approach them more cooperatively, see more value in engaging with them and voicing their concerns, and have lower levels of intergroup hatred and anxiety and more willingness to interact or compromise with members of outgroups." Peter Coleman, "Tired of Feeling Divided? What Americans Can Do to De-Polarize Our Nation," *Psychology Today,*

November 9, 2017, https://www.psychologytoday.com/us/blog/the-five-percent/201711/tired-feeling-divided.

2. Roxi Bahar Hewertson, *Lead Like It Matters...Because It Does! Practical Leadership Tools to Inspire and Engage Your People and Create Great Results* (New York: McGraw-Hill, 2014).
3. Roxi Bahar Hewertson, correspondence with the authors.
4. National Governors Association, "Disagree Better: Healthy Conflict for Better Policy," accessed November 25, 2023, https://www.nga.org/disagree-better/#about.
5. Neil Bradley, correspondence with the authors, November 27, 2023.
6. Arthur C. Brooks, *Love Your Enemies: How Decent People Can Save America from the Culture of Contempt* (New York: Broadside Books, 2019).

Acknowledgments

No book can be written without great support from those who helped directly with the book, others who have been essential to the authors' professional journeys, and of course family and friends.

A tremendous credit and thanks are due to Robin Dennis, our writing coach and editor, whose talent and experience have made an extraordinary and indispensable contribution to elevating the quality of what we present.

We are grateful to Wiley for believing in this book. Special thanks to our editor at Wiley, Kelly Talbot, and to Jeanenne Ray, associate publisher, and Casper Barbour, editorial assistant. We are most grateful to Paul Klein and Jennifer Smith for their help in connecting us to Wiley. Special thanks to Breelyn Stelle for her dedicated research and for helping to keep us organized.

Together, we both want to acknowledge all those whose stories or insights are part of the book. Thanks to Dave Baker, Ellie Bertani, Neil Bradley, Arthur Brooks, Judy Conti, Annie Gray, Roxi Hewertson, Marc Howard, Gisèle Huff, Melanie Leehy, Scott Melby, Sherry Davis Molock, Becky Pringle, Julie Ring, Lynn Schoch, Michael Sodini, Daren Swenson, Gwen Westerman, and the late Carla Willis and her husband Gregg Baker. Special thanks to Tom Dunne for sharing his stories, his help with the book, and all his terrific involvement with Convergence.

Special recognition is due Stuart Butler for great help with the book and for his deeply important role in elevating the work of Convergence both as a board member and as an invaluable originator and participant in various projects. Thanks to David Fairman and Pat Field of the Consensus Building Institute for their input on the book and their indispensable partnership on Convergence's work. Thanks also to others who provided valuable guidance for the book, including Monica Guzman, Jonathan Haidt, former Convergence board member Kelly Johnston, current Convergence board member Manu Meel, and Amanda Ripley.

Together, we offer thanks to many people who have been so helpful in the formation and success of Convergence Center for Policy Resolution. Special recognition is due to Aakif Ahmad, Convergence's co-founder and former chief operating officer; Rich Korn, our indispensable former board chair and organizational coach; Jean Molino, our deeply dedicated and capable long-term board chair; Dusie Cassata, our invaluable longest-standing staff member who is now in senior management; and Kelly Young, an early partner and extraordinary K–12 education project director. Much gratitude is due to the Akin Gump law firm for generous pro bono help to Convergence over many years and to one of their partners, John Jacob, who served so ably on our board for multiple terms.

Special thanks is due to Maja Kristin, our valued former board member and generous supporter. Deep thanks also to Richard Slifka, Stephen Heintz, and the Rockefeller Brothers Fund, and to David Einhorn, Jenn Hoos Rothberg, and Jon Gruber of the Einhorn Collaborative for their critically important support.

Many other people have greatly helped Convergence succeed, including current and former long-time board members Richard Alper, Bill Belding, Neil Bradley, Greg Campbell, Lisa Davis, Jessica Dibb, Michael Friedland, Peter Goldstone, Cherie Harder, the late David Lipsky, Linda Lorelle, Oliver Quinn, Leah Ray, Louise Phipps Senft, Riaz Siddiqi, Kellie Specter, Selika Josiah Talbott, Art Taylor, Lindsay Torrico, Rita Walters, Jeff Weissglass, Rebecca Westerfield, and Alison Acosta Winters. Others who helped greatly in the creation and success of Convergence include former US Representative Steve Bartlett, Lawrence Bathgate, Bill Bolling, Daniel Bowling, Rick Callahan, Claudia Carasso, Bob Chase, Toni Clark, Allan Cohen, Bruce Edwards, Susan Edwards, the late US Representative Vic Fazio, David Friedman, William Galston, Mark Gerzon, Chris Harte, Roxi Hewertson, the late Alan Jones, Steve Kayman, Howard Konar, Matt McKinney, Paulette Meyer, Matt Owens, Dennis Passis, Ron Pollack, Marc Racicot, Faith Roessel, Ambassador Dennis Ross, Debra Rubino, Larry Spears, the late Rob Stein, John Steiner, the late Senator Harris Wofford, and Mark Zitter.

The book is a tribute to the work of Convergence staff members and consultants over the years, including Lyn Bazzell, Amanda Broun, Demi Edwards, Julie Garel, Caryn Hederman, Isabel Hinestrosa, Susan Jerison, Russell Krumnow, Stephanie McGencey, Beth Miller, Hannah

Ollenburger, Sharona Shuster, Amy Slechta, Monica Snellings, Vicki Veenker, Sara Willi, and Susan Willie. We extend our gratitude to all current and former members of the Convergence board, Leadership Council, and staff.

From Mariah—I would like to thank the staff and volunteers at the Center for Conflict Resolution and the New York Peace Institute, where I benefited from formative training and invaluable experience in mediation. Thanks to my many wonderful former colleagues at the State of Minnesota, especially Dave Bartholomay, Commissioner Josh Tilsen, Commissioner Todd Doncavage, Commissioner Alice Roberts Davis, Assistant Commissioner Curt Yoakum, Commissioner Erin Campbell, Lauren Gilchrist, former Senate Majority Leader Roger Moe, and so many others. Thanks also to Mariann Johnson, Aimee Gourlay, Sharon Press, and Kathy Quick for their mentorship. I'm also grateful to the many participants in collaborative problem-solving processes that I've led who opened their hearts to each other and their minds to solutions that meet the needs of all involved.

I would like to thank my parents, Mark Levison and Christina Usher, for modeling deep understanding of all perspectives and care for all and for their unconditional love and support. Thanks to my sisters, Samantha and Lila Levison, for sharing our family values with me and for always making me laugh. My sons Soren and Everett are the center of my world and, even at their young ages, have been supportive of and patient with me as I wrote this book; every day they help me to hone my collaborative problem-solving skills. I'm forever grateful to my beloved husband, Kyle Onan, whose support is truly unwavering and whose love is my bedrock.

Finally, my thanks to my coauthor, Rob, whose superpower for genuinely connecting with his fellow human beings creates a web of people committed to collaborative problem-solving, including the many relationships and experiences that resulted in the creation of this book. Rob's care and jokes kept me going through the arduous process of writing a book, and his friendship is a tremendous blessing for which I am so grateful.

From Rob—Thanks to my family members, starting with my late parents, Blanche and Irving Fersh, for all their love and support. My wife, Sharon Markus, has been unwavering in her love and encouragement and anchors our family incomparably. Thanks go to all four of our children—Rachel, David (and his wife, Lynn), Ben, and Danny for being such a source of pride and grounding. Special thanks to Danny for his great help with the book and to Rachel for all her wonderful involvement with Convergence.

I am grateful to all my former colleagues at Search for Common Ground. My years there were invaluable in steeping me in the field of conflict transformation and indispensable to incubating Convergence. Thanks also to Tim Mealey and John Ehrmann of the Meridian Institute for their great partnership on the Health Care Coverage for the Uninsured project.

Special help with the book has also been provided to me by Andrew Yarrow, Jen Frye, and Steve Fiffer.

Final thanks are reserved for my coauthor and good friend Mariah Levison. I cannot imagine a better partner for this book. Although we are separated by decades in age and experience and by nearly half a continent, she and I have come to see the world in extraordinarily similar ways. She is one of the most insightful and skillful practitioners of collaborative problem-solving I have had the pleasure of working with over these past few decades. It has been an honor and a joy to collaborate with Mariah on this challenging task of creating a book that we hope will make a lasting, positive impact.

About the Authors

Robert Fersh

Rob Fersh was born, at an early age, in Poughkeepsie, New York, where he attended public schools until leaving for college at Cornell University. He chose Cornell's School of Industrial and Labor Relations because he was drawn to the field of mediation, and his experience at Cornell during tumultuous times (1968–72) made a deep impression on him to care about the world and want to make it better.

Following Cornell and a law degree from Boston University, Rob found employment in Washington, DC, working primarily on issues relating to hunger and poverty in the United States. He initially worked with state and local public welfare administrators and then served on the staffs of three congressional committees, always working on a bipartisan basis. In the middle of his congressional work, Rob also had a political appointment in the Carter Administration working as an assistant to the administrator of the Food and Nutrition Service of USDA.

After his congressional work, Rob was tapped in early 1986 to head the Food Research and Action Center (FRAC), a leading national anti-hunger organization. His work there led to an award for nonprofit leadership from the Prudential Foundation.

Starting in late 1997, Rob began an effort to create a new organization that would bring divergent stakeholders to a common table to find shared solutions to issues of critical national importance. After incubating this idea at the nonprofit organization Search for Common Ground, Rob founded Convergence Center for Policy Resolution in 2009 and remained its CEO until 2020. On his watch, Convergence successfully conducted multiple projects on a wide range of important public issues, and this work has since continued. Rob remains a board member of and an advisor to Convergence.

Rob is married to Sharon Markus, and together they have four children and three grandchildren. He resides in Bethesda, Maryland, where when not otherwise occupied, he is an avid golfer and keeper of friendships.

Mariah Levison

From a young age Mariah saw that most conflict, and the resulting bad behavior it too often generates, is driven by the fear that one won't be able to meet an important need because it seems incompatible with the demands of the other person or side. She could also see that this is usually a misperception and that there is a way to forge higher-ground solutions that meet the most important needs of all involved.

This insight led Mariah to become a mediator, working at non-profit dispute resolution centers in several cities before helping to reinstate and then lead the Minnesota State Office of Collaboration and Dispute Resolution. In that position Mariah used collaborative problem-solving processes to build consensus on complex and contentious state, tribal, and local issues; built the capacity of government to work well across difference; and facilitated the Minnesota Legislative Civility Caucus. In 2022 Mariah joined Convergence Center for Policy Resolution as the chief program officer and became president and CEO in February 2024.

Mariah's work in consensus building includes assessment, design, facilitation, mediation, collaborative processes, dialogue, public engagement best practices, restorative justice, and program development. Additionally, Mariah has been teaching these skills for 20 years in settings ranging from community to law schools and everything in between, domestically and abroad.

Mariah has a master's in international affairs with a focus on conflict management from Washington University in St. Louis.

When she isn't working, Mariah can be found biking, cross-country skiing, or reading books with her two young sons and husband in Minneapolis.

Index